Legal Theory Today
Law and Politics at the Perimeter

Legal Theory Today

Founding Editor

John Gardner, Professor of Jurisprudence, University College, Oxford

TITLES IN THIS SERIES

Law in its Own Right – Henrik Palmer Olsen and Stuart Toddington
Law and Aesthetics – Adam Gearey
Law as a Social Institution – Hamish Ross
Evaluation and Legal Theory – Julie Dickson
Risks and Legal Theory – Jenny Steele
A Sociology of Jurisprudence – Richard Nobles and David Schiff
Costs and Cautionary Tales: Economic Insights for the Law – Anthony Ogus
Legal Norms and Normativity – Sylvie Delacroix
Consent in the Law by Deryck Beyleveld and
Roger Brownsword

Forthcoming titles:

Law after Modernity by Sionaidh Douglas-Scott
Law and Ethics by John Tasioulas
Law and Human Need by John Stanton-Ife

Law and Politics at the Perimeter
Re-Evaluating Key Debates in Feminist Theory

Vanessa E Munro

·HART·
PUBLISHING

OXFORD AND PORTLAND, OREGON
2007

Published in North America (US and Canada) by
Hart Publishing
c/o International Specialized Book Services
920 NE 58th Avenue, Suite 300
Portland, Oregon
97213–3644
USA
Tel: +1 503 287 3093 or toll-free: (1) 800 944 6190
Fax: +1 503 280 8832
E-mail: orders@isbs.com
Website: www.isbs.com

© Vanessa Munro 2007

Vanessa Munro has asserted her right under the Copyright, Designs and Patents Act 1988,
to be identified as the author of this work.

All rights reserved. No part of this publication may be reproduced, stored in a retrieval system,
or transmitted, in any form or by any means, without the prior permission of Hart Publishing,
or as expressly permitted by law or under the terms agreed with the appropriate reprographic
rights organisation. Enquiries concerning reproduction which may not be covered by the above
should be addressed to Hart Publishing at the address below.

Hart Publishing, 16C Worcester Place, Oxford OX1 4LB
Telephone: +44 (0)1865 517530 or Fax: +44 (0)1865 510710
E-mail: mail@hartpub.co.uk
Website: http//:www.hartpub.co.uk

British Library Cataloguing in Publication Data
Data Available

ISBN 13: 978–1–84113–352–2

Typeset by Hope Services (Abingdon) Ltd.
Printed and bound in Great Britain by
TJ International Ltd, Padstow, Cornwall

Acknowledgements

I am much indebted to a great number of people who, in their different ways, have helped to ensure that this project has seen its way through to completion. Although this project builds only in a tangential way on my PhD thesis, I would like to thank my supervisor, Jane Mair, and Scott Veitch at the University of Glasgow for their feedback and support in the earliest stages of my research career. I would also particularly like to thank John Tasioulas for encouraging me, as an over-committed undergraduate student, to take the academic path seriously. I am grateful to both Hilary Charlesworth and Tom Campbell for welcoming me to the Australian National University during my PhD, and for their comments on some very early drafts of the discussion on MacKinnon and Foucault dealt with here. I am also grateful to a number of my colleagues at the University of Reading who displayed considerable generosity and support in the early stages in which the idea for this book was developed and proposed. In addition, I have benefited from the encouragement of several colleagues at King's College London, where I have been based during the period in which much of the latter work on the book was conducted. I would like to specifically thank those colleagues who have offered their time, advice and comments in reading drafts of sections of this book, in particular John Tasioulas, Sharon Cowan, John Stanton-Ife, and Alan Norrie. I would also like to thank Richard Hart for his considerable patience and support. On a personal note, there are a number of close friends and family members whose unending encouragement has been so important: they know who they are, and they know, I hope, that I am extremely grateful.

Earlier versions of Chapters four and five of this book were published respectively as 'On Power and Domination: Feminism and the Final Foucault' (2003) 2 (1) *European Journal of Political Theory* 79–99 and 'Resemblances of Identity: Ludwig Wittgenstein and Contemporary Feminist Legal Theory' (2006) 12 (2) *Res Publica* 137–62. In addition, sections of Chapter three have been drawn from work previously published as 'Legal Feminism and Foucault: A Critique of the Expulsion of Law' (2001) 28 (4) *Journal of Law and Society* 546–67.

Contents

Introduction   1

1 The Development and Dilemmas of Feminist Theory   11

Feminist Commonalities   11
Feminist Contestations   14
The Assimilation Model   14
   The Case For and Against Assimilation   15
   The Two Faces of Assimilation   19
Celebrating Difference   23
   The Case For and Against Celebrating Difference   24
The Rise of Dominance   28
   The Case For and Against Dominance   30
The Influence of Postmodernism   33
   The Case For and Against Postmodernism   36
Conclusion   39

2 Feminism(s), Law and Liberalism(s)   41

The Feminist Challenge to Legal Liberalism   43
   The Feminist Challenge to Liberalism's Method: Abstraction & Individualism   45
      Abstraction, Context & Hollow Legal Personhood   45
      Abstraction, Relationships and Relations of Power   47
   The Feminist Challenge to Liberalism's False Promise: Neutrality & Rationality   49
Out of the Shadows? A Re-evaluation of the Feminist Critique   51
   Individualism, Egoism & Community   54
   Abstraction, Context & Inequality   57
   Justice & Care: The Rationality of Emotions   59
Conclusion: A Return to Liberalism?   61

3 On Reform and Reforming Rights   63

From Theory to Strategy: Feminist Critique & Legal Reform   64
   The Case for De-Centering Law   64
   An Evaluation of the 'De-Centering' Thesis   68

Contents

Approaching Reform in the Third Way?	70
Feminist Reform and Women's Rights	73
The Feminist Challenge to Rights	74
Rights are too Individualistic	75
Rights are too Abstract	77
Rights and Wrong Assumptions	78
Towards the Reconstruction of Rights	81
Conclusion: On Rights & Reforming Rights	83

4 Power, Domination and Patriarchy   87

Perspectives on Power—Foucault v MacKinnon?	89
Perspectives on Power and the Possibility of Resistance	91
Perspectives on Power and the Role of Discourse	93
Perspectives on Power and the Deployment of Sexuality	94
Perspectives on Domination—Foucault *and* MacKinnon?	96
The Final Foucault and Domination	99
The Final Foucault and Resistance	102
The Final Foucault and Feminism	104
Conclusion	106

5 Womanhood, Essentialism and Identity   109

Setting the Scene: Essentialism and Difference	110
Strategic Essentialism	114
Iris Marion Young: Gender as Seriality	118
Back to the Rough Ground: Wittgenstein	123
Conclusion: 'False Prison' Breaks & Feminist Legal Theory	128

6 Equality, Respect and Feminist Futures   131

The Trouble(s) with Formal Equality	132
Re-formulating the Formal/Re-imagining Equality	134
Equality as Empowerment?	136
Equality Beyond Comparison?	139
Respect as an Alternative Moral Ideal	141
Respect, Sufficiency and Feminism	143
Respect Beyond Equality?	146
Conclusion: Toward A Respect Agenda	149

Concluding Remarks   151

Bibliography   155
Index   171

Introduction

The dawn of a new millennium has invited introspection. In the context of feminist legal and political theory, however, this critical stock-taking enterprise has yielded some disconcerting results. There is no doubt that the lives of many women have been improved, both materially and symbolically, by reforms pioneered by feminist campaigning. As a paradoxical testament to these successes, moreover, increasing numbers of young women are rejecting the feminist label, confident in their prospects for equality and seeing feminism as outdated and unnecessary in the modern world.

At the same time, though, gender gaps in the remuneration and promotion of employees remain, genuine shared parenting is rarely accomplished and barely supported by the state, and laws that seek to prohibit and punish the forms of violence predominantly visited upon women are too frequently ineffective. At a theoretical level, moreover, internal disagreements have come to mark the territory in which feminist analysis has been charted—tensions have arisen, for example, over how best to understand patriarchy, the utility of legal reform tactics, the legitimacy of woman-centred methods, the merits of grand-theorising and the contours of feminism's utopia.

The ferocity of these debates has intensified in recent times with the increasing reception of postmodern and pluralist analyses. Vehemently against the establishment of meta-narratives or essentialist accounts of generic womanhood, the postmodern insistence on subversion over critique, and on dislocation over collectivism, has put strain on an already fragile link between feminist theory and politics. Throughout the 1990s, the growing influence of postmodernism promoted a shift away from issues of exploitation and towards issues of identity. This, according to Fraser, has generated a condition in which there is:

> an absence of any credible overarching emancipatory project despite the proliferation of fronts of struggle; a general decoupling of the cultural politics of recognition from the social politics of redistribution; and a decentering of claims for equality in the face of . . . sharply rising material inequality.[1]

As a consequence, a growing reluctance 'to develop and embrace vigorous grand theory' has been identified amongst contemporary feminists, which

[1] N Fraser, *Justice Interruptus: Critical Reflections on the 'Post-Socialist Condition'* (London & New York, Routledge, 1997) at 3.

Introduction

has often been accompanied—or so it is argued—by an acute sense of 'nervousness when speaking critically about the situation of anyone other than one's own narrow cultural group.'[2]

Without denying the importance of these cultural and symbolic concerns, many other contemporary feminists, mindful of the 'bivalent' nature of gender, have become increasingly alert to the need for this focus on identity and recognition not to eclipse the equally important material reality of women's daily lives, in which the need to secure distributive justice in the allocation of social resources remains.[3] More generally, in a context in which the impetus behind feminism has traditionally been one grounded squarely in practical and political imperatives, the emerging disjunction between its theory and its activism has become a source of increasing concern. Commentators have frequently remarked on the disengagement of contemporary feminist legal and political theory from its reformist roots and have lamented the current 'paralysis' or 'brain drain' of an historically vibrant critical social movement.[4]

Set against this backdrop, this book offers a critical re-appraisal of contemporary feminist legal and political theory. It joins with an emerging body of feminist work that laments the disassociation of theory from politics, and that takes seriously both the divergent identities expressed by individual women and the complexity of their relationships with men, without rejecting thereby consideration of structural injustice or material inequality. In so doing, it re-visits key debates over the origins of patriarchy, as well as over the role of liberalism and the rule of law in its creation and perpetuation. What's more, it re-evaluates feminist calls for the abandonment or de-centering of legal reform strategies and rights-based claims. Critically reconstructing ideas of rights, justice and equality, it rejects 'attractively simple, monolithic theories in which everything is reduced to one explanatory concept'[5] without

---

[2] N Naffine, 'In Praise of Legal Feminism' (2002) 22 (1) *Legal Studies* 71 at 81.

[3] In some quarters, this postmodern seduction of feminism has been directly challenged—MacKinnon, for example, laments its preoccupation with talk about theory and with rehashing how theory should be done, which has left 'women's lives twisting in the wind' rather than re-theorising experiences of womanhood and patriarchy in the concrete—C MacKinnon, 'Symposium on Unfinished Feminist Business: Some Points Against Postmodernism' (2000) 75 *Chicago-Kent Law Review* 687 at 711.

[4] See eg, J Conaghan, 'Reassessing the Feminist Theoretical Project in Law' (2000) 27 (3) *Journal of Law and Society* 351; R Coward, *Sacred Cows: Is Feminism Relevant to the New Millenium?* (London, Harper Collins, 2000); N Naffine, 'In Praise of Legal Feminism,' above n 2; A Bottomley, 'Shock to Thought: An Encounter (of a Third Kind) with Legal Feminism' (2004) 12 *Feminist Legal Studies* 29; N Naffine, 'Shocking Thoughts: A Reply to Anne Bottomley' (2004) 12 *Feminist Legal Studies* 175; J Richardson, 'Feminist Legal Theory and Practice: Rethinking the Relationship' (2005) 13 *Feminist Legal Studies* 275; J Halley, *Split Decisions: How and Why to Take a Break from Feminism* (Princeton, Princeton University Press, 2006).

[5] N Lacey, *Unspeakable Subjects: Feminist Essays in Legal and Social Theory* (Oxford, Hart Publishing, 1998) at 31.

diminishing the normative condemnation of systematic domination that inspires feminist agitation or allowing the differences that exist between individual women to eclipse the grounds of their commonality. In order to do so, this book not only takes seriously the claims and commitments of the feminist movement, but also subjects its received wisdom to critical scrutiny and moves beyond its confines—drawing, as appropriate, on the work of 'mainstream' analytical jurists, as well as Foucault and Wittgenstein—to re-cast the terrain around key concepts of power, identity and equality within feminist theory.

An Outline of Subsequent Chapters

In Chapter one, then, the key claims and dilemmas of feminist theoretical analysis to date are outlined and opened up to critical scrutiny. Without rigidly pigeon-holing individual theorists into entrenched 'camps' of feminist thinking, discussion here reflects upon the different ways in which feminists have understood the nature of patriarchy—its origins and its perpetuation—and the role of sexual difference therein. The limitations of feminist reform agendas premised on formal equality and assimilation are examined and counter-posed to more sustained demands for structural reform, either in the name of celebrating women's unique perspectives and experiences or in the name of redressing the systematic subordination of women at the hands of men. The merits and demerits of these alternative approaches, typified in the work of Carol Gilligan[6] and Catharine MacKinnon[7] respectively, will be examined, setting the scene for the emergence of a postmodern turn in feminist thinking away from assertions of collective female experiences—be they positive or negative—as well as from mono-causal explanations of patriarchy and utopian agendas for reform.

---

[6] C Gilligan, *In a Different Voice: Psychological Theory and Women's Development* (re-issued Edition) (Cambridge, Harvard University Press, 1993). For further discussion and development of this approach, see also, eg, S Hekman, *Moral Voices, Moral Selves: Carol Gilligan and Feminist Moral Theory* (Cambridge, Polity Press, 1995); C Card (ed) *On Feminist Ethics and Politics* (Lawrence, University of Kansas Press, 1999); V Held (ed) *Justice and Care: Essential Readings in Feminist Ethics* (Boulder, Westview, 1995); M Labaree (ed) *An Ethic of Care: Feminist and Interdisciplinary Perspectives* (New York, Routledge, 1993); S Sevenhuijsen, *Citizenship and the Ethic of Care: Feminist Considerations on Justice, Morality and Politics* (London, Routledge, 1998).

[7] See in particular, C MacKinnon, 'Feminism, Marxism, Method and the State: An Agenda for Theory' (1982) 7 (3) *Signs* 515; C MacKinnon, 'Feminism, Marxism, Method and the State: Toward a Feminist Jurisprudence' (1983) 8 (2) *Signs* 635; C MacKinnon, *Feminism Unmodified: Discourses on Life and Law* (Cambridge, Harvard University Press, 1987); C MacKinnon, *Toward a Feminist Theory of State* (Cambridge, Harvard University Press, 1989); C MacKinnon, *Sex Equality* (New York, Foundation Press, 2001); C MacKinnon, *Women's Lives, Men's Laws* (Cambridge, Harvard University Press, 2005); C MacKinnon, *Are Women Human? And Other International Dialogues* (Cambridge, Harvard University Press, 2006).

Introduction

Without proposing resolution, discussion here highlights the extent to which this postmodern approach not only challenges the conceptions of power and gender identity that have animated many previous feminist accounts but also raises questions over the faith such approaches have often placed in the law and state as providing productive avenues for improvement. In so doing, it sets the stage for the subsequent chapters in which these key points of tension will be re-examined and re-evaluated.

Where the discussion in Chapter one is located at the more general level of feminist theoretical perspectives on the nature of patriarchy and the nature of sexual identity, Chapter two turns attention directly to the legal and the political, focusing specifically on feminist engagement with the liberal state, its methods and ideals. In a context in which much feminist commentary has been critical of the key tenets of the liberal tradition—lamenting in particular its tendency to abstraction and its assumption of individualism, as well as its tendency to mask substantive male privilege under a rhetorical veil that makes claims to neutrality and rationality—discussion here re-examines the contours of this challenge. Having done so, however, this chapter goes on to subject the critique of liberalism itself to scrutiny, highlighting the tendency in too much feminist work to 'lump together' disparate liberal approaches or to 'straw-man' its liberal target by creating a caricatured account that few, if any, individual liberal theorists would themselves advocate or defend. In this light, the recent attempts made by some thinkers—most notably Martha Nussbaum,[8] but also Susan Moller Okin,[9] Nicola Lacey[10] and, to some extent, Drucilla Cornell[11]—to revive engagement with liberal approaches will also be considered. Drawing

---

[8] In particular, M Nussbaum & A Sen, *The Quality of Life* (Oxford, Clarendon Press, 1993); M Nussbaum & J Glover (eds) *Women, Culture and Development* (Oxford, Clarendon Press, 1995); M Nussbaum, 'Capabilities and Human Rights' (1997) 66 *Fordham Law Review* 273; M Nussbaum, *Sex and Social Justice* (Oxford, Oxford University Press, 1999); M Nussbaum, *Women and Human Development: The Capabilities Approach* (Cambridge, Cambridge University Press, 2000); M Nussbaum, 'Rawls and Feminism' in S Freeman (ed) *The Cambridge Companion to Rawls* (Cambridge, Cambridge University Press, 2003); M Nussbaum, *Upheavals of Thought: The Intelligence of Emotions* (Cambridge, Cambridge University Press, 2003); M Nussbaum, *Frontiers of Justice: Disability, Nationality and Species Membership* (Cambridge, Harvard University Press, 2006).

[9] S Okin, 'Reason and Feeling in Thinking About Justice' (1989) 99 (2) *Ethics* 229; S Okin, *Justice, Gender and the Family* (New York, Basic Books, 1989); S Okin, 'Political Liberalism, Justice and Gender' (1994) 105 (1) *Ethics* 23; S Okin, 'Poverty, Well-Being and Gender: What Counts, Who's Heard?' (2003) 31 (3) *Philosophy and Public Affairs* 280; S Okin, 'Justice and Gender: An Unfinihsed Debate' (2004) 72 *Fordham Law Review* 1537.

[10] N Lacey 'Feminist Legal Theory' (1989) *Oxford Journal of Legal Studies* 9; N Lacey, 'Feminist Legal Theory Beyond Neutrality' (1995) *Current Legal Problems* 3; N Lacey, *Unspeakable Subjects: Feminist Essays in Legal and Social Theory*, above n 5.

[11] D Cornell, *At the Heart of Freedom: Feminism, Sex and Equality* (Princeton, Princeton University Press, 1998); D Cornell *Just Cause: Freedom, Identity and Rights* (New York: Rowman & Littlefield, 2000).

An Outline of Subsequent Chapters

on this literature to illustrate the extent to which feminism has too often not only misrepresented liberal ideals but also underestimated the potential value of those ideals to its own critical project, this discussion joins a growing movement in feminism that calls for a cautious re-evaluation of the merits both of liberal ideals of freedom, equality and respect, and of methods premised on abstraction and rationality.

The disillusionment with liberalism voiced by many feminist commentators has led, amongst other things, to a rejection of simple agendas for reform premised either on a pleading for recognition and inclusion by the state or on an invocation of its laws. Prominent voices within the feminist community have called for a de-centering of law and a rejection of legal reform strategies, which frequently involve reliance on rights.[12] To the extent that rights have typically been seen as emblems of liberal thinking, they too have been subjected to criticism by feminists for being too abstract, too individualistic, and only superficially productive as a means to challenge patriarchy. In Chapter three, the merits and demerits of the turn away from legal reform in general, and from rights-based strategies in particular, will be considered. In line with the pattern identified in the preceding chapter whereby a growing feminist movement towards re-evaluating the discarded remnants of liberalism has emerged, here too we can identify a contingent of contemporary feminists who have argued for a reassessment, reconfiguration and redeployment of rights-based analysis.[13] The arguments deployed by these feminists will be considered here and it will be argued that, at least in the current environment, there are a number of compelling reasons in favour of the retention of both legal reforms and rights claims for feminist purposes.

Where discussion in Chapters two and three is focused on defending the legitimacy of feminism's selective appropriation of liberal legal reform strategies, this leaves largely untouched some of the more foundational dilemmas posed by the rise of postmodernism that were outlined in Chapter

---

[12] In particular, C Smart, *Feminism and the Power of Law* (London, Routledge, 1989); C Smart, 'Law's Power, The Sexed Body and Feminist Discourse' (1990) 17 *Journal of Law and Society* 194; M Fineman, 'Challenging Law, Establishing Differences: The Future of Feminist Legal Scholarship' (1990) 42 *Florida Law Review* 25.

[13] See, eg, J Nedelsky, 'Re-conceiving Rights as Relationships' (1993) 1 *Review of Constitutional Studies* 1; M Minow & M Shanley, 'Relational Rights and Responsibilities: Re-visioning the Family in Liberal Political Theory and Law' (1996) 11 (1) *Hypatia* 4; R West, *Re-Imagining Justice: Progressive Interpretations of Formal Equality, Rights and the Rule of Law* (Aldershot, Ashgate Publishing, 2003); E Kiss, 'Alchemy or Fool's Gold? Assessing Feminist Doubts About Rights' in M Shanley and U Narayan (eds) *Reconstructing Political Theory: Feminist Perspectives* (Pennsylvania, University of Pennsylvania Press, 1997); S Palmer, 'Feminism and the Promise of Human Rights: Possibilities and Paradoxes' in S James & S Palmer (eds) *Visible Women: Essays on Feminist Legal Theory and Political Philosophy* (Oxford, Hart Publishing, 2002); S Mullally, *Gender, Culture and Human Rights: Reclaiming Universalism* (Oxford, Hart Publishing, 2006).

Introduction

one. More specifically, key questions regarding how we understand women's predicament under patriarchy, and indeed of whether we can talk at all about the predicament of women (plural) in such (singular) terms, have yet to be fully (re)considered. These questions, the answers to which determine the feasibility and contours of any collective feminist movement mobilised for structural change, will be the primary focus of attention in Chapters four and five.

In Chapter four, the postmodern challenge to mono-causal explanations of patriarchy and grand-scale theories of feminist reform grounded in a revolution in the gender power structure will be examined. Feminists attracted to this postmodern account have often explicitly acknowledged their indebtedness to the work of Michel Foucault,[14] and have argued that his account provides a dramatically different conception of power relations to that implicated within the radical feminist frameworks of Catharine MacKinnon and others. Such theorists have suggested, moreover, that the model thus provided by Foucault is not just different but also preferable in its ability to recognise both the subtlety of the operation of modern power—the multiplicity of the networks and relations that it creates—and the scope for perpetual resistance thereto that it affords even to those who are subjected to power.[15]

Building on this discussion, in this chapter, the key points of divergence between Foucault's conception of power and that of MacKinnon will be re-examined, as—equally importantly—will be their points of convergence. In particular, without denying the many benefits that are afforded by the more nuanced understanding of power that Foucault's work yields, it will be argued here that his own position does not in fact reject the notion of domination that is so central to MacKinnon's feminism 'unmodified'. More specifically, drawing upon Foucault's latter works, this chapter will argue that Foucault's own account was capable not only of acknowledging domination where it existed, but also of condemning it, and of advocating strategies designed to overcome it—without suggesting that power itself can be obliterated. To the extent that this offers an invigorated account of power which avoids the determinism and essentialism associated with

---

[14] See in particular, M Foucault, *The Archaeology of Knowledge* (trans A Sheridan) (New York, Harper Colophon, 1972); M Foucault, *The History of Sexuality Volume I* (London, Penguin 1976); M Foucault, *Discipline and Punish: The Birth of the Prison* (Trams A Sheridan) (London, Vintage 1979); M Foucault, *Power / Knowledge: Selected Interviews and Other Writings 1972—77* (ed C Gordon) (New York, Pantheon, 1980); M Foucault. 'The Ethics of Care of the Self as a Practice of Freedom' (1987) 12 *Philosophy and Social Criticism* 6.

[15] See, eg, J Butler, *Gender Trouble: Feminism and the Subversion of Identity* (London & New York, Routledge, 1990); J Butler, *Bodies That Matter: On the Discursive Limits of Sex* (London & New York, Routledge, 1993); J Butler, *The Psychic Life of Power* (Stanford, Stanford University Press, 1997); J Butler, *Excitable Speech: A Politics of the Performative* (London & New York, Routledge, 1997); J Butler, *Undoing Gender* (London & New York, Routledge, 2004).

An Outline of Subsequent Chapters

MacKinnon's work, without rendering all power relations normatively equivalent or foreclosing the possibility of resistance, it will be argued that it provides a productive vision for feminist theory and practice.

Of course, the value thus afforded to conceiving of power at the structural or macro level also depends on the legitimacy of talking about women (or indeed men) in collective terms. While some feminist commentators have remained staunchly committed to the insistence that women *qua* women share a common essence, experience, predicament or perspective, the postmodern influence in contemporary thinking has led many other feminists to reject this claim. Highlighting the myriad diversity of individual women's lives, and drawing attention to the complex ways in which axes of social stratification such as race, class, sexuality, etc cut across and intersect with gender, these theorists have called for a rejection of essentialism, and with it an abandonment of efforts to identify any quality that may be seen to bind women together as a coherent and mutually identifying collective. In a context in which this has created real difficulties for a feminist politics that is fundamentally grounded in a claim to the uniqueness and commonality of women's position, a number of feminists have sought ways of avoiding this double-bind. In Chapter five, the notion of strategic essentialism associated with Gayatari Spivak[16] and Diana Fuss,[17] as well as the idea of gender as seriality put forward by Iris Young,[18] will be examined. In preference to these models, an approach building on Wittgenstein's idea of 'family resemblance' will be outlined and defended.[19] Re-thinking the unity of the concept of 'woman' as something that does not require rigid definitional limits, it is argued that this approach charts a useful course between radical deconstruction of collective gender identity on the one hand and descriptive essentialism on the other.

Building both on this more nuanced understanding of patriarchal power and the emergent potential for ongoing engagement with women as a (familial) collective concept, discussion in the last chapter returns to the issue of equality that has been so central to feminist theory and politics. Having re-capped on the shortcomings identified with the formal equality approach—which seeks women's inclusion whenever they can prove themselves to be like men—discussion here will examine some of the ways in which contemporary feminists have sought to redeploy equality more effectively. The notion of equality as acceptance associated with Christine

---

[16] G Spivak, *In Other Worlds: Essays in Cultural Politics* (New York, Methuen Press, 1987).

[17] D Fuss, *Essentially Speaking: Feminism, Nature and Difference* (New York, Routledge, 1989).

[18] I Young, 'Gender as Seriality: Thinking about Women as a Social Collective' (1994) 19 (3) *Signs* 713, reproduced in I Young, *Intersecting Voices: Dilemmas of Gender, Political Philosophy and Policy* (Princeton, Princeton University Press, 1997).

[19] L Wittgenstein, *The Philosophical Investigations* (trans G Anscombe) (Oxford, Blackwell, 2000).

Introduction

Littleton will be considered,[20] as will the model of equality as empowerment which can be found in the work of both Catharine MacKinnon and—albeit from a quite different perspective—Davina Cooper.[21] While the benefits offered by this re-engagement with equality will be acknowledged, it will be argued in this chapter that equality is a concept that ultimately cannot escape the comparative. Yet, it is precisely this which renders it ill-suited to achieving the ultimate goal of feminist politics, which is grounded in an absolute commitment to ensuring that women's lives go well, and is best reflected, it will be suggested, in the ideal of respect. Drawing on the work of Derek Parfitt,[22] Harry Frankfurt[23] and Peter Westen,[24] discussion here will draw out the differences and similarities between equality and respect, while at the same time providing an explanation for the tenacity of egalitarianism in the feminist landscape. Under this analysis, feminist calls for equality (and specifically equality of power) will emerge ultimately not as pursuing an end in itself, but rather as a means to the end of securing respect for women and their choices, individually and collectively.

Law and Politics at the Perimeter?

According to Halley, the challenge posed by 'post-feminism' has typically led feminist thinkers to insist on two possible, and polarised, outcomes: 'either feminism is reinstated as the pervasive ground commitment of all left sexuality projects, or it is buried alive'.[25] While this book rejects the claim that society has entered a 'post-feminist age,' it does not trivialise the dilemmas that contemporary feminist theory faces and nor does it support the contention that patriarchy is a monochrome phenomenon. It is not that this book objects in principle to 'spending some time outside (feminism) exploring theories of sexuality, inhabiting realities, and imagining political goals that do not fall within its terms'—far from it.[26] Equally, this book, while setting much of its discussion in the context of the rise of post-modernism, does not suggest that the difficulties feminism faces can be

---

[20] C Littleton, 'Reconstructing Sexual Equality' (1987) 75 *California Law Review* 1279.

[21] D Cooper, 'And You Can't Find Me Nowhere? Relocating Identity and Structure Within Equality Jurisprudence' (2000) 27 (2) *Journal of Law and Society* 249; D Cooper, *Challenging Diversity: Rethinking Equality and the Value of Difference* (Cambridge, Cambridge University Press, 2004).

[22] D Parfitt, 'Equality and Priority' in A Mason (ed) *Ideals of Equality* (Oxford, Blackwell, 1998).

[23] H Frankfurt, 'Equality as a Moral Ideal' (1987) 98 (1) *Ethics* 21; H Frankfurt, 'Equality and Respect' in *Necessity, Volition and Love* (Cambridge, Cambridge University Press, 1999).

[24] P Westen, 'The Empty Idea of Equality' (1982) 95 (3) *Harvard Law Review* 537; P Westen, *Speaking of Equality: An Analysis of the Rhetorical Force of Equality in Moral and Legal Discourse* (Princeton, Princeton University Press, 1990).

[25] J Halley, *Split Decisions: How and Why to Take a Break from Feminism*, above n 4 at 11.

[26] J Halley, *Split Decisions: How and Why to Take a Break from Feminism*, above n 4 at 10.

attributed to postmodernism in any causal way, since, as Halley points out, they are as much caused by the shortcomings (including the 'paranoid structuralism')[27] of pre-existing approaches.

At the same time, though, this book disagrees fundamentally with Halley's conclusion that feminism is sturdy enough to be put at risk, and more specifically, that the dangers of demobilisation, demoralisation, cooption by regressive forces or the legitimation of women's injuries, which she recognises are posed by 'taking a break from feminism', can be tolerated. Despite the unprecedented level of acceptance that feminist analysis now enjoys within academic and policy discourse, serious harms continue to be routinely perpetrated upon women all over the globe. In this context, then, the title of this book is designed to ward against the feminist movement becoming 'a victim of its own success,' allowing its accomplishments either to 'undercut the urgency of further struggle' or to mask the extent to which feminist claims, even in the new millennium, continue to operate too often at the perimeter.[28]

---

[27] J Halley, *Split Decisions: How and Why to Take a Break from Feminism*, above n 4 at 188.
[28] D Rhode, *Speaking of Sex: The Denial of Gender Inequality* (Cambridge, Harvard University Press, 1997) at 14.

1
The Development and Dilemmas of Feminist Theory

Feminism, as a political and theoretical movement, is committed at its most fundamental level to highlighting the historical and contemporary sites of women's exclusion and/or subordination, to exploring the material, structural and ideological conditions that create and perpetuate this condition, and to making demands for their eradication.[1] But, as will become clear over the course of this chapter, the cohesion that underpins and informs this abstract feminist 'mission statement' is often significantly reduced when theorists move on from here to seek out detailed analyses of women's position in specific contexts or to develop concrete strategies for reform.

These feminist contestations are important not only because of the difficult practical dilemmas that they pose, but also because of the theoretical and sociological questions that they raise. At the same time, though, in our rush as commentators to categorise divergent 'camps' of feminist analysis, it is vital that we do not lose sight of the basic and fundamental convictions that continue to animate and unite theorists across these divides. Before moving on to examine the contours of these internal debates in more detail, evaluating their implications for both feminist theory and politics, it is useful, therefore, to take a moment to expressly draw out surviving points of commonality.

Feminist Commonalities

What diverse feminist approaches share is a core belief that the value, integrity and justice of our historical and present day society, and its practices and institutions, is undermined by a pervasive tendency to privilege the interests and experiences of men over women. In turn, this generates a further nexus of unity, reflected in a deeply felt frustration (if not anger) at

---

[1] A similar exposition of the core feminist commitments can be found in the work of several authors: See, eg, C Dalton, 'Where We Stand—Observations on the Situation of Feminist Legal Thought' (1987) 3 *Berkeley Women's Law Journal* 1 at 2; H Wishik, 'To Question Everything: The Inquiries of Feminist Jurisprudence' (1985) 1 *Berkeley Women's Law Journal* 64; D Reaume, 'What's Distinctive About Feminist Analysis of Law?' (1996) 2 *Legal Theory* 265; or J Halley, *Split Decisions: How and Why to Take a Break from Feminism* (Princeton, Princeton University Press, 2006) at 17–18.

the ways in which women have been excluded, marginalised, silenced, misrepresented, patronised, or victimised by public institutions that reflect and represent the perspectives of their fore-*fathers* and their male progeny.

The claim that society, and its institutions, are patriarchal is central to feminist analysis. Significantly, this does not necessarily imply that women and their interests have been ignored. Rather, the claim is often, more accurately, that the processes through which women's interests have been (re)presented, historically and currently, have been mediated (or 'refracted')[2] by male interpretations and understandings. It is argued, moreover, that this process has not been one of neutral translation, but one of at best clumsy misinterpretation and at worst cynical and deliberate misrepresentation.

Throughout history, public discourse has been almost exclusively conducted by men, from their (largely unacknowledged) gendered perspective. The membership of social institutions in the legal, political and economic sphere has been (and continues to be) predominantly male. Conceptions of women's nature and social role have been derived primarily from men's perspectives, rather than women's. This is not to say that these men have been essentially incapable of adopting the perspective of women, or at least of striving to understand it better. But it is to say that, for the most part, they have not done so. Women's identity and appropriate social role has been defined instead in light of men's understanding of what this is, or of what this should be (which invariably reflects what it has always been). Women are identified with domestic and family life, with reproduction and with passive but accessible (hetero)sexuality. In line with this, constructions of 'femininity' have emerged that valorise women's vulnerability and naivety, and these have been complemented by constructions of 'masculinity' that valorise men's chivalry and protectiveness (while, paradoxically and simultaneously, sanctioning selective acts of masculine aggression).

Not only does this generate an understanding of gender or sex difference that boasts the conceptual neatness of a male/female binary, it also maps conveniently on to another dichotomy that helps to legitimate the exclusion of women from areas of life to which they are, apparently by their own nature, not suited. This second binary, which divides the so-called 'public' and 'private' spheres, when propped up by patriarchal logic, has been deployed to re-affirm the connection of women to domesticity and of men to civil and political life. According to feminist critics, it has deterred women's involvement in the terrain of the workplace or politics, even where formal restrictions to participation have been removed, and has frequently rendered women mere spectators to a public forum in which men (mis)represent their interests.

---

[2] L Finley 'Breaking Women's Silence in Law: The Dilemma of the Gendered Nature of Legal Reasoning' (1989) 64 *Notre Dame Law Review* 886.

Thus the boundaries of what constitute the 'public' and the 'private', and the allocation of men and women thereto, although presented under patriarchy as inevitable and natural, emerge, under a feminist analysis, as deeply political and inherently constructed. Those with power in society, mostly men, have relegated sexual and familial situations, in which women are most vulnerable, to the private sphere. Notably, while the actors in this sphere are not free from construction or normative regulation, the realm of the private is one that the law intrudes into with reluctance (at least in liberal societies). This in turn raises difficult questions about the impact of the public/private distinction, and in particular about the assertion underpinning it that preserving privacy helps to ensure equal freedom for everyone.[3]

This recognition of the constructed, partial and politicised nature of these binaries between masculinity and femininity, and between public and private spheres, promotes a critique of prevailing social institutions. The (mutually re-affirming) interaction between these binaries generates not only a kind of experiential incompleteness in public discourse, reflecting the non-representation of women's experiences in terms true to them as authors, but also a circular system in which the internal logic of this partiality is legitimated. As Pateman explains, therefore, it emerges that the construction both of 'sexual difference' itself *and* of 'sexual difference as political difference' are central to the processes of patriarchy.[4]

Amongst the key objectives for feminists seeking to undermine patriarchy, then, is a commitment to redressing this tendency for women's experiences to be 'refracted' through male definitions, thereby systematically excluding them from the political or public realm. To do so, feminists frequently assert the need to 'start from the perspective of women',[5] examining existing doctrines, practices and structures in this light. In consequence, techniques such as 'consciousness-raising' and 'asking the woman question' have been deployed to attend to the ways in which social standards have silenced or distorted the concerns that are more typical of women than of men.[6]

By asking women to articulate their individual experiences and to engage in an interactive process that makes sense of those experiences in light of the narratives of other women, these techniques provide an important foundation for women's collective action. What's more, they play a vital role

---

[3] For an overview of this critique and its feminist implications, see eg, R Gavison, 'Feminism and the Public/Private Distinction' (1992) 45 *Stanford Law Review* 1 or T Higgins, Revisiting the Public-Private Distinction in Feminist Theorising' (2000) 75 *Chicago-Kent Law Review* 847.

[4] C Pateman, *The Sexual Contract* (Cambridge, Polity Press, 1988) at 16.

[5] L Finley, 'The Nature of Domination and the Nature of Women: Reflections on Feminism Unmodified' (1988) 82 *Northwester University Law Review* 352 at 352.

[6] K Bartlett, 'Feminist Legal Methods' (1990) 103 *Harvard Law Review* 829. For discussion of the use and value of specialist feminist legal methods, see eg, C Littleton, 'Feminist Jurisprudence: The Difference Method Makes' (1989) 41 *Stanford Law Review* 751 or M Mossman, 'Feminism and Legal Method: The Difference It Makes' (1986) *Australian Journal of Law and Society* 103.

in fusing the theoretical and political, since it is on the basis of these autobiographical accounts of women's concerns and values that feminism's reformist calls for their inclusion, equality, or empowerment are erected. At the same time, though, it is clear that difficulties arise when it comes to moving beyond these basic ideological foundations and techniques in order to draw conclusions about women's nature, to develop concrete analyses of patriarchy or to devise strategies for woman-centred reform. Amongst feminists, concerns abound, for example, that the female perspective will reflect little more than women's indoctrination in, or negotiation of, patriarchal expectations, or that these techniques will pressurise women to translate their experiences in ways that are politically, rather than experientially, correct. It is the emergence of such cautionary counsel that sets the stage for the internal debates that have marked feminist analysis.

Feminist Contestations

Over the course of the following sections, this chapter will examine the nature of these debates in detail. More specifically, it will reflect upon the different ways in which women's inequality is theorised and addressed in some of the most prominent feminist responses, and will examine the divergent understandings of the nature of patriarchy, and of femininity, reflected therein. Seeking to avoid rigidly 'pigeon-holing' feminist positions, this discussion will be framed in terms of the debates within, rather than the 'schools' of, feminist thinking. While such debates undoubtedly chart the territory in which the 'schools' of feminism (frequently labelled as 'liberal', 'cultural', 'radical' and 'postmodern') have emerged, it is hoped that focusing directly on them will avoid attributing too much commonality to any one 'school' and permit a more complex analysis of those (conceptually rich) theories, which defy simplistic categorisation by adopting variable positions on key debates.

The Assimilation Model

One feminist response to the problem of patriarchy outlined above has been to attribute the prevailing institutions' disinterest in, or distortion of, women's experiences and needs to the inherent partiality of the male perspective. According to this approach, women have been excluded from public discourses and institutions largely because men have set the standards for inclusion, and in so doing have tended (mistakenly but not necessarily maliciously) to presume that women's nature and/or their traditional involvement in domestic life render them ill-suited to participation.

On this account, the roots of patriarchy lie primarily in a failure to include women in public institutions, rather than in any inherent inability of those institutions to recognise or protect women's unique interests and experiences. In turn, therefore, the solution lies in listening to, and taking seriously, women's own evaluation of their capabilities and goals, together with their frustration at being excluded from opportunities that are open to men. Such an approach, it is argued, will build directly on the silenced or misunderstood perspectives of women, drawing attention in particular to their ability to operate alongside (and like) men in the public sphere. This will highlight, to those in power and to others, the unfounded rationale for the exclusion of women that underpins the patriarchal social, legal, economic and political structure, and will in turn bring about reform of that structure in ways that permit scope for women's increased and enduring involvement. With these reforms in place, moreover, it is submitted that women will take advantage of the new opportunities thus afforded for assimilation, participating in public equally with men, and rising to positions of power in which they can counteract the legacy of inequality.

In concrete terms, this approach has often been distilled down to a fundamental commitment that better representation of women's rights and interests can be secured simply by including women in pre-existing structures and institutions. To the extent that women are able to operate in a manner comparable with men, they are to be treated as equal, and accorded the same entitlements. As a corollary to this, disparate treatment of the genders is to be approached with suspicion, pending justification on the basis of a real, and demonstrable, difference. Underpinning this analysis, therefore, are two guiding ideological commitments—firstly, to the basic value of the pre-existing public structures and institutions; and secondly, to a formal conception of equality as requiring treating like case alike. As will become apparent over the course of the following discussion, however, it is these very foundations of the assimilation model that have been the central target of challenge from other feminist responses.

The Case For and Against Assimilation

On first sight, this assimilation model offers an appealing basis for feminist analysis and reform. For one thing, its faith in the ability of pre-existing structures and institutions to support feminist visions permits operation within, rather than outwith, prevailing political discourse. This has a number of strategic advantages in terms of galvanising support for, and decreasing resistance against, a specific cause. In addition, as Wasserstrom points out, this approach's suspicion of group-related differentiation exposes the arbitrariness of many social distinctions, such as those based on gender, that have hitherto been taken to be natural and inevitable, and its reliance on treating like alike affords a clear standard by which to measure the (in)justice of social institutions and practices.[7] What's more, it provides a strong

---

[7] R Wasserstrom, 'On Racism and Sexism' in R Wasserstrom (ed), *Today's Moral Problems* (New York: MacMillan, 1985). Originally printed as 'Racism, Sexism, and Preferential Treatment' (1977) 24 (3) *UCLA Law Review* 581.

political platform and inspirational mentality for feminist campaigning orientated around the simple but powerful assertion that 'anything men can do, women can do'.[8]

Certainly, this conception of equality and the assimilation reform agenda it promotes has been reflected in some high profile strikes against the patriarchal orthodoxy. The case for women's suffrage was, for example, facilitated by feminist campaigns highlighting the similarities between men and women as the basis for securing equal voting rights. Likewise, and in more recent times, women's access to higher education and their inclusion in the workplace have been successfully pursued through an approach that highlights the lack of any justification, grounded in gender difference, for not appointing, remunerating and promoting women on equal terms with men.

But despite the high profile reforms that have been facilitated by this assimilationist logic, many feminists have become increasingly disillusioned with this approach. In particular, they have argued that this approach, by conceiving of instances of sex inequality as 'blips' in an otherwise legitimate system, and by failing to take account of situations in which the genders are not 'similarly situated', fails to bring about the kind of deep-seated reform required to realise substantive gender equality. Central to the concerns raised by these feminist critics is the way in which this approach only permits the receipt of benefits to women who position themselves as akin to men. This demands assimilating women in an unchanged male sphere, or as Young puts it:

> coming into the game after it has already begun, after the rules have been set, and having to prove oneself according to those rules and standards.[9]

As critics point out, however, this does nothing to address the partiality of the status quo, as it has been defined and institutionalised by men. Indeed, this approach's commitment to the fundamental legitimacy of pre-existing public structures and institutions leads it to uncritically sidestep the difficulties thus presented. In so doing, this approach risks endorsing patriarchal values that are endemic in, rather than incidental to, those structures and institutions. It is this tendency to make limited demands on the basic institutions of society that leads Cornell to conclude that this assimilation approach cannot 'bring justice to the millions of women around the world who demand it.'[10]

---

[8] C MacKinnon, 'Reflections on Sex Equality Under Law' in L Kauffman (ed), *American Feminist Thought at Century's End: A Reader* (Oxford, Blackwell, 1993) at 370–1. Originally at (1991) 100 (5) *Yale Law Journal* 1281. See also C MacKinnon, *Sex Equality* (New York, Foundation Press, 2001).

[9] I Young, *Justice and the Politics of Difference* (Princeton, Princeton University Press, 1990) at 164.

[10] D Cornell, *At the Heart of Freedom—Feminism, Sex and Equality* (Princeton, Princeton University Press, 1998) at 5.

The implications of this arguably unduly conservative approach are increasingly apparent when we reflect on the characteristics of the women it is most likely to assist. Indeed, as MacKinnon points out, those who will do best under this approach are those 'who have been able to construct a biography that somewhat approximates the male norm, at least on paper.'[11] Clearly, when those women are denied an opportunity that is open to men, it looks most like injustice or inequality. But, and here is the 'rub' for many other feminist thinkers, the more structurally unequal society gets, the fewer such women will be permitted to exist. This, then, is what can be seen as the paradox of assimilation—the more entrenched gender inequality becomes, the less likely it is that this approach will be able to do anything about it.

Reflecting on these shortcomings has led a number of feminists to conclude that this approach ultimately perpetuates a structure and ideology under which patriarchal partiality appears as neutrality. The assimilation strategy conceals 'the substantive way in which man has become the measure of all things.'[12] Not only does it fail to engage with the glaring question of:

> why (a woman) should . . . have to be the same as a man to get what a man gets simply because he is one?[13]

it also fuels a personally and politically damaging self-denigration amongst women, as their perpetual failure to live up to what is presented to them (by patriarchy and by some feminists) as a neutral standard lends a self-fulfilling air to their disadvantaged social position.[14]

These criticisms of the approach's apparent theoretical naivety and conservatism are bolstered, furthermore, by the existence of social research on the disappointing outcomes of feminist reforms grounded in this assimilation mentality.[15] Extending the franchise to women has not, for example, led to an equal political representation of, or by, women. The most recent figures available indicate that only 25.6 per cent of members of the European Parliament, and 19.5 per cent of the UK House of Commons, are women.[16] What's more, it is by no means clear that the increase which has occurred in the levels of women's involvement in the political sphere over recent decades (which extended, amongst other things, to the election

---

[11] C MacKinnon, *Feminism Unmodified: Discourses on Life and Law* (Cambridge, Harvard University Press, 1987) at 37–8.
[12] C MacKinnon, *Feminism Unmodified: Discourses on Life and Law*, ibid at 34.
[13] C MacKinnon, *Feminism Unmodified: Discourses on Life and Law*, ibid at 37.
[14] I Young, *Justice and the Politics of Difference*, above n 9 at 165.
[15] P Cain, 'Feminism and the Limits of Equality' (1990) 24 *Georgia Law Review* 803; See also, eg, Z Eisenstein, *Feminism and Sexual Equality: Crisis in Liberal America* (New York, Monthly Review Press, 1984); M Fineman, *The Illusion of Equality: The Rhetoric and Reality of Divorce Reform* (Chicago, University of Chicago Press, 1991).
[16] http://www.womenandequalityunit.gov.uk/public_life/parliament.htm.

and re-election of the UK's first female Prime Minister) has in any way generated more 'female-friendly' laws or policies.

Likewise, passing laws demanding equality of opportunity for women has not ensured equality of outcome, even in situations in which women can prove themselves to be 'similarly situated'. In the workplace, the position of men and women remains far from equal. While there has been a steady increase in the representation of women within the British workforce, much of this has occurred in the part-time sector, where rates of pay, and levels of skill involved, tend to be lower.[17] In addition, women who are in full-time employment in the UK currently earn only 83 per cent of the average earnings of their male counterparts.[18] Thus, it seems that this approach, by placing faith in pre-existing institutions and practices and by assuming that inequality can be remedied simply by permitting women's inclusion in the public sphere, may have been unduly optimistic over the translation of formal policy into substantive results.

Beyond this frustration at the model's unfulfilled promise in those contexts in which it has been officially adopted, moreover, many feminists have also expressed concern regarding the limited application of this approach, and in particular over its inability to deal with situations that involve biological and abiding sex difference. The focus of this approach on the similarities between men and women, and its attendant refusal to recognise intrinsic gender differences as affording anything other than a justification for unequal treatment, has, it has been argued, rendered it ill-equipped to deal with those situations in which the sexes are not, and can never be, 'similarly situated'.

The classic example here, of course, is that of pregnancy. Pure biology dictates that men cannot fall pregnant and thus can never experience the peculiar concerns that arise from the prospect of conceiving, the practice of being pregnant, or the consequences of childbirth. Yet, the attendant questions of reproductive autonomy, maternity leave and the availability of flexible work-family policies are ones that affect most, if not all, women in some way. Despite this, the assimilation model has a 'paradigm trauma'[19] when it encounters pregnancy—here is a situation in which a demonstrable gender difference exists, and in which, therefore, there can be no call for equal treatment on the basis of women's ability to operate like men. But this has left feminists who support assimilation with little choice but

---

[17] The increase in women's full-time employment between 1971 to 1995 was only 3%, compared to an increase of 75% in part-time employment: S Walby, *Gender Transformations* (London, Routledge, 1997) at 31–2.

[18] Equal Opportunity Commission, 2006: *Facts About Women and Men in Great Britain* at http://www.eoc.org.uk/pdf/facts_about_GB_2006.pdf. See also D Grimshaw and J Rubery, *The Gender Pay Gap: A Research Review* (Manchester, Equal Opportunities Commission, 2001) at 3.

[19] C MacKinnon, *Feminism Unmodified: Discourses on Life and Law*, above n 11 at 36.

to either 'minimise' the issue of pregnancy and its impact on women's (in)equality as 'unimportant' or to construct it in a manner akin to a male experience (analogising it to an illness, for example).[20] The difficulty with both strategies, of course, is that they fail to pay attention to what many see as the centrality of childbearing and childrearing, both to women's experiences and values, and to the structure of patriarchal society itself.

It is not only in regard to the specific issue of pregnancy, moreover, that this problem arises. Indeed, the failure of this approach to recognise the existence of any kind of structural gender inequality beyond biology is equally problematic. In particular, it has been argued that this approach, by adopting a largely formal conception of equality and an assimilation mindset to securing women's inclusion, fails to pay enough attention to the engrained effects of cultural pressure and social conditioning. In so doing, it fails to recognise the extent to which stereotypes operating upon women in the so-called private sphere, for example regarding woman's 'natural' role as maternal caregiver, can impact negatively upon her sense of the appropriateness or desirability of involvement in the workplace, or in the public sphere more broadly.

A study conducted for *The Guardian* newspaper in 1997 found, for example, that women spent almost twice as long on household chores as men (even when they were in full-time employment);[21] yet studies also indicate that this kind of situation is seen as satisfactory and even 'natural' by 80 per cent of women.[22] To the extent that such tensions exist between the assimilation model's rhetoric of equal opportunity and women's existential reality of unequal social roles, it is perhaps unsurprising that the practical outcomes of this approach have not been as significant as expected, even in those (public) areas in which no prima facie barriers to women's participation remain.

The Two Faces of Assimilation

To the extent that such criticisms of the assimilation approach, in particular those related to its limited application, give ground for legitimate feminist concern, it is worth noting that there are two possible models for assimilation—which Young identifies as conformist and transformational.[23] In the approach discussed thus far, there is no doubt that a more conformist mindset has prevailed, according to which the aim is primarily to secure women's inclusion alongside men on a 'level playing field' of opportunity.

---

[20] C MacKinnon, 'Reflections on Sex Equality Under Law' in L Kauffman (ed), *American Feminist Thought at Century's End: A Reader*, above n 8 at 370–1.

[21] *The Guardian*, 7 Oct 1997—See N Charles, *Gender in Modern Britain* (Oxford, Oxford University Press, 2002) at 50.

[22] See, eg, J Martins and C Roberts, *Women and Employment: A Lifetime Perspective* (London, Department of Employment/OPCS, 1984).

[23] I Young, *Justice and the Politics of Difference*, above n 9 at 165.

This requires treating women *as if* they were men, in a context in which the standard for inclusion nonetheless purports to be neutral or androgynous.

As the discussion in the previous section highlights, however, a number of difficulties have been identified with this approach, both at the theoretical and practical level. Despite this, however, some feminists have argued that there remains scope for resurrecting the ideal of assimilation, in particular by supplanting or supplementing this conformist version with a transformational reform agenda. The merits and demerits of this dual approach, and of the new genre of transformational assimilation that thereby emerges, will be discussed in detail over the course of this section.

Like its conformist counterpart, transformational assimilation seeks to render women equal in the world without recourse to radical reconstruction. As such, it offers no fundamental critique of the rhetoric or ideological claims to neutrality professed by pre-existing social institutions and practices, and casts no doubt on their potential to represent and protect, fully and fairly, women's interests. That said, however, it accepts that these institutions and practices have fallen short of their own standards in their treatment of particular marginalised groups. Thus, the aim of both these genres of assimilation is ultimately the same, ie to make irrelevant group differences as unimportant in reality as the prevailing institutional rhetoric purports them to be (without changing those institutions).[24] But while the conformist approach has been criticised for its blindness to the different starting positions from which men and women 'enter the game' and for its exclusive focus on a (limited) conception of equality, which demands simply that likes are treated alike, the transformational approach acknowledges the need for a careful consideration of background context and a re-structuring of the treatment afforded to those who are deemed to be different.

Unlike its conformist counterpart, therefore, this approach takes seriously the engrained and abiding differences that it encounters between marginalised and dominant groups, and sees the enterprise of redressing the impact of those differences on securing entitlements or recognition as central to achieving genuine equality. In concrete terms, this means that where the conformist approach is limited to situations of sameness between the genders, the transformational approach can support regimes of special protection or affirmative action dealing with situations of gender difference.

For a number of feminists, many of whom have been reluctant to reject assimilation in favour of a more radical critique of prevailing norms, this transformational approach facilitates a social justice that lives up to its rhetoric of equal treatment for all. The transformational approach, by permitting selective recognition of, and compensation for, sexual difference, has the potential to be more sensitive to context than its conformist counterpart. In line with this transformational spirit, a number of feminists have,

---

[24] I Young, *Justice and the Politics of Difference*, above n 9 at 165–6.

therefore, campaigned for programmes of 'special rights' for women, to be deployed alongside the conformist (or 'sameness') model in situations where sexual difference cannot be ignored or reasoned away without injustice or misrepresentation.

Certainly, this supplementation of the conformist approach with a transformational model of assimilation, which offers special protection measures to respond to sexual difference, has the potential to deal with the feminist dilemma over pregnancy discussed above. At the same time, though, the more general wisdom or utility of this move is debatable. In particular, by accepting uncritically those questions that seek to arrive at a definitive list of sexual differences, it has been argued that this approach allows the forum for feminist activism to become inappropriately narrowed.[25] Thus, the problem with the transformational approach lies in its failure to move beyond the project of assimilation. Indeed, as Scales puts it, this kind of incorporation mentality, which claims that women can achieve equality by simply grafting their voices (where distinctive from men's) onto the pre-existing system via a programme of special rights:

> presumes that we can whip the problem of social inequality by adding yet another prong to the already multi-pronged legal tests.[26]

This, however, continues to leave unaddressed many of the concerns that feminists have expressed regarding the entrenched patriarchal values endemic within the prevailing social, legal, political and economic structure. Thus, the problem with transformational assimilation, just as much as conformist assimilation, is that it assumes that 'male supremacy is simply a random collection of irrationalities in an otherwise rational coexistence,'[27] despite the claims of other feminists to the existence of insidious and organised patriarchal bias.

Related to this, moreover, it can also be argued that by narrowing the focus of analysis in this way, this transformational approach re-affirms the tenacity of the male norm as the measuring rod for social, political, economic and legal entitlement. As Minow explains, the concept of difference is itself a relational one—since I am no more different from you than you are from me, the concept of difference only makes sense when invoked as a comparison.[28] What is left crucially unarticulated in the transformational approach, however, is the reality that the benchmark for comparison remains, as in conformism, a male one. Despite its acknowledgement that

---

[25] A Scales, 'The Emergence of a Feminist Jurisprudence' (1986) 95 *Yale Law Journal* 1373.
[26] A Scales, 'The Emergence of a Feminist Jurisprudence', *ibid* at 1382.
[27] A Scales, 'The Emergence of a Feminist Jurisprudence', *ibid* at 1382.
[28] M Minow, 'Justice Engendered' (1987) 101 *Harvard Law Review* 10. See also M Minow, *Making All the Difference—Inclusion, Exclusion and American Law* (Itacha, Cornell University Press, 1990).

some differences between men and women cannot be ignored, the transformational approach continues to adopt a largely uncritical perspective, which is too often blind to the fact that the viewpoint from which the extent and relevance of those differences is determined is male-defined.[29] It is women's differences from men that need to be accommodated and protected through special regimes, rather than men's differences from women. Thus, the male perspective remains the unquestioned, but silent, norm and the female perspective remains the deviation. As MacKinnon puts it, while the gender neutrality of the conformist approach consciously reflects the male standard and the special protection rule of the transformational approach consciously reflects the female, in the final analysis 'masculinity, or maleness, is the referent for both.'[30]

These difficulties with the transformational approach have led some feminist commentators to return to an exclusive reliance on the conformist genre of assimilation. As Williams argues, feminists pursuing the goal of assimilation may ultimately find themselves faced with an uncomfortable choice between *either* pursuing equality on the basis of similarity between the sexes *or* pursuing special treatment on the basis of difference. Aware that, as the criticisms of the transformational approach have illustrated, 'difference' in this context will typically be constructed and interpreted to mean *women's* difference,[31] Williams argues that, notwithstanding its own problems, the conformist model, with its focus on securing women's inclusion on the basis of their sameness to men, remains preferable.

But in a context in which, as we have seen, many feminists are equally dissatisfied with the conformist and transformational approaches, it may be that it would in fact be better to abandon the call to assimilation altogether. Indeed, despite the formal and symbolic successes that have been achieved by politicising the exclusion of 'similarly situated' women from the public sphere, it might credibly be argued that a more critical engagement with prevailing institutions and practices is required in order to bring about substantive equality. What is needed, in the words of Fineman, is a theory that does more than 'merely open doors to institutions designed with men in mind.'[32]

For many feminists, developing this kind of approach demands doing more than simply acknowledging and overcoming instances of real gender difference where they exists (as in the transformational approach). Indeed,

---

[29] M Minow, 'Justice Engendered', *ibid* 28.

[30] C MacKinnon, *Feminism Unmodified: Discourses on Life and Law*, above n 11 at 34.

[31] W Williams, 'First Generation' (1989) *University of Chicago Legal Forum* 99; See also W Williams, 'The Equality Crisis: Some Reflections on Culture, Courts and Feminism' (1982) 7 *Women's Rights Law Reporter* 175.

[32] M Fineman, 'Feminist Theory and Law' (1995) 18 *Harvard Journal of Law and Public Policy* 349 at 352. See also G Brock & S James (eds) *Beyond Equality and Difference* (London, Routledge, 1992).

it requires replacing altogether the prevailing conception of this difference as a deviation to be compensated, with a vision of it as a specificity to be celebrated. While both the conformist and transformational variants of assimilation have, in their different ways, denied that sexual difference can itself be positive or desirable,[33] this alternative approach seeks to consciously embrace women's difference from men, celebrating the unique perspective that it yields and calling for reform (rather than mere extension) of pre-existing practices and institutions in this light. Over the course of the next section, we will examine the parameters, merits and demerits of this approach in more detail.

Celebrating Difference

At the centre of this shift in feminist thinking towards the celebration, rather than mere toleration or compensation, of women's difference from men is the work of developmental psychologist Carol Gilligan.[34] The primary motivation behind Gilligan's work, published in the early 1980s, was to disprove the assertion, originating in the work of Lawrence Kohlberg,[35] that women's moral development arrests at an earlier stage than men's, reflected in the female tendency to be less adept at reasoning via abstract rules and universal principles. Gilligan's work sought to challenge this claim by questioning its implicit assumptions about the context of completed moral development. Conducting a series of experiments on children, Gilligan observed that young boys and girls do in fact approach dilemmas requiring moral reasoning in distinctive ways. Little boys tend to reason via an 'ethic of justice', which prioritises abstraction, impartiality, detachment, rights and autonomy. By contrast, little girls tend to reason via an 'ethic of care', which prioritises the concrete, partiality, connection, relationships and responsibility. On the basis of this finding, Gilligan asserted that female moral reasoning is *different*, but not deficient. She called on prevailing social structures to embrace this ethic of care alongside the dominant ethic of justice, arguing that its values of community, nurturance and responsibility are at least as worthy of protection as autonomy, self-reliance and individuation.

This empirical finding from Gilligan, and the normative assertion that she derived from it, has had a profound influence on feminist thinking. It has long-since been acknowledged by many feminists that women stand in a different relation to others than do men. As West has pointed out, for example, women are both materially and existentially connected to, rather than separate from, the rest of human life, and while the welcomeness of this may

---

[33] I Young, *Justice and the Politics of Difference*, above n 9 at 165–6.
[34] C Gilligan, *In a Different Voice: Psychological Theory and Women's Development* (Cambridge, Harvard University Press, 1993).
[35] L Kohlberg, *The Philosophy of Moral Development* (San Francisco, Harper & Row, 1981).

vary as between individual women, it is a fact that uniquely frames all women's experiences and perspectives.[36] Equally, though, this is a peculiar reality which has been ignored, silenced or denigrated by the prevailing patriarchal frameworks and institutions. Women, unlike men, become pregnant, thereby assuming an intimate connection with their foetus that is imprinted through the process of gestation and childbirth. And thereafter, it is women, rather than men, who assume the dominant share of caring work in relation to the child, and indeed in relation to other dependents. As Chodorow asserts, this reality (of women's mothering) is central to the sexual division of labour and has a profound effect 'on women's lives, on ideology about women, on the reproduction of masculinity and sexual inequality.'[37] Indeed, O'Brien argues that so profound is this connection through pregnancy that it is men's alienation from it that sparks patriarchy itself.[38]

This claim that the roots of patriarchy lie in a conscious and structured marginalisation and devaluing of women's unique experiences has received considerable support. Unlike the assimilation model discussed in the previous section, feminists who adopt this approach identify a deliberate and sinister aspect to the historical and present-day exclusion of women from prevailing (patriarchal) structures. The affirmation of typically male experiences and interests as being of greater value than their female counterparts emerges as more than an innocent oversight stemming from the partiality of the male perspective. It results from a complex and engrained process through which female concerns and modes of thinking are not only overlooked but belittled on the basis that they are inadequate or inappropriate, and certainly insufficient to grant access to the sites of social power. Thus, feminist reform, if it is to bring about equality, must concentrate not only on affording the opportunity for women's inclusion in the institutions of public life, but also on radically re-imagining those institutions and the values that underpin them.

The Case For and Against Celebrating Difference

Building on the feminist commitment to listen to, and take seriously, the ways in which women express their concerns and priorities, the approach inspired by Gilligan's work has generated a strand of 'relational' feminist thinking. This approach not only recognises the values associated with women, seeking to incorporate them in pre-existing structures, but also celebrates those values, demanding reform of guiding institutions in their light. As Rhode puts it, it insists 'that these values *be* valued.'[39]

---

[36] R West, 'Jurisprudence and Gender' (1988) 55 *University of Chicago Law Review* 1.

[37] N Chodorow, *The Reproduction of Mothering: Psychoanalysis and the Sociology of Gender* (Berkeley, University of California Press, 1978) at 11.

[38] M O'Brien, *The Politics of Reproduction* (London, Routledge & Kegan Paul, 1981).

[39] D Rhode, *Justice and Gender* (Cambridge, Harvard University Press, 1989) at 309.

The objective, then, is not simply to include women, or to celebrate their experiences, but rather, in so doing, to *change* men's experiences and to bring about reform in the contexts of work, family and politics. Thus, this approach can be seen to boast a number of potential advantages over its assimilation alternative. Most obviously, it 'turns the tables' on a patriarchal logic which has denigrated the concerns more typical of women and builds directly on the foundation of women's own experiences to demand that these be valued on their own terms. In so doing, it symbolically and practically reclaims the feminine as a site of power rather than oppression. And this in turn promotes a clear agenda for political reform centred around restructuring social life to accord value to the feminine and to the modes of reasoning associated with it.

Despite the considerable appeal of this approach, however, a number of concerns can be, and have been, raised. For one thing, the empirical merits of the claim that all (or even most) women reason in a different voice, and more specifically in the voice of care, has been questioned. It is highly debatable whether all women do in fact bear the characteristics of relational thinking—care, self-sacrifice, nurture. In addition, it is striking that Gilligan's own conclusions are drawn from a very small and potentially unrepresentative sample. Notably, in fact, subsequent psychologists who have conducted similar experiments have questioned how different the voices of the genders really are.[40] To this extent, then, it may be that the 'jury is still out' on the question of whether a direct correspondence between women and the ethic of care can be sustained, despite the fact that the very justification for relational thinking lies in the claim that it affirms women's own perspective, hitherto silenced by patriarchy.[41]

Of course, it could perhaps be reasonably argued that, in the absence of cast iron empirical evidence discounting the assertion that women reason via an ethic of care, there are still good grounds to suspect that women will, on the whole, experience and reason about things in a different way from men. Certainly, it seems feasible to expect that both men's and women's shared childhood experience of being under the primary protection of women would have some impact upon our (adult) moral orientation,[42] as would the vastly greater amount of child-raising and home-keeping in which women are typically engaged.[43] But to the extent that this is true, it begs another (arguably more problematic) question, namely can or should we take this voice at face value?

---

[40] D Rhode, *Justice and Gender*, *ibid* at 309–10.

[41] R West, *Caring for Justice* (New York, New York University Press, 1997) at 18.

[42] R West, *Caring for Justice*, *ibid*. See also N Chodorow, *The Reproduction of Mothering*, above n 37.

[43] C Gilligan, 'Reply to Critics' in M Larrabee (ed), *An Ethic of Care: Feminist and Interdisciplinary Perspectives* (New York & London, Routledge, 1993) at 207.

As Rhode acknowledges, any resonance between the ethic of care and the voice of women may, at least in part, 'be the product of internalised gender stereotypes that have contributed to women's disadvantage.'[44] Thus, it has been argued that the relational approach risks affirming that which has distinguished women from men, without questioning the extent to which those characteristics, and their consequences, are 'really' women's own, rather than something attributed to women by a self-serving male supremacy. More specifically, in support of this concern, MacKinnon has highlighted the possibility that 'women value care because men have valued us according to the care we give them' and that 'women think in relational terms because our existence is defined in relation to men.'[45] In this light, it would seem that for women to follow the call of relational feminism, affirming their difference from men as if this provides the key to gender equality, could prove counter-productive.

Even if these epistemological and empirical concerns regarding the legitimacy of women's relational voice can be met, moreover, a number of feminists have also identified the existence of strategic grounds for concern implicated in this relational approach. Although it is true that this approach sets out to operate more subversively than assimilation, it is not altogether clear whether simply celebrating women's distinctiveness, and adding the female voice of care as a supplement to the male voice of justice, is sufficient to bring about the kind of substantial reforms required to ensure gender equality. For one thing, this approach assumes a one-way projection of women's influence. In other words, it assumes that women's participation will reshape the structure and substance of public decision-making whilst ignoring the possibility that involvement in this sphere may operate to modify or distort women's voice itself.[46] Thus, it is argued that this relational approach may prove to be just as overly-optimistic, and ultimately conservative, as the assimilation model it rejects.

What's more, there is a danger that the methods and rhetoric of the relational approach will, in the final analysis, undermine the official demand for women's greater involvement. After all, Gilligan's description of gender difference can, in some senses at least, be read simply as an updated version of the Victorian ideology of domesticity, according to which women's abdication from the public sphere is painted as a 'virtue', valorisation of which facilitates their economic and social marginalisation.[47] In this light, then, the relational approach does nothing necessarily to challenge the relegation of women to the private sphere, a process which, as we have seen, has been

---

[44] D Rhode, *Justice and Gender*, above n 39 at 310.

[45] C MacKinnon, *Feminism Unmodified: Discourses on Life and Law*, above n 11 at 39.

[46] For further discussion of this concern, see D Rhode, *Justice and Gender*, above n 39 at 311.

[47] J Williams, 'Deconstructing Gender' (1989) 87 *Michigan Law Review* 797.

identified by many feminists as central to patriarchal domination. Drawing on this concern, Abrams has noted the ways in which this mentality may be used 'to celebrate the rejection of the workplace by women who leave their jobs to care for their children.'[48] Similarly, O'Neill has questioned the ability of this approach to say or do anything about the political and economic contexts of women's lives, concluding that in the final analysis:

> an ethics of caring and relationships will be adequate only if we assume lives that are confined to the nursery or the boudoir.[49]

Significantly, the concern here is not only that this will leave women and their unique perspective firmly entrenched in the private sphere, but also that the polarity which this approach encourages between the virtues of justice and care may in itself render those women more vulnerable to abuse. By sidelining the significance of justice within feminist ethics, this relational approach risks surrendering women to an ever-encroaching dictate to care for others. Not only does this fail to acknowledge the extent to which justice and care, rights and responsibilities, are in themselves ideologically and practically inter-dependent, it also results in an ethical programme that is ill-equipped to respond to important questions about the distribution of care—Whom should we care for? How much should we care for them? And perhaps most importantly, should we care for others at the expense of caring for ourselves?[50] Without a conception of justice as located within, rather than opposed to, care, the relational approach threatens to valorise self-sacrifice as the vocation of femininity. But this is problematic. As Houston puts it:

> when I reflect on the history of women I realise how much our caring has nurtured and empowered others. I see how good it has been, for others. However, I also see how terribly costly it has been for women.[51]

Thus, this relational approach, like the assimilation approach discussed above, has attracted considerable criticism from feminists who nonetheless remain committed to the core project of highlighting, challenging and undermining the existence of patriarchy. What generates these criticisms is competing conceptions of the origins of patriarchy, of the 'true' nature of femininity, and of the most desirable and productive route to reform. The relational approach, by demanding reform of, rather than inclusion in, pre-existing institutions and structures, represents a step towards the kind

---

[48] K Abrams, 'Ideology and Women's Choices' (1990) 24 *Georgia Law Review* 761 at 765–6.

[49] O O'Neill, Friends of Difference (1989) 11 (7) *London Review of Books* 20.

[50] E Kiss, 'Justice', in A Jaggar and I Young (eds), *A Companion to Feminist Philosophy* (Oxford, Blackwell Publishing, 2000) at 491.

[51] B Houston, 'Prolegomena to Future Caring' in M Brabeck (ed) *Who Cares?: Theory, Research and Educational Implications of the Ethic of Care* (New York, Praeger, 1989). Quoted in R Rhode, *Theoretical Perspectives on Sexual Difference* (New Haven, Yale University Press, 1990) at 171.

of critical analysis, the absence of which in the assimilation model was lamented. But its valorisation of the feminine voice that it finds under patriarchy, coupled with its assumption that equality can be achieved by infusing an ethic of care into public life, without deconstructing the prevailing ethic of justice, have been the subject of concern. In the following section, we will turn to another possible response to the problems of patriarchy; a response that seeks to overcome some of these difficulties.

The Rise of Dominance

Animated both by the failure of reforms premised on assimilation (conformist or transformational) to move beyond an unstated reliance on masculinity as the benchmark for entitlement, and by the tendency of the relational approach to inappropriately valorise a femininity that is derived from, and supportive of, patriarchy, a number of feminist commentators have sought out more radical ways of conceptualising the causes of, and strategies for combating, gender inequality. Influenced by Marxist analyses of power, domination and hegemony, this response has conceived of the problem of patriarchy as stemming not so much from the inadvertent partiality of the male perspective, nor even from the deliberate denigration of the feminine as such, but rather from the resolute determination of men as a group to maintain a position of power and privilege over women, through any means.

Under this account, patriarchy emerges as a problem of male dominance, rather than a question of women's sameness to or difference from men.[52] Indeed, as MacKinnon puts it, 'difference is the velvet glove on the iron fist of domination.'[53] In other words, while the assimilation and relational approaches have, in their different ways, identified gender difference first and assumed that the social power disparities of patriarchy are built on top of those differences, this approach inverts that dynamic, assuming that domination was established first, with gender differences only subsequently being constructed as significant in order to justify and maintain this pattern of patriarchal power.[54] In this light, the question of whether female differ-

---

[52] As MacKinnon puts it, 'in rape crisis centres, battered women's shelters, incest support groups, and organisations of former prostitutes against prostitution, for example, nobody experiences anything so taxonomic and generic and neutral and analytic and abstract and empty as sameness and difference. . . . Their screams of pain and terror are not generally valorised as a "different voice". Their difference lies in being on the bottom.' C MacKinnon, *Toward a Feminist Theory of State* (Cambridge, Harvard University Press, 1989) at 219. For further discussion of this approach, see also C MacKinnon, 'Feminism, Marxism, Method and the State: An Agenda for Theory' (1982) 7 (3) *Signs* 515; 'Feminism, Marxism, Method and the State: Toward a Feminist Jurisprudence' (1983) 8 (2) *Signs* 635.

[53] C MacKinnon, *Toward a Feminist Theory of State*, ibid at 219.

[54] As MacKinnon puts it, 'differences are inequality's post hoc excuse, its conclusory artefact, its outcome presented as its origin, the damage that is pointed to as the justification for doing the damage after the damage has been done, the distinctions that perception is socially

ence is affirmed or denied is irrelevant, since what matters is the way in which those differences are defined by relationships of power; and feminist approaches (such as those above) which fail to acknowledge this ultimately 'neutralise, rationalise, and cover disparities of power, even as they appear to criticise or problematise them.'[55]

What is significant in this approach, then, is not just the emphasis on domination rather than difference as the root cause of gender inequality, but also the extent to which the conception of patriarchy which emerges out of this account is so all-embracing. Instances of inequality are no longer 'blips' in an otherwise legitimate system, but part of a complex, pervasive network that infiltrates every aspect of our gendered existence. As MacKinnon explains:

> sex inequality questions are questions of systematic domination, of male supremacy, which is not at all abstract and anything but a mistake.[56]

Thus, this approach builds upon the felt experiences of powerlessness and marginalisation expressed by individual women to posit the existence of a collective condition of oppression. Apparently central to the maintenance of this oppression, moreover, is the regulation of female sexuality, and more specifically, of men's access to that sexuality. Indeed, as MacKinnon explains, 'sexuality is to feminism what work is to Marxism: that which is most one's own, yet most taken away.'[57] Social relations of gender are created around, and expressive of, notions of female sexuality that have been constructed and imposed by patriarchy, and yet these constructions have come to assume an air of inevitability, 'creating the social beings we know as men and women, as their relations create society.'[58]

Allied to this conception of the pervasiveness of patriarchal power, therefore, is an awareness of the subtlety of its operation: male dominance is 'metaphysically perfect.'[59] The patriarchal logic that constructs and disempowers women infiltrates deeply and deviously into the structures and institutions that regulate social life. As a result, inclusion within, or addition to, these structures and institutions will never be sufficient to bring about true gender equality. On the contrary, a radical reform is required which can only be brought about through a revolution in the arrangements of gender power. The fact that gender inequality is grounded in domination and subordination means that feminism must seek the empowerment of women, on their own terms, free of oppression and false consciousness. Accordingly,

organised to notice because inequality gives them consequences for social power'—C MacKinnon, *Feminism Unmodified: Discourses on Life and Law*, above n 11 at 8.

[55] C MacKinnon, *Toward a Feminist Theory of State*, above n 52 at 219.
[56] C MacKinnon, *Feminism Unmodified: Discourses on Life and Law*, above n 11 at 42.
[57] C MacKinnon, *Toward a Feminist Theory of State*, above n 52 at 3.
[58] C MacKinnon, *Toward a Feminist Theory of State*, above n 52 at 3.
[59] C MacKinnon, *Toward a Feminist Theory of State*, above n 52 at 116–7.

improvement in the conditions of women's daily lives emerges only when women seize power from men, when they regain control over the meaning, access to and regulation of their sexuality, and when they expose the partiality of patriarchal norms and institutions.

The Case For and Against Dominance

This emerging understanding of patriarchy as dominance clearly provides a powerful impetus for feminist political activism and reform. Certainly, in resisting the temptation towards strategically attractive, but arguably short-sighted, assimilation, it offers a 'productive counterpoint which generates further feminist discourses.'[60] In addition, the suggestion here that:

> discrimination law, if it is going to improve the social position of women, must also be fundamentally concerned with power differentials[61]

has been well-received. Cornell, for example, has specifically commended this approach for exposing the reality that reforms designed to secure gender equality will inevitably fail if they neglect questions of how female sexual identity is constructed through a gender hierarchy in which women are subordinate to men.[62] In addition, the insistence that feminism cannot generate a theory of equality that envisions the end of domination:

> without confronting the relationship between sex and sexuality, as these have become constitutive of the gender identity imposed upon women by patriarchy

has been widely supported by other feminist thinkers.[63]

Despite this, however, the dominance approach has also been the subject of considerable criticism. For one thing, the claim that women are universally and essentially victimised by men, although central to this approach, is empirically questionable. Not only do feminists who adopt this dominance model rarely provide evidence which would support the generalisability that they assert for this claim, they also ignore the experiences of many women who derive positive value from their interaction with men, and who do not regard their intimate heterosexual relations as premised on a domination-subordination dynamic. Those who seek to defend this analysis may, of course, attribute these divergent expressions of femininity to patriarchal 'false-consciousness', but as Abrams observes, to do so would be to suggest knowledge about the 'truth' of femininity that can be determined without attention to women's own accounts—not only does this replicate the patriarchal tendency to silence women's expressed perspectives, it also runs

---

[60] C Smart, *Feminism and the Power of Law* (London & New York, Routledge, 1989) at 72.
[61] L Finley, 'The Nature of Domination and the Nature of Women: Reflections on Feminism Unmodified', above n 5 at 358.
[62] D Cornell, 'Sexual Difference, the Feminine and Equivalency (1991) 100 *Yale Law Review* 2247.
[63] D Cornell, 'Sexual Difference, the Feminine and Equivalency', *ibid* at 2248.

counter to the feminist commitment to take seriously the standpoint and narratives of individual women.[64] In addition, moreover, it adopts too narrow a view of privilege, assuming that the experience of being a 'victim' is the only one that gives access to 'truth'.[65]

Related to this concern about the legitimacy of the claim that all women are essentially oppressed is a specific concern about the attendant suggestion that the extent of women's oppression is constant across time and culture. Indeed, this approach has been heavily criticised by a number of commentators who note its failure to pay attention to the existence of power disparities *between* women, often as a result of the intersection of other axes of social stratification (such as race, class, or sexual orientation). While talking about women in collective terms assists in the development of monocausal and grand-scale theories of gender oppression, critics argue that it obscures important differences among women, ignoring the entirely plausible possibility that women are not all subordinate to men in the same way, or to the same degree. As Crenshaw puts it, feminists adopting this approach too often:

> ignore how their own race functions to mitigate some aspects of sexism, and moreover, how it often privileges them over, and contributes to, the domination of other women.[66]

Applying this insight, critics have drawn attention to the ways in which power relations grounded on race intersect with gender relations, creating a more complex structure within which some (black) women find themselves oppressed at the hands of other (white) women, or at least find themselves less empowered.[67]

In addition, moreover, this claim within the dominance approach that the common experience of women under current patriarchal conditions is one of oppression faces criticism on account of its determinism, and in particular its failure to provide any scope for transcending the status of perpetual victim. This approach apparently assumes that patriarchal ideology affects women's perspectives and decisions in consistent and predictable ways—women absorb its dictates wholesale, as blank sheets on which patriarchal scripts can be written. As MacKinnon puts it, 'the perspective from the male standpoint enforces women's definition, encircles her body, circumlocutes

---

[64] K Abrams, 'Ideology and Women's Choices' above n 48 at 770. See also K Bartlett, 'MacKinnon's Feminism: Power on Whose Terms?' (1987) 75 *California Law Review* 1559.

[65] K Bartlett, 'Feminist Legal Methods' above n 6.

[66] K Crenshaw, 'Demarginalising the Intersectionality of Race and Sex: A Black Feminist Critique of Antidiscrimination Doctrine, Feminist Theory and Antiracist Politics' in A Phillips (ed), *Feminism and Politics* (Oxford, Oxford University Press, 1998) at 326–7.

[67] A Harris, 'Race and Essentialism in Feminist Legal Theory' (1990) 42 *Stanford Law Review* 581. See also, M Mahoney, 'Whiteness and Women, In Practice and Theory: A Reply to Catharine MacKinnon' (1993) 5 *Yale Journal of Law and Feminism* 217.

her speech and describes her life.'[68] Not only is this kind of 'ideologically determinist' approach questionable on its own terms,[69] but it also denies any positive value in the attributes that one might associate with conventional femininity.[70] The women who populate this approach are always victims, always constructed by men, always lacking a sexual identity beyond patriarchy. But as Cornell points out, this leaves the dominance approach in danger of 'reifying the historical experience of a group of women into a "second nature" that is then attributed to all women.'[71] Even if women's sexual difference has been the terrain upon which gender power relations have been scripted, this does not mean that this is the only way in which sexual difference could be used or deployed. It is imperative, therefore, that feminists focus not only on what 'woman' is under current conditions, but also on what 'woman' would be if she had the space to re-imagine her femininity. While locating that space, and valorising what emerges from it, does not require us to deny male power, it does require us to make sure that we avoid the temptation inherent in the dominance approach to insist 'that we are only what men have made us to be.'[72]

This overly-deterministic understanding of the operation of patriarchy is problematic, moreover, not only in relation to its conception of women, but also in relation to its conception of men. After all, as Rhode points out, patriarchy cannot be understood solely as an instrument of men's interests, since, as a threshold matter, what constitutes those interests is not self-evident.[73] In addition, it has been argued that the kind of monolithic vision of patriarchy generated by the dominance approach is in itself unhelpful, since:

> a framework that can characterise all state interventions as directly or indirectly patriarchal offers little practical guidance in challenging the conditions it condemns.[74]

Thus, it would seem that the totalising tendency in this approach, while generating a powerful feminist rhetoric centred on the existence of 'an unshakeable, objective, unmodified reality, the reality constructed by the male gaze,'[75] risks a one-dimensional analysis of patriarchy and a dualistic style of we/them politics that impedes would-be sympathisers and misrep-

---

[68] C MacKinnon, *Toward a Feminist Theory of State*, above n 52 at 114.
[69] K Abrams, 'Ideology and Women's Choices', above n 48.
[70] D Cornell, 'Sexual Difference, the Feminine and Equivalency', above n 62.
[71] D Cornell, 'The Doubly Prized World: Myth, Allegory and the Feminine (1990) 75 *Cornell Law Review* 644 at 668.
[72] D Cornell, 'The Doubly-Prized World: Myth, Allegory and the Feminine', *ibid* at 693.
[73] D Rhode, 'Feminism and the State' (1994) 107 *Harvard Law Review* 1181.
[74] D Rhode, 'Feminism and the State', *ibid* at 1185.
[75] D Cornell, 'The Doubly-Prized World: Myth, Allegory and the Feminine', above n 71 at 687.

resents the problem that women face: a problem, surely, that is not simply that men act 'freely' while women do not, but that *both* men and women are constructed by gender in different ways.

This critique of the dominance approach is significant not only at the theoretical level, but also at the practical level of feminist reform. Indeed, without reformulation, the dominance approach appears to run into concrete problems—in particular, if women are essentially and inevitably disempowered under the present system, then how can women gain the power with which to rise up and defeat patriarchy? As Cornell expresses it, if 'women as a gender are defined as victims, as fuckees, as voiceless,' and if 'the feminist "point of view" is an impossibility within our system of male dominance,' it seems impossible for this approach 'to provide the condition for repair.'[76] Given the strong relationship between feminist theory and feminist politics, the potential paralysis imposed by this dominance approach is deeply concerning. That said, however, it is clear that many theorists who adopt this approach have not felt unduly burdened. MacKinnon herself, for example, has campaigned tirelessly for reforms (most famously her anti-pornography ordinance) that speak on behalf of women, claiming their disempowered status and using it as a basis of empowerment.

The extent to which this reform programme is in keeping with the theoretical tenor of the dominance approach is something we will consider again in Chapter three. For present purposes, however, this blossoming disjunction between theory and politics, which arises in the context of the dominance approach, is itself significant, since it also emerges as a key issue in the remaining feminist response to patriarchy to be considered in this chapter, namely that associated with the rise of postmodernism.

The Influence of Postmodernism

While the dominance approach has proven influential in a number of ways, we have seen that both its conception of the essence of female oppression and of the unilateral imposition of patriarchal power have generated considerable disquiet. In particular, this approach has proven problematic for those feminist theorists who wish to take seriously the narratives of individual women who affirm their femininity, or who testify to oppressions that do not fit the patriarchal domination mould, for example oppression at the hands of other women or as a result of race or sexual orientation.

The problem here is not just that the dominance approach excludes these non-conforming narratives, but that in so doing it sets up a claim to the 'truth' of femininity that relegates those narratives to the status of distortions

---

[76] D Cornell, 'Sexual Difference, the Feminine and Equivalency', above n 62 at 2256.

Development and Dilemmas of Feminist Theory

or 'distractions'.[77] In a context in which many feminists consider the notion of the female subject itself to be the result of social construction, greater caution may be needed to ensure that the patriarchal claim to the 'truth' of femininity is not simply replaced with another (equally illegitimate) feminist one. As Frug explains, the stable binary between male and female identities set up and affirmed under the dominance approach is fundamentally fictitious and denies both 'the semiotic character of sex differences and the impact that historical specificity has on any individual identity.'[78] There can, in reality, be no single story of women's oppression, since each woman's experience is unique, emerging from her own life situation and perspective. Likewise, there can be no single theory of equality that will work to the benefit of all women. By failing to acknowledge this, both the dominance, and the relational, responses display a fundamental flaw. This is a flaw, moreover, that cannot be remedied by 'tacking' on to these approaches a greater attention to women's diversity, since this in itself does little to undermine their conviction that 'a unitary truth' would nonetheless emerge.[79]

On this account, then, what is required to avoid these shortcomings is a feminist response that pays closer attention to the context of individual women's lives and that acknowledges the complexities of the power relations that frame that context. Such a response accepts the dominance approach's assertions that patriarchy is primarily a matter of power, rather than of difference or discrimination, and that women's role and identity is constructed by those relations of gender power. But it diverges in its understanding of the nature of those power relations as fluid and complex, rather than stagnated, one-dimensional and coherent, and in its attendant understanding that each woman's construction by patriarchal power relations can never be complete, predicted or exactly replicated. Underlying this approach, therefore, are two core assertions—firstly, that the context-dependent nature of power relations renders each woman's experience of gender inequality unique; and secondly, that the complexity of power relations renders accounts of patriarchy as a monolithic structure of male domination inadequate. Together, these assertions generate a further conclusion, namely that strategies for securing women's equality must be sensitive to the subtle operations of power, and tailored to the particularities of the people and situations they target.

---

[77] C Smart, *Feminism and the Power of Law*, above n 60 at 77–8. For further discussion of this postmodern critique of dominance, see also, eg, J Flax, *Thinking Fragments: Psychoanalysis, Feminism and Postmodernism in the Contemporary West* (Berkeley, University of California Press, 1990); L Nicholson (ed) *Feminism/Postmodernism* (London & New York, Routledge, 1990); or M Eichner, 'On Postmodern Feminist Legal Theory' (2001) 36 *Harvard Civil Rights—Civil Liberties Law Review* 1.

[78] M Frug, 'A Postmodern Feminist Legal Manifesto (An Unfinished Draft)' (1992) 105 *Harvard Law Review* 1045 at 1046–7. See also M Frug, *Postmodern Legal Feminism* (London & New York, Routledge, 1992).

[79] C Smart, *Feminism and the Power of Law*, above n 60 at 77–8.

The Influence of Postmodernism

Many feminist theorists who seek to cultivate this kind of response have been influenced in recent times by the rise of postmodernism. Encouraging a shift away from the theoretical perspectives of modernity, which often assume progressive models of social development and humanistic conceptions of subjectivity as existing beyond societal influence, postmodernism emphasises the processes through which personal identity is constructed and signified.[80] In turn, this facilitates the replacement of the 'stable' and 'coherent' (female) self who has typically populated feminist analyses with a subject that is 'constituted from multiple institutional and ideological forces that, in various ways, overlap, intersect and even contradict each other.'[81]

Judith Butler, for example, uses the insights of postmodernism to challenge the belief, inherent in the feminist approaches above, that:

> there is some existing identity understood through the category of woman, who not only initiates feminist interests and goals within discourse, but constitutes the subject for whom political representation is pursued.[82]

Building on Foucault's claim that the individual is not a pre-given entity seized upon by the exercise of power but itself a product of power relations, she argues that female identity (individually and collectively) is 'a site of contest, a cause for anxiety' within which it is impossible to separate out 'gender from the political and cultural intersections in which it is invariably produced and maintained.'[83] Similarly, Cornell, despite adopting an approach which differs from Butler's in several respects, also indicates some scepticism about feminist claims to a pre-given, essential gender identity. As she expresses it, since:

---

[80] While postmodernism is, perhaps by definition, a difficult theoretical position to distil down to basic principles, Benhabib's description is instructive. For her, 'postmodernism heralded the end of history, understood as a cumulative, progressive, coherent sequence; postmodernism announced the end of man, and reduced the anthropological subject to a vanishing face in the sand, a disappearing signifier, a fractures, centreless creature; postmodernism trumpeted the end of philosophy and of master narratives of justification and legitimation.' S Benhabib, 'Sexual Difference and Collective Identity: The New Global Constellation' in S James and S Palmer (eds) *Visible Women: Essays on Feminist Legal Theory and Political Philosophy* (Oxford, Hart Publishing, 2002) at 137. See also S Benhabib & D Cornell (eds) *Feminism as Critique: On the Politics of Gender* (Minneapolis, University of Minnesota Press, 1987); S Benhabib, *Situating the Self: Gender, Community and Postmodernism in Contemporary Ethics* (Cambridge, Polity Press, 1992).

[81] K Bartlett, 'Anglo-American Law', in A Jaggar and I Young (eds), *A Companion to Feminist Philosophy*, above n 50 at 538.

[82] J Butler, *Gender Trouble: Feminism and the Subversion of Identity* (London & New York, Routledge, 1990) at 1. For further discussion of this approach, see J Butler, *Undoing Gender* (London & New York, Routledge, 2004).

[83] J Butler, 'Subjects of Sex/Gender / Desire' in A Phillips (ed), *Feminism and Politics*, above n 66 at 275. See also J Butler, *Bodies that Matter: On the Discursive Limits of Sex* (New York, Routledge, 1993); J Butler, *The Psychic Life of Power* (Stanford, Stanford University Press, 1997); J Butler, *Excitable Speech: A Politics of the Performative* (London & New York, Routledge, 1997).

we cannot separate the 'truth' of woman from the fictions in which she is represented, and through which she portrays herself,

we will never know once and for all who or what 'woman' is.[84]

While this poses deep theoretical and practical problems for most of the feminist responses examined in this chapter, for those who subscribe to postmodernism, this presents considerable opportunities. The fact that gender identity is always constructed and contested means that it contains the potential for new interpretations. Shifts are actualised, on this account, not by transcending power relations, but by embarking on a process of 'playful' resistance against imposed social roles and expectations. Representations and constructions of the feminine (and indeed the masculine), though fictitious and inherently unstable, can never be avoided. Thus, fruitful feminist reform does not seek women's liberation from patriarchy as such, but accepts our immersion in the networks of gender power and draws on those networks, and the fictions they contain, to generate alternative ways of being male and female.

The Case For and Against Postmodernism

The theoretical nuances provided by this postmodern account certainly afford a sophisticated understanding of the operation of power relations, and of its constructive effect on experiences and manifestations of gender identity. In addition, this approach can boast some advantages over alternatives grounded in male dominance, since it accredits the narratives of individual women (whatever their content), provides an account of women as potentially other than 'perpetual victims' and facilitates a reform agenda that can operate within the prevailing power structure, rather than having to postpone its moment of victory until the occurrence of a 'triumphant' revolution.

Despite this, however, a number of difficulties have been identified with the postmodern account, and in particular with its application to feminist analysis. For one thing, it has been argued that embracing the myriad situated realities of individual women in all their diversity and complexity will make it increasingly difficult to identify points of commonality between women or to build a single theory of women's structural subordination.[85] This, of course, poses considerable problems for feminism as a movement, particularly given the importance of a shared sense of womanhood to its collective mobilisation. But as Walby notes, just because 'gender relations *could* potentially take an infinite number of forms' does not mean that they do. Indeed, it might be argued that 'in actuality, there are some widely repeated

---

[84] D Cornell, 'The Doubly-Prized World: Myth, Allegory and the Feminine', above n 71 at 675.

[85] A Assiter, *Enlightened Women: Modernist Feminism in a Postmodern Age* (London & New York, Routledge, 1996) at 108.

The Influence of Postmodernism

features and considerable historical continuity' such that the signifier 'woman' can be seen to have adequate constancy and coherence to warrant its ongoing useage.[86] In Chapter five of this book, this is an argument that we will return to consider in detail.

In addition, it has been argued that the postmodern insistence on the localised nature of all norms threatens to render it incapable of sustained critical judgement, particularly of the sort that is central to feminism—ie that 'some forms of social organisation are just plain unjust, or that some beliefs are plain false.'[87] Fricker, for example, warns that feminists who try to challenge or change the status quo by appeal to arguments that are grounded in a general or objective standard of reason will find themselves branded under this approach as 'guilty of discursive terrorism.'[88] But this deeply undermines the platform from which feminist critique often speaks and highlights the fundamental conservatism of the postmodern approach. As she puts it, while:

> at an aesthetic level, postmodernism may be a champion of creativity, playfulness and perpetual movement, at the level of critical thought, it replaces the progressive dynamic of reason with a lugubrious critical stasis.[89]

Similarly, Weir suggests that what feminists may lose in the turn to postmodernism are the tools through which to identify:

> any meaningful differentiation among unreflective, deliberate, dogmatic, defensive, anxious, ironic, playful or parodic performances of gender, and any understanding of the ways in which these interact and conflict.[90]

In defence of the postmodern position, however, a number of commentators have highlighted the extent to which this approach can, in fact, support feminist activism. According to Hutchison, for example, although postmodernism does not provide any blueprint for reform as such, it allows individuals to exercise agency in making decisions about their world and

---

[86] S Walby, 'Post-Post-Modernism? Theorizing Social Complexity' in M Barrett & A Phillips (ed), *Destabilizing Theory: Contemporary Feminist Debates* (Cambridge, Polity Press, 1992) at 36.

[87] M Fricker, 'Feminism in Epistemology: Pluralism without Postmodernism' in M Fricker & J Hornsby (eds), *The Cambridge Companion to Feminism in Philosophy* (Cambridge, Cambridge University Press, 2000) at 150. For further discussion of this point, see also N Fraser, 'Foucant on Modern Power: Empirical Insights and Normative Confusions' (1981) 23 *Praxis International* 272; N Fraser, 'Foucault: A Young Conservative?' (1985) 96 (1) *Ethics* 165; or N Harstock, 'Foucault on Power: A Theory for Women?' in L Nicholson (ed), *Feminism / Postmodernism*, above n 77.

[88] M Fricker, 'Feminism in Epistemology: Pluralism without Postmodernism' in M Fricker & J Hornsby (eds), *The Cambridge Companion to Feminism in Philosophy*, ibid at 150.

[89] M Fricker, 'Feminism in Epistemology: Pluralism without Postmodernism' in M Fricker & J Hornsby (eds), *The Cambridge Companion to Feminism in Philosophy*, ibid at 150.

[90] A Weir, *A Sacrificial Logic: Feminist Theory and the Critique of Identity* (London, Routledge, 1996) at 127.

about the identities that they wish to make or remake on the basis of experiential truths.[91] Thus, it can be seen to open up space for transformative action that empowers and affirms an individual's sense of self without reliance on a monolithic claim to authority and/or truth derived from universal reason.

Of course, the difficulty with this defence is that it continues to assume that every individual has the same power with which to undertake these affirming and transformative activities when it is precisely the fallacy of this supposition that feminism has sought to highlight. The representation of power as highly dispersed in many postmodern accounts might be read to preclude the possibility that one social group can be systematically oppressed by another. But according to Walby, this dispersal, when coupled with a postmodern de-emphasis on material and economic relations makes the analysis of gender 'overly free-floating.'[92] In turn, it generates a feminist reform agenda that is centred upon localised subversion or resistance, rather than collective progress, and that seems ill-equipped to justify the impetus to change other than on the basic premise that there is a value in fluctuation for its own sake.[93]

In Chapter four, the merits and demerits of these claims regarding the relationship between postmodernism and feminism (in terms of concepts of power and resistance) will be examined in detail. For current purposes, though, suffice to say that, to the extent that critics have identified a tendency for postmodernism to reduce politics to the level of personal transformation, a notable feminist 'backlash' has recently emerged. A vocal proponent of this backlash, MacKinnon has not only challenged the wisdom of too close an allegiance between feminism and postmodernism, but has disputed the claim that provides the basis for this allegiance, namely that other feminist approaches (including her dominance one) assume a 'mono-causal' explanation of sex inequality. Postmodern theorists who interpret such accounts as suggesting that gender is all that there is, or that gender can explain everything, are, she argues, quite simply mistaken. As she puts it:

> postmodernism natters on about how feminism privileges gender, but seldom says what that means. . . . If these critics mean that feminists think gender matters a lot, and often read situations in terms of dynamics of gender hierarchy, and refuse to shut up about gender as a form of domination, they're right.[94]

---

[91] A Hutchison, 'Inessentially Speaking (Is there Politics After Postmodernism?)' (1991) 89 *Michigan Law Review* 1549 at 1553.

[92] S Walby, 'Post-Post-Modernism? Theorizing Social Complexity' in M Barrett & A Phillips (ed), *Destabilizing Theory: Contemporary Feminist Debates*, above n 86 at 35.

[93] N Fraser, 'False Antitheses: A Response to Benhabib and Butler' in S Benhabib, J Butler, D Cornell & N Fraser (ed), *Feminist Contentions* (London & New York, Routledge, 1995) at 59.

[94] C MacKinnon, 'Symposium on Unfinished Feminist Business: Some Points Against Postmodernism' (2000) 75 *Chicago-Kent Law Review* 687 at 696–7.

But in that case, postmodernists need to provide a clearer account of *why* feminists are wrong to focus on gender in this way. The fact that postmodernism has been unable to provide this account, she argues, reflects its inability to engage with oppressive and systematic power relations, and with the concrete realities of women's lives. The tendency in postmodern analysis to theorise gender as a 'discursive practice' or 'performance' is problematic, she argues, not only because it diverts attention from the violence that is central to gendered existence, but also because it ignores the peculiarity of gender norms, the weightiness of their imperatives, and the import of their consequences in the event of non-compliance.

Conclusion

Phillips has argued that:

> there is a curious cycle within feminism that starts with exposing the once-invisible woman (attacking the many ways in which her needs, concerns or interests have been submerged under those of men or mankind), but then gets frustrated with what comes to be experienced as an obsessive preoccupation with sex difference, and wishes it could submerge those women again.[95]

Over the course of the previous sections, this chapter has charted the stages of this cycle and the debates which have mobilised it in more detail. While the assimilation model has focused its attention on making women visible, we have noted the ways in which some feminists have become frustrated with its inherent limitations, in particular its tendency to rest at the point of formal equality between the genders in the public sphere. Both the relational and dominance approaches, in their turn, have sought a more deep-seated critique of patriarchy and a more ambitious programme for reform.

While the relational approach has proven problematic in its uncritical valorisation of women's caring characteristics, the dominance approach has proven problematic in its determined denigration of femininity as a mere repository for patriarchal scripts of victimhood. Frustrated by the unfounded assertions of a coherent and shared female identity, and by a binary understanding of power as a commodity held by all men and denied to all women, some feminists have, as we have seen, developed the insights of postmodernism to generate a subversive agenda for reform, grounded in a recognition of gender as one category of difference among many others. As noted in the discussion above, however, this approach has posed some troubling dilemmas for those committed to the feminist collective political agenda, and has threatened to isolate individual women, or as Phillips puts it, to render them invisible once more.

---

[95] A Phillips, 'Feminism and the Politics of Difference, Or, Where Have All the Women Gone?' in S James and S Palmer (eds) *Visible Women: Essays on Feminist Legal Theory and Political Philosophy*, above n 80 at 11.

Development and Dilemmas of Feminist Theory

The developments in feminist analysis outlined in this chapter have often been depicted in terms of a linear progression, with each emerging debate and each new response representing a refinement that will ultimately yield an ideal feminist vision of the origins of patriarchy, of the nature of 'true' femininity and equality, and of the best route to reform. Seeing these developments more in terms of a cycle than a line is, however, not only apt, but also productive for feminist analysis. Indeed, in this light, it is perhaps no accident that we can identify a recent resurgence of feminist interest in liberal ideals, as well as a frustration at the abstraction of postmodernism, and a return to more radicalised conceptions of patriarchy as male dominance.[96] In the following chapters, we will examine these trends in more detail, reflecting on the dilemmas that they pose and the challenges that they present. The hope is that, as feminism circles around these points of contention, it does not directly re-trace its steps, but rather spirals towards a theoretically stronger and political brighter future.

---

[96] See eg, J Marshall, *Humanity, Freedom and Feminism* (Aldershot, Ashgate Publishing, 2005); S Mullally, *Gender, Culture and Human Rights: Reclaiming Universalism* (Oxford, Hart Publishing, 2006); R West, *Re-Imagining Justice: Progressive Interpretations of Formal Equality, Rights and the Rule of Law* (Aldershot, Ashgate Publishing, 2003); C MacKinnon, *Are Women Human? And Other International Dialogues* (Cambridge, Harvard University Press, 2006).

2
Feminism(s), Law and Liberalism(s)

While Durkheim's assertion that law provides an unproblematic index of social solidarity[1] has rightly been challenged,[2] it is widely accepted that examining the nature and remit of law in a society can provide a useful insight into various aspects of broader social relations. Law operates variously as a mechanism for social control as well as a normative system that stipulates the standards of expected behaviour and expresses popular condemnation of non-compliance through its sanctions. As a result, it is widely accepted that the substantive dictates of law, as well as the discourses that we use to invoke, evaluate and justify those dictates, can provide 'a convenient lens through which to examine critically the production and interaction of power and knowledge.'[3] It should come as no surprise, therefore, that feminists have frequently engaged with law and legal critique, and that in so doing they have been informed by their peculiar perspectives on power relations, gender identity and sexual difference.

The various feminist views on the nature of patriarchal power discussed in the previous chapter have, of course, had a significant bearing on this analysis of law, particularly in regard to claims about its origins and future potential. Those feminist thinkers who attribute patriarchy to historical marginalisation or innocent oversight have, for example, emphasised the extent to which legal institutions and principles (grounded as they are in rules of precedent and tradition) have been crafted and articulated primarily by men. According to Finley, for example, it is significant that throughout history 'the primary linguists of law have almost exclusively been men' and that:

> men have shaped it, they have defined it, they have interpreted it, and given it meaning consistent with their understandings of the world.

It is as a result of this, she argues, that the voices of others have been marginalised and that one form of (masculine) reasoning has been privileged, despite the equally feasible alternatives.[4]

---

[1] E Durkheim, *The Division of Labour in Society* (trans W Hall) (London, MacMillan, 1948) at 68.
[2] S Lukes & A Scull, *Durkheim and the Law* (Oxford, Martin Robertson, 1983).
[3] A Hutchison, 'Inessentially Speaking (Is There Politics After Postmodernism?)' (1991) 89 *Michigan Law Review* 1549 at 1555.
[4] L Finley, 'Breaking Women's Silence in Law: The Dilemma of the Gendered Nature of Legal Reasoning' (1989) 64 *Notre Dame Law Review* 886 at 892.

Feminism(s), Law and Liberalism(s)

For these feminists, then, the law's partiality towards masculine values and interests can be remedied by enlarging the parameters of its vision and cognition. But while the aim here is not just to 'tack' women onto theories about law, but also thereby to transform dominant notions of what constitutes an 'objective' or 'normative' perspective,[5] for those feminist theorists who sense a deeper, conscious and strategic imposition of patriarchy, this approach remains inadequate. Such theorists have argued that sex inequality does not simply provide the context in which our historical and contemporary legal system operates, but also provides the very condition for it. Thus, under this more radical analysis, sex inequality is not only reproduced by the law but is also in turn justified by a jurisprudence that supports uncritically the existing order of things.[6] As a result, redressing patriarchy requires more than including female experiences in order to challenge the law's partiality; it entails a deep-seated restructuring of social power relations to empower women vis-à-vis men.

To the extent that these different approaches emerge from distinct explanations of the origins of patriarchy and thus generate divergent proposals for reform, through law and beyond, it is important that we pay attention to their specificity.[7] That said, however, when it comes to substantive points of disillusionment with the dominant liberal ideals and methods that have informed the contemporary legal framework, it is clear that there has been a notable consensus amongst these various theorists. Indeed, despite the different routes used to reach and to depart from this point, feminist commentators have frequently found themselves in agreement over what they take to be the key failings of liberalism. More specifically, as we will see, they have isolated concerns about the individualism and abstraction inherent in liberal method (and reflected in its conception of the legal subject) as well as about the masking of the substantive (male) partiality of liberal values under a veil of neutrality and rationality.

---

[5] M Mossman, 'Feminism and Legal Method—the Difference it Makes' (1986) *Australian Journal of Law and Society* 103 (reproduced in M Fineman and N Thomadsen (eds), *At the Boundaries of Law—Feminism and Legal Theory* (London & New York, Routledge, 1991) at 283–300.

[6] V Kerruish, *Jurisprudence as Ideology* (London, Routledge, 1991) at 194. For discussion of this radical approach see in particular C MacKinnon, 'Feminism, Marxism, Method and the State: An Agenda for Theory' (1982) 7 (3) *Signs* 515; C MacKinnon, 'Feminism, Marxism, Method and the State: Toward a Feminist Jurisprudence' (1983) 8 (2) *Signs* 635; C MacKinnon, *Feminism Unmodified: Discourses on Life and Law* (Cambridge, Harvard University Press, 1987); C MacKinnon, *Toward a Feminist Theory of State* (Cambridge, Harvard University Press, 1989).

[7] For further discussion of this tension between diversity and coherence in feminist analysis, and its implications for the way in which the feminist critique of law is depicted, see, eg, the recent engagement between Naffine and Bottomley—N Naffine, 'In Praise of Legal Feminism' (2002) 22 (1) *Legal* Studies 71; A Bottomley, 'Shock to Thought: An Encounter (of a Third Kind) with Legal Feminism' (2004) 12 *Feminist Legal Studies* 29; N Naffine, 'Shocking Thoughts: A Reply to Anne Bottomley' (2004) 12 *Feminist Legal Studies* 175.

The Feminist Challenge to Legal Liberalism

As Phillips has noted, then, 'the relationship between feminism and liberalism has always been an uneasy one.' Initially, she argues, this was because liberals were often reluctant to engage feminism, and in particular to see through the implications of their new understanding of politics for women's lives. Latterly, however, she suggests that this tension has been as much at feminism's insistence, with theorists deploying the term 'liberal' as 'shorthand for everything stodgy, unambitious, and dishonest.'[8] In this chapter, we will look in more detail at the claims against liberalism made by feminist commentators when occupying these points of consensus. Having done so, however, later sections will move on to subject these common objections to liberalism to critical scrutiny, both in order to evaluate their respective merits and demerits and also to consider their implications for the future of feminist legal and political theory.

The Feminist Challenge to Legal Liberalism

Clearly, the concept of law is by no means monolithic and the enterprise of defining its essence is one that has preoccupied jurists for many centuries. Nonetheless, in analysing law in modern society, feminists have come to identify a range of claims, implicated within so-called 'liberal legalism', that, they argue, have been characteristically invoked. These include the assertion of law's distinctiveness, which entails that the methods, aspirations and values of law can be distinguished and kept separate from those of politics, economics, morality, etc. In addition, the assertion of law's determinacy has been identified, which entails that solutions to social problems can be reached by applying legal rules in a principled, disinterested, and rational way.

Following sceptics like Holmes[9] and Llewellyn,[10] and joining forces with critical legal theorists like Unger[11] and Kennedy,[12] feminist scholarship on law has often disputed both the logical coherence and the practical feasibility of each of these claims.[13] In particular, building on the insistence that law is a thinly veiled version of political controversy, feminist analysis

---

[8] A Phillips, 'Feminism and Liberalism Revisited: Has Martha Nussbaum Got It Right?' (2001) 8 (2) *Constellations* 249 at 249.
[9] O Holmes, 'The Path of Law' (reprinted) (1996) 110 *Harvard Law Review* 991.
[10] K Llewellyn, 'A Realistic Jurisprudence: The Next Step' (1930) 30 *Columbia Law Review* 431; K Llewellyn, 'Some Realism about Realism' (1931) 44 *Harvard Law Review* 1222.
[11] R Unger, 'The Critical Legal Studies Movement' (1983) 96 *Harvard Law Review* 561.
[12] D Kennedy, *A Critique of Adjudication* (Cambridge, Harvard University Press, 1997); D Kennedy, *Sexy Dressing: Essays on The Power and Politics of Cultural Identity* (Cambridge, Harvard University Press, 1993).
[13] For further discussion of the relationship between feminist and realist/critical approaches, see eg, M Davies, *Asking the Law Question* (Sydney, Law Book Company, 1994); R West, *Re-Imagining Justice: Progressive Interpretations of Formal Equality, Rights and the Rule of Law* (Aldershot, Ashgate, 2003).

Feminism(s), Law and Liberalism(s)

has tended to highlight the extent to which prevailing legal norms and mechanisms are underpinned by a range of patriarchal biases and privileges that perpetuate women's exclusion or oppression whilst simultaneously purporting to be neutral, natural and inevitable. Thus, many feminists have questioned the traditional emphasis on objectivity, rationality and neutrality attributable to the liberal rule of law ideal by suggesting that the values thus elevated to the status of neutral absolute are simply partial projections of the male psyche. What's more, they have highlighted the extent to which the law, rather than being a discrete and autonomous social practice, actively reflects, constructs and reinforces the gendered patterns of power that are manifest in the wider social, political and economic context.

As noted in the previous chapter, then, the feminist claim here is not that women have been completely excluded from the legal form of life. Indeed, 'the partial inclusion of women was, and remains, important for the law's legitimacy.'[14] Rather, the point is that women have been recognised as legal persons only for certain purposes and, importantly, only where that recognition has served to reinforce, or at least not damage too seriously, patriarchy.[15] Thus, women have been entitled to maintenance from their husbands during marriage but the establishment of regimes of communal property has often been resisted; and women have been deemed capable of consenting to marriage, even under familial or cultural pressure, whilst being simultaneously denied the reproductive autonomy afforded by an unqualified legal right to abortion.

In addition, even in those contexts in which the law has recognised women as persons deserving of protection and empowerment in their own right, the legal interventions in question have often been, in MacKinnon's words, 'unconstructive, to say the least.'[16] Reforms in law aimed at protecting women from sexual assault have, for example, permitted reliance on dubious socio-sexual stereotypes and created the illusion of legal redress in a context in which only the most violent of stranger rapes (which are statistically also the rarest) secure convictions.[17] Similarly, laws against domestic violence, which is a highly gendered phenomenon, have been

---

[14] N Naffine, 'In Praise of Legal Feminism', above n 7 at 77–8. See also N Naffine, 'Can Women Be Legal Persons?' in S James & S Palmer (eds) *Visible Women: Essays on Feminism Legal Theory and Political Philosophy* (Oxford, Hart Publishing, 2002).

[15] For further discussion of this see generally, N Naffine & R Owens (ed) *Sexing the Subject of Law* (London, Sweet and Maxwell, 1997).

[16] C MacKinnon, 'Law in the Everyday Life of Women' in C MacKinnon (ed), *Women's Lives, Men's Laws* (Cambridge, Harvard University Press, 2005) at 33.

[17] For further critique, see, eg, S Estrich, *Real Rape* (Cambridge, Harvard University Press, 1987); S Lees, *Carnal Knowledge: Rape on Trial* (London, Penguin, 1996); S Schulhofer, *Unwanted Sex: The Culture of Intimidation and the Failure of Law* (Cambridge, Harvard University Press, 1998); C MacKinnon, *Feminism Unmodified* and *Toward a Feminist Theory of State*, above n 6.

inadequately enforced and often fail to properly reflect, or respond to, the harm experienced by its victim.[18]

Building on this analysis, numerous feminist scholars have also submitted that this marginalisation of women's experiences from the remit of law has been reflected not only in practical legal interventions, but also in mainstream jurisprudential theory. Rhode, for example, has pointed out that 'inattention to gender is striking in much contemporary liberal work.'[19] And likewise, Minow has emphasised the extent to which conventional legal theory has 'treated as marginal, inferior and different any person who does not fit the normal model of autonomous, competent individual.'[20] The various ways in which feminist commentators allege that liberalism has secured and legitimised this marginalisation will be examined over the following sections.

The Feminist Challenge to Liberalism's Method: Abstraction & Individualism

Where feminist method has tended to prioritise the concrete and to rely on contextual analysis, liberal legal analysis has tended to operate, according to its critics, at a highly abstract level. Liberal legalism, it is argued, purports to analyse and address social problems by removing actors from their everyday environment, stripping them of the characteristics and relationships that influence their choices, and placing them in a sterile legal world populated by similar persons where complex dilemmas are resolved by detached models of distributive justice and invocation of self-interested and conflict-oriented claims. According to many of liberalism's critics, no theorist has exemplified this approach, or courted its problematic consequences, more than Rawls.

Abstraction, Context & Hollow Legal Personhood

In *A Theory of Justice*, John Rawls presents a model, consciously invoking the spirit of liberalism, through which to ensure the fair distribution of assets and opportunities in a society composed of individuals with diverse talents and diverse levels of luck.[21] For Rawls, the path to this distribution lies in the use of a device, which he calls 'the veil of ignorance'. This veil

---

[18] For further critique, see, eg, R Dobash & R Dobash, *Women, Violence and Social Change* (London & New York, Routledge, 1992); S Edwards, *Policing Domestic Violence* (Manchester, Manchester University Press, 1989); C Hoyle, *Negotiating Domestic Violence: Police, Criminal Justice and Victims* (Oxford, Oxford University Press, 2000).

[19] D Rhode, *Justice and Gender* (Cambridge, Harvard University Press, 1989) at 316. See also D Rhode, *Theoretical Perspectives on Sexual Difference* (New Haven, Yale University Press, 1990); D Rhode, *Speaking of Sex: The Denial of Gender Inequality* (Cambridge, Harvard University Press, 1997).

[20] M Minow, *Making All the Difference—Inclusion, Exclusion and American Law* (Itacha, Cornell University Press, 1990) at 9–10. See also M Minow, *Not Only for Myself: Identity, Politics and the Law* (New York, New Press, 1997).

[21] J Rawls, *A Theory of Justice* (Oxford, Clarendon Press, 1971) [See also J Rawls, *A Theory of Justice* (revised edition) (Oxford, Oxford University Press, 2000)].

of ignorance operates to strip individuals back to an original position in which they are unaware of those factors about their social standing and personal ability that may influence their conception of what would be just. Without the knowledge of whether they are a pauper or a prince in the world beyond, Rawls hypothesises that people, whom he assumes to be both risk-averse and self-interested, would settle on a distribution that ensures that they would be adequately catered for either way. While this does not entail a strictly socialist distribution, it does entail an egalitarian model within which any differences in distribution will only be justifiable where they can be seen to operate to the advantage of the worst off.

While this Rawlsian model of distribution has undergone some important revisions since its first airing,[22] the approach to resolving social problems that it reflects has been identified by many commentators as characteristic of liberal thinking, and as exhibiting a number of its most serious flaws.[23] In particular, critics have challenged its tendency to remove from persons behind the veil of ignorance the very characteristics and concerns that render them properly human.[24] This, it is submitted, has generated a hollow conception that fails to reflect the realities of human subjectivity and which, in its turn, has facilitated the creation and perpetuation of an unrealisable and unattractive model for social justice. Indeed, as Young has noted:

> while Rawls insists on the plurality of selves as a necessary starting point for a conception of justice, the reasoning of the original position is nevertheless monological.[25]

This is not only because the constraints imposed in the original position rule out any meaningful differences between participants but also because they rule out scope for proper discussion—participants behind the veil of ignorance reason from identical assumptions and, since they are mutually disinterested, they have no interest in one another's point of view. To the extent that this replicates what she sees as a general liberal tendency to view legal actors as abstract, socially detached entities, Young suggests that this

---

[22] See, eg, J Rawls, *Political Liberalism* (New York, Columbia University Press, 1996); J Rawls, *The Law of Peoples* (Cambridge, Harvard University Press, 1999).

[23] For a more general critique of Rawls' theory, see, eg, M Sandel, *Liberalism and the Limits of Justice* (Cambridge, Cambridge University Press, 1982); C Taylor, *Sources of the Self* (Cambridge, Harvard University Press, 1989).

[24] For further discussion of this feminist engagement with Rawls see, eg, S Benhabib, *Situating the Self: Gender, Community and Postmodernism in Contemporary Ethics* (Cambridge, Polity Press, 1992); S Okin, *Justice, Gender and the Family* (New York, Basic Books, 1989); M Nussbaum, 'Rawls and Feminism' in S Freeman (ed) *The Cambridge Companion to Rawls* (Cambridge, Cambridge University Press, 2003); A Baier, 'The Need for More than Justice' in V Held (ed) *Justice and Care: Essential Readings in Feminist Ethics* (Boulder, Westview, 1995); A Jaggar, *Feminist Politics and Human Nature* (Totowa, Rowman and Littlefield, 1983).

[25] I Young, *Justice and the Politics of Difference* (Princeton, Princeton University Press, 1990) at 101.

rules out the possibility for a focus in law and justice on communication rather than conflict, as well as on relationship rather than individualism, and on concern for others rather than self-interest. But this, she and others have argued, is lamentable, since such an atomistic vision sits at odds with the reality of our daily lives in which we do attribute significance to community and cannot fail to be inter-dependently situated in relational and co-operative networks.[26]

Drawing on this critique and developing Gilligan's insight that it is the masculine voice, deemed to be unemotional, impersonal and objective, which coincides with our cultural expectations of justice, subsequent feminist theorists have sought to highlight the ways in which this has impoverished liberalism's conception of both social living and law.[27] The 'feminine' voice, which perceives of social reality in terms of interconnected dynamics held together on a morality of continuity, communication and interdependence, it is argued, represents a model that should play a more prominent role in informing our legal thinking. While the masculine voice, reflected in the liberal imagination, has forced us to express arguments in de-contextualised and abstract formulae, the possibility remains, therefore, for a legal theory that is more cognisant of context and that focuses on particularity, cooperation and connection.

Supporters of such an approach argue that its adoption would not only constitute a dramatic improvement in terms of its representation of competing perspectives on social living, but would also provide a more complete and adequate theory of justice. Indeed, as West puts it:

> if it is true . . . that the act of caring for others to whom we are connected in some way is central to our moral lives, then our capacity for care should be at the centre of our understanding of our public and legal, as well as private and personal, virtues, and . . . it should be central to the meaning of legal justice.[28]

Thus, the feminist call to engage with relational thinking can be seen to take law beyond its liberal confines and also, in so doing, to preserve 'the law's soul' by bringing it back to its purpose, which is 'to enhance rather than ignore, the rich diversity of life.'[29]

Abstraction, Relationships and Relations of Power

Of course, the legal person that many feminists identify as populating the realm of conventional liberal theory has not only been abstracted from specific relationships with others, but has also been abstracted from the social, political and economic context within which s/he operates. This too

---

[26] R West, 'Jurisprudence and Gender' (1988) 55 *University of Chicago Law Review* 1.
[27] C Worden, 'Overshooting the Target—A Feminist Deconstruction of Legal Education' (1984) 34 *American University Law Review* 1141.
[28] R West, *Caring for Justice* (New York, New York University Press, 1997) at 9.
[29] A Scales, 'The Emergence of a Feminist Jurisprudence' (1986) 95 *Yale Law Journal* 1373 at 1387.

is a relational context but its structural setting highlights broader power disparities. Critics have often argued that liberal theory, by elevating legal analysis above these concerns, improperly represents itself as unaffected by the concrete power relations that impinge on other systems of social control. While such an approach serves to bolster claims to law's distinctiveness and determinacy, critics have suggested that it tends to prevent liberal theorists from asking the most pertinent questions about social justice, and thereby masks the extent to which other (condoned but unjust) power relations are permitted to remain intact.[30]

The extent to which abstraction from concrete power struggles is a standard tool in the armoury of liberal legalism has been regularly remarked upon by feminist commentators. Certainly, the work of leading liberal thinkers can be seen to provide fuel for these concerns. Rawls, for example, asks participants in the original position to leave behind knowledge of their social standing, gender, and capacities. Thus, the power disparities reflected in these distinctions are rendered irrelevant within the Rawlsian model; and while the rationale for this may have been well-intentioned, it has been argued that the upshot is that they are simply left unchallenged in the resultant theory. Likewise, feminist critics have pointed out that 'questions of membership and power are quite simply not on the theoretical agenda'[31] in Dworkin's work, the reason for this allegedly being that their inclusion would undermine the abstract ideals that animate the liberal approach. In the same way that focussing on the concrete of daily life may undermine the consensus that Rawls has constructed through the original position, it is suggested that insistence on the political nature of the attribution of legal meaning ultimately casts doubt on the very idea of a single interpretive community from which Dworkin asserts that law derives its legitimacy.[32]

From a feminist perspective, of course, this alleged refusal on the part of leading liberal theorists to engage with questions of power is deeply problematic. Discussion in the previous chapter has illustrated the extent to which differential power distributions between the sexes have been identified and challenged by feminist work. Indeed, for some feminist commentators, the issues of justice and power are inevitably and inextricably linked. As Minow puts it, justice is not 'abstract, universal or neutral' but:

> the quality of human engagement with multiple perspectives framed by, but not limited to, the relationships of power in which they are formed.[33]

---

[30] N Lacey, 'Theories of Justice and the Welfare State: A Feminist Critique' in *Unspeakable Subjects: Feminist Essays in Legal and Social Theory* (Oxford, Hart Publishing, 1998) at 69–70.
[31] N Lacey, 'Community in Legal Theory: Idea, Ideal or Ideology?' in Lacey *Unspeakable Subjects, ibid* at 147.
[32] N Naffine, 'In Praise of Legal Feminism', above n 7 at 75.
[33] M Minow, 'Justice Engendered' (1987) 101 *Harvard Law Review* 10 at 16.

The Feminist Challenge to Legal Liberalism

As a result, it is unsurprising that theories of justice which do not appear to engage with power struggles, that assume an equal distribution of social power, or that isolate the axes of power from consideration have been met with sustained feminist criticism. In their place, Kiss has argued that:

> feminists should champion approaches to justice that are more contextual, that acknowledge theorising from a particular position or perspective, and that pay more attention to issues like violence, domination and cultural injustice.[34]

This, of course, is in keeping with a feminist spirit that has demanded that we individualise law and attend to the complex ways in which power constructs legal norms, creating the illusion of consensus and limiting the alternatives.

The Feminist Challenge to Liberalism's False Promise: Neutrality & Rationality

It is an established tenet of liberal legalism, reflected amongst other things in its rule of law ideal, that law sets up standards of behaviour that are to be applied impartially, and thus fairly, to all those before it. Feminist critics of liberalism have argued, however, that while partiality and perspective are officially frowned upon under this model, liberal law is effectively 'embedded in a patriarchal framework that equates abstraction and universalisation from only one group's experiences as neutrality.'[35]

For some feminists, this propensity to universalise the particular through the guise of impartiality is the result of unintentional oversight. Meanwhile, for others, it results from the factual impossibility of impartiality as an ideal. As Young explains, for example, situated perspectives, derived from particular histories and experiences, will inevitably 'rush to fill the vacuum created by counterfactual abstraction,' while failing to be recognised as subjective when voiced from a culturally privileged position.[36] At the same time, however, for some other feminists, there is a more calculating dimension to this process. Indeed, the claim to neutrality is seen by some as contrived to mask the truth of women's oppression and as operating in furtherance of deliberate male domination. Such a perspective is represented by MacKinnon, for example, who asserts that:

> the liberal state coercively and authoritatively constitutes the social order in the interests of men as a gender—through its legitimising norms (including neutrality), forms, relations to society and substantive policies.[37]

---

[34] E Kiss, 'Justice', in A Jaggar and I Young (eds), *A Companion to Feminist Philosophy* (Oxford, Blackwell, 2000) at 492–3.

[35] L Finley, 'Breaking Women's Silence in Law: The Dilemma of the Gendered Nature of Legal Reasoning' above n 4 at 897.

[36] I Young, *Justice and the Politics of Difference*, above n 25 at 115.

[37] C MacKinnon, *Toward a Feminist Theory of State*, above n 6 at 161–2.

Feminism(s), Law and Liberalism(s)

Whether inevitable, selfishly pursued or inadvertently maintained, the situation thus uncovered by feminists is presented as unjust. It reinforces oppression by rendering inferior those marginalised groups whose experiences do not and cannot measure up to the norms constructed by the privileged group as neutral. Not only does this generate amongst members of the group a sense of individual and collective failure, it presents serious obstacles to change, since:

> if oppressed groups challenge the alleged neutrality of prevailing assumptions and policies and express their own experience and perspectives, their claims are heard as those of biased, selfish special interests.[38]

In seeking to see through the 'mists of neutrality' created in this process, feminist scholarship has, amongst other things, deconstructed:

> law's claims to be enunciating truths, its pretensions to neutral or objective judgement, and its construction of a field of discrete and hence unassailable knowledge.[39]

It has unpicked the liberal claim that law is a closed system, administered in a neutral and detached manner by a profession trained in the practice of a specific form of rationality. What's more, it has highlighted the ways in which law's pretence to coherence has prevented those on the periphery from entering into its domain and speaking in terms that are comprehensible to it.

Drawing attention to the partiality of the law's purportedly neutral perspective and illustrating the extent to which the agenda for what counts as knowledge in legal theory is supported by specific (male) claims to power and 'truth', feminist analysis has sought out new forms of rationality with which to challenge the liberal orthodoxy. In so doing, it has focused on the conflicts that lurk on the underside of the official liberal story of law's coherence. Feminists have highlighted, for example, the fundamental choice that underpins the law's definition of the injury in rape from the point of view of the man's (rather than the woman's) understanding,[40] or its decision to accredit hot-headed and jealousy-fuelled homicide with a mitigating plea of provocation while treating women's slow-burn response to abuse with suspicion.[41]

---

[38] I Young, *Justice and the Politics of Difference*, above n 25 at 116.

[39] N Lacey, *Unspeakable Subjects*, above n 30 at 7.

[40] See, eg, C MacKinnon, *Towards a Feminist Theory of State*, above n 6 at 183: '(t)o attempt to solve (the problem of rape) by adopting reasonable belief as a standard without asking, on a substantive social basis, to whom the belief is reasonable and why . . . is one-sided: male-sided.' For discussion in UK context, see also N Lacey, 'Beset by Boundaries: The Home Office Review of Sexual Offences' (2001) *Criminal Law Review* 3; J Temkin & A Ashworth, 'The Sexual Offences Act 2003: Rape, Sexual Assault and the Problems of Consent' (2004) *Criminal Law Review* 328; E Finch & V Munro, 'Breaking Boundaries: Sexual Consent in the Jury Room' (2006) 26(3) *Legal Studies* 303.

[41] See, eg, K O'Donovan, 'Defences for Battered Women Who Kill' (1991) 18 *Journal of Law and Society* 219; A McColgan, 'In Defence of Battered Women Who Kill' (1993) 13 *Oxford Journal of Legal Studies* 508; D Nicholson and R Sanghvi, 'Battered Women and Provocation: The Implications of R v Ahluwaila' (1993) *Criminal Law Review* 728.

Re-evaluation of the Feminist Critique

Although this has often been thought of as characteristically deconstructive or 'trashing' activity, Lacey highlights the more productive aspects of this practice. In particular, she notes that the unearthing of such contradictions:

> forms part of an intellectual and political strategy—of exposing law's indeterminacy, of emphasising its contingency, and of finding resources for its reconstruction in those doctrinal principles and discursive images which are less dominant, yet which fracture and complicate the seamless web imagined by orthodox legal scholarship.[42]

Thus, while it is true that this deconstructive method has performed a largely negative function in the hands of other critical scholars, in the hands of feminists, she argues, it can, and should, be coupled with a reformist agenda and a utopian vision of gender equality.

The role that law has to play in facilitating this prescriptive agenda will be considered in the next chapter. Before doing so, however, there is one preliminary question to be addressed, namely: to the extent that this feminist critique sets out to challenge the traditional (liberal) insistence on an abstract and detached subject who populates a legal realm characterised by neutrality and rationality, is it justified in calling for the abandonment, or even radical reconstruction, of liberalism per se? Or in other words, are these feminist objections to liberalism adequately convincing, both on their own terms and in terms of their resultant call for the rejection of a liberal approach to law?

Out of the Shadows? A Re-evaluation of the Feminist Critique

While the feminist criticisms of liberal legalism discussed above forcefully highlight many of the values and priorities that prima facie appear to have been marginalised in law and conventional legal theory, it will be argued over the following sections that there are also a number of reasons why this critique may be considered problematic. Indeed, to the extent that it lodges a wholesale challenge to liberalism, it will be argued—drawing on the work of some contemporary feminists who have sought to 'buck' the trend of this anti-liberal analysis—that there are good grounds for caution.

Amongst other things, it is important to note from the outset that commentators who support this critique tend, in developing their alternatives, to invoke values that are presumed to be antithetical to those prioritised in liberal legalism. The difficulty with this, however, is that it leads to precisely the kind of dualistic thinking that feminist method has typically purported to reject. Building on this concern, it has been pointed out that, while the call to re-contextualise legal subjectivity may be a welcome one, feminists should not allow it to eclipse the possibility that, in some areas at least, legal

---

[42] N Lacey, *Unspeakable Subjects*, above n 30 at 11.

reasoning is already relational (albeit perhaps in the more negative sense that 'it privileges certain kinds of relationships: such as proprietary, object relations'[43]). Similarly, in the context of theories of justice, commentators have cautioned that 'feminists must not succumb to a sweeping (and ironically, highly abstract) preference for 'context' over 'abstraction,'' which would undermine their critique.[44]

Underpinning these cautionary comments regarding the feminist challenge to liberal legalism is a more general concern that critical scholarship on law has at times been guilty of 'straw-manning' its liberal target. Indeed, as Lacey has pointed out, while analytical legal theory has been the focus for much of the rejection of the alleged objectivity and neutrality of law, 'feminist scholars have in fact engaged in rather little direct debate with traditional jurisprudence.'[45] In a context in which the precise tenets of liberal legal theory are somewhat illusive, and in which the diversity of approaches congregating under the banner of liberalism can be bewildering, it is understandable that feminists have been tempted to attribute to liberalism as a movement more coherence than it in fact exhibits, and to leave aside more complex engagement. Nonetheless, as Nussbaum points out, the danger in speaking so broadly about 'liberalism' in a context in which 'liberalism is not a single position but a family of positions' is one that has plagued various feminist criticisms and debates.[46]

Of course, emphasising the diversity of liberalism is not to suggest that an approach that can be characterised as liberal does not exist; clearly it does, and it has had a profound influence on contemporary values. Nonetheless, there is some concern that feminist analysis, much like its critical legal studies forerunner, has focussed its attention on defining liberalism in oppositional terms, setting it up too thinly as a target for critique, without first engaging fully with its complexities, subtleties and distinctions. Certainly, there has been a discernable tendency in otherwise thoughtful feminist analysis to 'lump together' a range of diverse liberal thinkers—often with little recognition of the myriad ways in which their approaches differ from one another and with no serious evaluation of the extent to which such differences may interface with feminism.[47] West, for example, when challenging the tendency to describe the human predicament as one of 'natural

---

[43] N Lacey, *Unspeakable Subjects*, above n 30 at 6.

[44] E Kiss, 'Justice', in A Jaggar and I Young (eds), *A Companion to Feminist Philosophy*, above n 34 at 495.

[45] N Lacey, 'Closure and Critique in Feminist Jurisprudence: Transcending the Dichotomy or a Foot in Both Camps?' in *Unspeakable Subjects*, above n 30 at 169. There have, however, been occasional and notable exceptions to this rule—not only Lacey, but also, eg, M Davies, *Asking the Law Question*, above n 13; V Kerruish, *Jurisprudence as Ideology*, above n 6.

[46] M Nussbaum, *Sex and Social Justice* (Oxford, Oxford University Press, 1999) at 57.

[47] N Lacey, 'Closure and Critique in Feminist Jurisprudence: Transcending the Dichotomy or a Foot in Both Camps?' in *Unspeakable Subjects*, above n 30 at 169.

equality and mutual antagonism' conflates 'Hobbes, Ackerman, Dworkin, Rawls and the rest of the liberal tradition.'[48]

This lack of engagement with the liberal tradition on its own terms threatens, however, to substantially weaken the feminist critique. For one thing, it renders it a challenge to a caricatured theoretical position that, it might be argued, is not in fact supported by anyone. Indeed, even the suggestion that liberalism makes claims to law's distinctiveness and determinacy, which constituted a core starting point for much critical as well as feminist engagement, is disputable. While it may be true that the strict formalist logic challenged by the Realists in the 1920s and 1930s did advocate this position, it is by no means clear that any contemporary liberal theorist would continue to support this kind of approach. Dworkin, for example, would not contend that the law is distinct from other systems of social control—indeed his very theory of the nature of law in modern, liberal society is one characterised by the centrality of legal principles that find their substantive content and weight in the moral realm.[49] Equally, while Dworkin might be more inclined to support the claim to law's determinacy (reflected in his 'single right answer' thesis),[50] other liberal theorists, for example Hart, would clearly reject it. It is well established in *The Concept of Law* that, despite Hart's liberal pretensions and commitment to the rule of law ideal, there remains an inevitable 'penumbra of uncertainty' in regard to legal rules that sits alongside their 'core of settled meaning', leaving forever open the possibility of legal indeterminacy and necessitating some role for judicial discretion.[51]

In addition, moreover, it is not just that this lack of detailed feminist engagement with traditional theory has facilitated the adoption of dubious received wisdom about the liberal position on law's determinacy and distinctiveness, but also that it threatens to do a disservice to those liberal frameworks that may already offer the potential for a more sympathetic and more feminist understanding of the rule of law. According to Nussbaum, for example, there is no question that liberalism, at least of a certain kind, can be defended and deployed productively for feminist purposes. As she explains:

> the deepest and most central ideals of the liberal tradition are ideas of radical force and great theoretical and practical value . . . although liberalism needs to learn from feminism if it is to formulate its own central insights in a fully adequate manner.[52]

More specifically, Nussbaum suggests that at the heart of Kantian and classical Utilitarian liberalism lies a fundamentally valuable intuition about human beings:

---

[48] R West, 'Jurisprudence and Gender' (1988) 55 *University of Chicago Law Review* 1 at 64.
[49] R Dworkin, *Law's Empire* (London, Fontana Press, 1986).
[50] R Dworkin, *Taking Rights Seriously* (London, Duckworth Press, 1977).
[51] H Hart, *The Concept of Law* (2nd edn, with Postscript) (Oxford, Clarendon Press, 1994).
[52] M Nussbaum, *Sex and Social Justice*, above n 46 at 56.

namely, that all, just by being human, are of equal dignity and worth, no matter where they are situated in society, and that the primary source of this worth is a power of moral choice within them, a power that consists in the ability to plan a life in accordance with one's own evaluation of ends.[53]

This intuition is reflected, albeit in divergent ways, in the work of many liberal theorists. And thus, while feminists may be right to point out that 'malestream' liberal theorists have not adequately problematised women's subordination, there is untapped potential in their core premise. As a result, she argues, the problems identified by feminists can be read as much as a failure of liberalism to live up to its principles than as a reason to reject it altogether. Indeed:

there seems to be no reason why the gender bias of existing social roles would not be recognised by the contractors in Rawls' original position as a source of injustice . . . [and] similar conclusions about the injustice of traditional gender roles can be reached if we ask whether these roles pass Dworkin's test of fairness.[54]

In making these claims, Nussbaum adds her voice to a growing movement of feminists who have argued that too much critical analysis, advertently or otherwise, has 'caricatured or misunderstood liberal thought.'[55] Unconvinced by the conventional feminist critique of liberal legalism for being too individualistic, too abstract and too preoccupied with a form of rationality that marginalises the role of emotion and care in moral and political life, these theorists have sought, in a number of ways, to develop more sympathetic readings of key liberal texts. In the following sections, we will consider this work and its attempted defence of liberalism in detail.

Individualism, Egoism & Community

In response to feminist concerns about liberalism's alleged tendency to focus on the individual and thereby to prioritise asocial egoism, Nussbaum emphasises that the essence of liberalism is in fact fundamentally relational, since it is about respect for *others* as individuals. This can be seen, she argues, not only in the work of Dworkin, who talks of the need to treat each person with equal concern and respect, but also in the work of Rawls against whom so much of the feminist challenge has been directed.

Such an interpretation of Rawls has also been bolstered by Okin who argues that it would be wrong to think that the motivation behind his theory lay in an overtly individualistic agenda, since in fact it lay in a communally grounded concern about co-operation in the face of the vagaries of a social and natural life lottery. On this interpretation, the aim of the veil of igno-

---

[53] M Nussbaum, *Sex and Social Justice*, above n 46 at 57.
[54] W Kymlicka, *Contemporary Political Philosophy: An Introduction* (2nd edn) (Oxford, Oxford University Press, 2002) at 385.
[55] S Okin, 'Justice and Gender: An Unfinished Debate' (2004) 72 *Fordham Law Review* 1537 at 1544.

Re-evaluation of the Feminist Critique

rance is not to render individuals hollow, self-interested and indistinguishable, but to encourage them to engage with forms of life other than their own without prejudice. As Okin explains, those behind the veil of ignorance are self-interested only in the sense that because they do not know what interests they have, they must consider the interests of all equally. Thus, a proper interpretation of Rawls' theory will establish that the veil of ignorance is a heuristic device rather than a blueprint for social interaction,[56] and that what it offers for actual people, who know who they are, is a model for guiding their deliberations not by rational egoism but by empathy and engagement with the points of view of others.[57]

To the extent that this analysis suggests that the popular feminist concern that a Rawlsian approach to justice will generate a society of atomistic, self-interested and profoundly alienated individuals is misplaced, it also raises the question of whether there might not in fact be some value to feminism in this non-egoist perception of the individual as self-sufficient and detachable (if not detached) from social context. The normative goal of self-sufficiency is not one that women should dismiss too lightly, especially since the process of women's individuation is a difficult one, fraught with the danger of subservience to others. Developing this idea further, Cornell draws on the work of another key liberal thinker, Ronald Dworkin, to illustrate the ways in which liberalism might have a vital role to play in facilitating women's individuation.

For Cornell, Dworkin's dual assertions that each of us has equal intrinsic value and that each of us is uniquely responsible for our own life are of considerable worth to feminist analysis. Not only do they chime with the feminist focus on equality, defined as 'treatment of each of us as an equal and not just equal treatment,'[58] but they also reflect the relational insight that being responsible for one's life does not, and cannot, entail a kind of abstract, metaphysical freedom.[59] On the contrary, as Dworkin explains, while:

> you, rather than anyone else, have the right and the responsibility to choose the ethical values that you will try to embody in your life,[60]

this does not entail that you select those values from an abstract or disconnected vantage point.

To the extent that these understandings of freedom and of the individual are useful ones, Cornell suggests that they should not be rejected out of hand by a feminist critique that inappropriately assumes a radical notion of

---

[56] S Okin, 'Justice and Gender: An Unfinished Debate', *ibid* at 1544.

[57] S Okin, 'Reason and Feeling in Thinking about Justice' (1989) 99 (2) *Ethics* 229 at 246.

[58] D Cornell, *At the Heart of Freedom—Feminism, Sex and Equality* (Princeton, Princeton University Press, 1998) at 60. This position is developed by Dworkin in *Taking Rights Seriously*, above n 50.

[59] D Cornell, *At the Heart of Freedom*, *ibid* at 63–4.

[60] R Dworkin, 'The Roots of Justice', unpublished manuscript at 28–9; referred to in D Cornell, *At the Heart of Freedom*, above n 58 at 63.

Feminism(s), Law and Liberalism(s)

liberal autonomy or some highly individualised notion of the liberal self. What's more, Cornell goes on to suggest that, if anything, there is a tendency in Dworkin's account to downplay rather than overstate the importance of individuation in ethical life. Dworkin, theorising from a position in which masculine individuation is a culturally sanctioned process, fails, she argues, to see the 'vulnerability of individuation' from women's point of view. As a result, therefore, he pays inadequate attention to the fact that this individuation process 'needs legal, political, ethical and moral recognition if it is to be effectively maintained.'[61] In order to remedy this, Cornell supplements his analysis with the invocation and protection of a prior moral space for female individuation and equivalent evaluation, which she refers to in her work as 'the imaginary domain'.

In a related fashion, albeit relying on Rawls' work rather than Dworkin's, Okin has joined with Nussbaum and Cornell in suggesting that, contrary to conventional feminist wisdom, one of the main problems with the liberal account of justice may be not that it is too individualistic, but rather that in its views of the family, it is not individualistic enough. Rawls' analysis, at least in its initial form,[62] hypothesised that parties in the original position would be heads of families, thereby assuming that they:

> even if otherwise assumed to be motivated by rational self-interest, could be expected, altruistically, to take into account the interests of other members of their own families.[63]

When situated in a context in which feminist analysis has questioned whether male heads of household can in fact be so trusted, this is a troubling assumption that 'makes the family opaque to claims of justice.'[64] While Okin takes Rawls to task for failing to foresee this shortcoming, therefore, she seeks to establish that it is in fact perfectly in keeping with the spirit of his liberalism to 'conclude that families are the quintessential place for justice' and that other virtues, such as generosity and self-sacrifice, should not be relied upon unless built upon justice.[65]

Contrary to the standard feminist criticisms, then, Cornell, Nussbaum and Okin all suggest that what liberalism really requires when it insists that the individual be taken as the basic unit of political thought is that we recognise the reality that:

---

[61] D Cornell, *At the Heart of Freedom*, above n 58 at 63–4.

[62] In 1997, he published an essay stating that his theory was designed 'to secure equal justice for women and children' in the family while simultaneously asserting that the principles of distribution discovered 'are to apply to (the basic) structure, but are not to apply directly to the internal life of the many associations within it, the family among them'—J Rawls, 'The Idea of Public Reason Revisited', (1997) 64 (3) *University of Chicago Law Review* 765, reprinted in S Freeman (ed) *Collected Papers* (Cambridge, Harvard University Press, 1997) at 596.

[63] S Okin, 'Justice and Gender: An Unfinished Debate', above n 55 at 1552.

[64] J English, 'Justice Between Generations' (1977) 31 *Philosophical Studies* 91 at 95.

[65] S Okin, 'Justice and Gender: An Unfinished Debate', above n 55 at 1564.

Re-evaluation of the Feminist Critique

each person has a course from birth to death that is not precisely the same as that of any other person; that each person is one and not more than one, that each feels pain in his or her own body.[66]

This in turn entails a recognition that 'the demands of a collectivity or a relation should not as such be made the basic goal of politics' since collectives, such as the state and the family, are composed of individuals 'who always continue to have their separate brains and voices, however much they love one another.'[67]

To the extent that this suspicion of social collectives has been frowned upon by communitarian theorists, as well as by feminists influenced by communitarianism, there remains scope for challenge. Nonetheless, it appears that suspicion does not entail dismissal in the manner often assumed. Thus, Nussbaum, Okin and Cornell suggest that liberal theory may in fact pay greater respect to its principles by acknowledging the relevance of community, context and relationship. What's more, it may do so without running into the communitarian trap, of direct concern to feminists, of resigning individuals to the dictates of those collective environments.[68]

Abstraction, Context & Inequality

Turning her attention to feminist concerns regarding the abstraction allegedly inherent in liberal thinking, Nussbaum argues that it is mistaken to think that liberalism has ever entailed 'unrealistic and ahistorical abstraction.' Indeed, as she points out:

> liberals standardly grant that the equality of opportunity that individuals have a right to demand from their governments has material prerequisites, and that these prerequisites may vary depending on one's situation in society.[69]

This, she reflects in her own liberal analysis, through the notion of capabilities and through the suggestion that what liberalism really seeks is not just the fair distribution of resources but rather the assurance that those resources will be operative in promoting the capacity of diverse people to choose and pursue a life in accordance with their own thinking.[70]

---

[66] M Nussbaum, *Sex and Social Justice*, above n 46 at 62.

[67] M Nussbaum, *Sex and Social Justice*, above n 46 at 62.

[68] For further discussion of the difficult relationship between feminism and communitarianism see, eg, N Lacey, 'Community in Legal Theory—Idea, Ideal or Ideology' in *Unspeakable Subjects*, above n 30; M Friedman, 'Feminism and Modern Friendship—Dislocating the Community' (1989) 99 *Ethics* 275; S Hekman, *Moral Voices, Moral Selves* (Cambridge, Polity Press, 1995); E Frazer & N Lacey (eds), *The Politics of Community: A Feminist Critique of the Liberal-Communitarian Debate* (Hemel Hempstead, Harvester Wheatsheaf, 1993).

[69] M Nussbaum, *Sex and Social Justice*, above n 46 at 68.

[70] For further discussion of the capabilities approach and its relation to liberalism, see M Nussbaum, *Women and Human Development: The Capabilities Approach* (Cambridge, Cambridge University Press, 2000) and *Frontiers of Justice: Disability, Nationality and Species Membership* (Cambridge, Harvard University Press, 2006). For a more critical engagement, see

To support this claim, Nussbaum draws directly upon the work of Rawls, which as we have seen, demands that social arrangements be readjusted to ensure that people do not derive advantage from morally irrelevant characteristics. While commentators like Okin and Nussbaum have criticised Rawls for talking about individuals, whilst presuming them to be both male and heads of household, they have also nonetheless defended the original position as a useful idea that 'forces one to question and consider traditions, customs and institutions from all points of view.'[71] In addition, Phillips has suggested that, when properly fostered, the Rawlsian model may be productive for feminist goals, since it permits 'a realisation that a major precondition for a just society is the elimination of inequalities between men and women.'[72]

What is significant here, of course, is that such a realisation is distinctly concrete. To the extent that it demands engagement with the morally irrelevant characteristics from which social advantage yields, both prior to and beyond the veil of ignorance, it requires:

> extensive scrutiny of the history of group hierarchy and subordination, rejecting abstractness at this point as incompatible with a fully equal treatment.[73]

Indeed, it can be argued that what motivates Rawls' theory in the first place is this concern about concrete (and often systematic) disparities in the social distribution of resources as between persons, or groups of persons, who should, in fact, be treated equally. Thus, it is submitted that a deeper engagement with Rawls' work will yield the realisation that it does not in fact entail abstraction from concrete social contexts in any way that feminists should find problematic (at least not once sex and gender issues have also been factored into the constraints imposed in the original position). Indeed, the difference, as Nussbaum explains, comes down to one of *how*, rather than *if*, this concrete context, and the power relations it entails, should be factored in.[74]

At the same time, though, a number of commentators have moved beyond highlighting the role of the concrete within liberal theory to questioning more fundamentally whether it is in fact wise for feminists to reject appeals to abstraction out of hand in any event. After all, as Kiss has pointed out, 'if the aim of feminist justice is inclusion of everyone in moral

---

S Okin, 'Poverty, Well-Being and Gender: What Counts, Who's Heard?' (2003) 31(3) *Philosophy and Public Affairs* 280.

[71] S Okin, 'John Rawls: Justice as Fairness—For Whom?' in M Shanley and C Pateman (eds) *Feminist Interpretations and Political Theory* (Cambridge, Polity Press, 1994) at 190.

[72] A Phillips, 'Universal Pretensions in Political Thought' in M Barrett & A Phillips (ed), *Destabilizing Theory: Contemporary Feminist Debates* (Cambridge, Polity Press, 1992) at 18.

[73] M Nussbaum, *Sex and Social Justice*, above n 46 at 69.

[74] M Nussbaum, 'Rawls and Feminism' in S Freeman (ed) *The Cambridge Companion to Rawls*, above n 24.

Re-evaluation of the Feminist Critique

and social life' then this surely entails constructing a general (ie abstract) point of view which encompasses everyone and that provides 'justice for all regardless of their particular experiences or identities.'[75] Since those who seek to change the world always need concepts that can give them a critical distance from the relations they challenge, it has been argued, furthermore, that feminists should be mindful of the distance they inevitably lose by challenging the vestiges of abstract individualism, universal values and impartial justice.[76] Thus, Mullally, for example, has emphasised the importance of 'reclaiming' universalism, arguing that 'reconstruction must continue to appeal to universal norms and principles, if feminism is to retain its critical, emancipatory edge.'[77] Similarly, Kiss counsels that, while feminists should 'urge vigilance against hasty and unreflective claims of impartiality' and 'stress the challenges of moral theorising in a world of difference and hierarchy,' they should not overstate this 'by claiming that impartiality is always dangerous or that it has no place within feminist ideals of justice.'[78]

Thus, when it comes to the feminist challenge of liberalism's purported reliance on abstract methods and its deployment of a suspect claim to impartiality facilitated thereby, there appears to be some cause for caution, and for more thorough evaluation. According to Nussbaum, there is nothing inherent in liberal goals or ideals that entail abstraction—indeed, at a more fundamental level, even Rawls' theory, which has been seized upon by many feminists as exemplifying abstraction par excellence, is motivated by and grounded in concrete contexts and tangible dilemmas about power relations, social hierarchies and resource inequalities. What's more, to the extent that Rawls' approach, and those of other prominent liberal theorists, may invoke techniques of abstraction in order to pursue their concrete goals, it is submitted that this should not necessarily be viewed as problematic. After all, such techniques ensure not only that distance is maintained between a critical project and its subject but also that people are recognised and treated as equals, despite their diversity.

Justice & Care: The Rationality of Emotions

In response to the alleged tendency within liberalism to prioritise a masculine mode of rationality in which emotions are denigrated, and in which a sharp distinction is maintained between ethics of justice and care,[79]

---

[75] E Kiss, 'Justice', in A Jaggar and I Young (eds), *A Companion to Feminist Philosophy*, above n 34 at 496.

[76] A Phillips, 'Universal Pretensions in Political Thought' in M Barrett & A Phillips (ed), *Destabilizing Theory*, above n 72 at 17.

[77] S Mullally, *Gender, Culture and Human Rights: Reclaiming Universalism* (Oxford, Hart Publishing, 2006) at 1.

[78] E Kiss, 'Justice', in A Jaggar and I Young (eds.), *A Companion to Feminist Philosophy*, above n 34 at 496.

[79] O O'Neill, 'Friends of Difference' (1989) 11 (7) *London Review of Books* 20.

Feminism(s), Law and Liberalism(s)

Nussbaum points out that even liberal theorists like Kant, who may have had a deficient conceptualisation of emotion,[80] were 'far from dismissing emotions from their normative picture of the moral life.'[81]

For Kant, what mattered was that emotions should not be unreflective in their influence, which entailed insistence on a process whereby emotions were subject to rational appraisal. While some feminists, for example Noddings, have been highly critical of this insistence, suggesting that it represents 'an imposition of a male norm of cool rationality on the natural vigour of the passions,'[82] Nussbaum reminds us that that there is good cause for women to be wary of emotion, particularly where that emotion is expected to take the form of care, nurturance of others and self-sacrifice.[83] Indeed, as she puts it:

> indiscriminate self-giving-away seems a very bad idea, especially for women, who have frequently been brought up to think that they should sacrifice their well-being to others without demanding anything for themselves.[84]

Nussbaum emphasises, moreover, that this insistence on subjecting emotion to scrutiny in no way entails that emotion per se is irrelevant in a rational liberal framework or that justice must inevitably be viewed as antithetical to care. On the contrary, the relevance of emotions in liberal theory can be traced back beyond its Enlightenment incarnation to the work of Aristotle. In *The Rhetoric*, for example, Aristotle offers a subtle analysis of emotions such as anger, fear and pity. He suggests that these emotions should be recognised as playing a crucial role in an individual's rational response to life contexts and asserts that a human being cannot think or act virtuously without being possessed of the passions appropriate to the situation:

> far from seeing them as obstacles to good reasoning, Aristotle makes proper passivity and passional responsiveness an important and necessary part of good deliberation.[85]

To the extent that this defence of the rationality of emotions sits alongside a consideration of the importance of friendship and an acknowledgement that none of us are separated in a hard or impenetrable way, it parallels, moreover, moves that Okin and others have identified in Rawls' work. Building on her suggestion that the meaning of Rawls' theory is

---

[80] For further discussion, see R Schott, *Feminist Interpretations of Immanuel Kant* (Pennsylvania, Pennsylvania State University Press, 1997).
[81] M Nussbaum, *Sex and Social Justice*, above n 46 at 73.
[82] M Nussbaum, *Sex and Social Justice*, above n 46 at 74.
[83] R West, *Caring for Justice*, above n 28 at 81.
[84] M Nussbaum, *Sex and Social Justice*, above n 46 at 76.
[85] Aristotle, *The Rhetoric*. Discussed by M Nussbaum in *The Fragility of Goodness: Luck and Ethics in Greek Tragedy and Philosophy* (Cambridge, Cambridge University Press, 1986) at 307; See also M Nussbaum, *Upheavals of Thought: The Intelligence of Emotions* (Cambridge, Cambridge University Press, 2003).

Conclusion: A Return to Liberalism

captured by the image of empathetic, benevolent individuals rather than mutually disinterested maximisers, Okin argues that his account builds as much upon an ethic of care as upon any 'abstracted and rationalistic ethic of justice.'[86] Similarly, McClain has argued that Rawls's theory envisions 'a society where recognition of interdependency leads to mutual respect' and where that respect entails not isolationism but 'an almost tender-hearted solicitude for one another.'[87] This recognition of the role of empathy situates Rawls, it is argued, in line with, rather than opposed to, the Gilligan-inspired vision of relational ethics that has animated much feminist critique of liberalism. What's more, it represents a departure from the Kantian account of emotion in which, as we have seen, 'any feelings that do not follow from independently established moral principles are morally suspect.'[88]

Thus, it is argued that, contrary to the standard feminist critique, many liberal theorists are in fact willing and able to accept that care and justice are always related. What's more, the way in which these ethics are combined in some accounts may be preferable for feminist purposes. Indeed, by insisting that the contextual capacity for care cannot and should not supplant the role of more abstract principles, some versions of liberalism may in fact facilitate a complementarity between the concrete and the abstract, between care and justice, and between emotion and rationality. This is important, since as West points out, while:

> the zealous pursuit of justice, or of some attribute of justice—be it institutional consistency, personal integrity or impartiality—when unconstrained by the demands of an ethic of care, will fail as a matter of justice as well as a matter of care . . . the zealous pursuit of some attribute of care—nurturance, compassion, or particularity—when unconstrained by the demands of an ethics of justice will fail as a matter of care not less than as a matter of justice.[89]

Conclusion: A Return to Liberalism?

There can be no doubt that feminist critique has played an important role in improving our vision beyond the 'mists of neutrality', and in particular in highlighting the ways in which at least some elements of liberalism have facilitated the misrepresentation of legal decision-making as detached from power disparities and patriarchal agendas. At the same time, though, as discussion in the latter part of this chapter has indicated, there has been a marked tendency for feminist theorists engaged in this critical project to accredit too much unanimity to the liberal perspective and to exaggerate the contrast between that perspective and their own position. Granted, as Kiss

---

[86] S Okin, 'Justice and Gender: An Unfinished Debate', above n 55 at 1545.
[87] L McClain, 'Atomistic Man Revisited: Liberalism, Connection and Feminist Jurisprudence' (1992) 65 *Southern California Law Review* 1171 at 1209.
[88] S Okin, *Gender, Justice and the Family*, above n 24 at 98–9.
[89] R West, *Caring for Justice*, above n 28 at 88.

points out, this is not always a bad thing, since 'sharp phrasing can be intellectually clarifying.'[90] But, ultimately, this 'straw-manning' of the liberal target poses a number of dangers to feminist analysis of law, both in terms of undermining the credibility of its critique on its own terms and in terms of preventing the discovery of potentially productive conceptual tools even amongst the ruins of the most conventional of liberal accounts.

To be sure, this project of re-evaluating strands of liberal analysis should not generate uncritical endorsement. The specific liberal theories under scrutiny may require careful and substantial modification to render them of assistance to feminism, and in some cases the assistance achieved may be at best partial or transient.[91] At the same time, though, it has been argued in this chapter that blanket demonisation of liberal thinking does, and should, generate some disquiet. Recognising the complexity and diversity of its contemporary manifestations, Phillips, for example, has conceded that feminist opposition to liberalism, in the contexts of both legal and political theory, 'threatens to become something of a mantra.'[92] In this context it is incumbent upon feminist scholars to re-evaluate the legitimacy of their challenge, the faithfulness of their representation of its target, and the extent to which women's interests might be better promoted by selective appropriation of certain liberal methods or ideals.

Sceptics may argue, of course, that it is a 'public relations' exercise designed to bolster the ideologies of patriarchy and liberalism, but the fact that some liberal thinkers—most notably Rawls—have been receptive to feminist engagement can be seen to attest powerfully both to the artificiality of liberalism/feminism dichotomies and to the potential for productive reformulations. Not only is there considerable value in theoretical terms in investigating these avenues further, but there are also compelling political and strategic reasons for embarking on this enterprise. Indeed, as we will discuss in the next chapter, in a context in which the rhetoric of liberal legalism is both well-established and typically unreceptive to demands framed by competing discourses, there is considerable pragmatic wisdom in feminists re-visiting this approach—if not necessarily with a view to rescuing liberalism per se, then at least with a view to protecting feminism against decline from a position of engaged critique to one of politically stymied and legally silenced mere oppositionalism.

---

[90] E Kiss, 'Justice', in A Jaggar and I Young (eds), *A Companion to Feminist Philosophy*, above n 34 at 493.

[91] For critical perspectives on Okin's reformation of Rawls, eg, see N Lacey, 'Theories of Justice and the Welfare State: A Feminist Critique' in *Unspeakable Subjects*, above n 30 at 65; S Benhabib, *Situating the Self*, above n 24, at 167; D Cornell, *At the Heart of Freedom*, above n 58 at 91; I Young, *Justice and the Politics of Difference*, above n 25 at 105. See also, A Phillips, 'Feminism and Liberalism Revisited: Has Martha Nussbaum Got It Right?' above n 8; S Mullally, *Gender, Culture and Human Rights: Reclaiming Universalism*, above n 77.

[92] A Phillips, 'Feminism and Liberalism Revisited: Has Martha Nussbaum Got It Right?' above n 8 at 250.

3
On Reform and Reforming Rights

The previous chapter critically evaluated some of the key concerns that have been expressed by feminist critics of liberal legalism. In particular, it illustrated the extent to which many feminist theorists, despite their considerable internal diversity, have shared concerns in regard to the role of liberalism—and specifically its methodological abstraction and substantive claims to impartiality and neutrality—in perpetuating and disguising patriarchy. At the same time, though, latter stages of this discussion also highlighted the emergence of a counter-trend within some sections of feminist analysis. Without necessarily trivialising the concerns of previous critics, this counter-movement supports a more nuanced and complex depiction of the liberal enterprise and has demanded a critical re-appraisal of the scope for more productive feminist engagement with key liberal methods and ideals. While the outcomes of this re-visioning and re-deployment of liberalism have yet to be fully charted, let alone evaluated, it was suggested that there are a number of compelling reasons (both in terms of theoretical rigour and pragmatic politics) for pursuing this avenue further.

To the extent that the move away from an unquestioning reliance on liberalism discussed in the last chapter has also marked a move away from a relatively simple style of politics in which there is 'an easy and very direct inference from theory/analysis to policy/strategy,'[1] disagreements have increasingly emerged between feminists over the value of legal reform itself. As the framework of liberal politics, and crucially the role of legal theory within it, has been problematised and scrutinised, law has no longer been represented as 'a straightforwardly useable tool for feminist legal strategy.'[2] And this, in turn, has had a significant impact upon the unanimity with which feminist theorists have been willing and able to support political or practical agendas for reform grounded in a turn to law. It is this engagement between feminism and law (or more specifically legal reform) that will be the focus of discussion in this chapter. Drawing attention to the ways in which many feminists have sought to reject reliance on legal reform techniques (including the use of rights analysis), the following sections will also examine the counters forwarded by those feminists who, although not blind to the

---

[1] N Lacey, 'Feminist Legal Theory Beyond Neutrality' in *Unspeakable Subjects: Essays in Feminist Legal and Social Theory* (Oxford, Hart Publishing, 1998) at 195–6.

[2] N Lacey, 'Feminist Legal Theory Beyond Neutrality' in *Unspeakable Subjects, ibid* at 195–6.

dangers inherent in invoking law or rights, nonetheless stand by their theoretical and practical potential. In important ways, then, this chapter can be seen to provide a concrete case study for examining the previous theoretical discussion around feminism's engagement with liberalism more broadly.

From Theory to Strategy: Feminist Critique & Legal Reform

There is no doubt that the feminist relationship to legal reform strategies grounded in a commitment to the rule of law ideal has been fluctuating and complex. For feminist theorists and activists, in all their diversity, law has been a contested and contradictory domain of social and political struggle. While 'the initial transmutation of the feminist impulse into law lost a lot in translation' such that early feminist engagement 'tended to accept reigning legal assumptions and method,'[3] more recent critique has identified the myriad ways in which the law is itself implicated within the construction of gender relations. While for some feminists, the law nonetheless remains a productive site through which to advance social change, for others the law has been identified as irredeemably patriarchal. As a result, there is profound disagreement, and even ambivalence, amongst feminists over how far the law can be relied upon to change gender relations, as well as over whether strategic attempts to use law to bring about change, in the end, simply operate to reaffirm law's power.

The Case for De-Centering Law

Central to the case against the feminist use of legal reform strategies is the belief that such strategies will, almost inevitably, be futile or counter-productive. Since the goal of feminism is not to replicate the social and legal categories that inform the status quo, the measure of success of its activism lies in the changes that it secures. Yet, many critics have argued that the law, through its reliance on dubious legitimising norms and methods that serve the interests of men, is resistant to feminist reform. Thus Flax, for example, has pointed out that 'we cannot re-vision the world with the tools we have been given,'[4] and Wishik has noted that 'the analytical frames of patriarchal law are not the spaces within which to create visions of feminist futures.'[5]

---

[3] C MacKinnon, 'Reflections on Sex Equality Under Law' in L Kauffman (ed), *American Feminist Thought at Century's End: A Reader* (Oxford, Blackwell, 1993) at 369. Originally printed at (1991) 100 (5) *Yale Law Journal* 1281.

[4] J Flax, 'Mother-Daughter Relationships: Psychodymanics, Politics and Philosophy' in H Eisenstein and A Jardine (eds), *The Future of Difference* (New Brunswick, Rutgers University Press, 1990) at 38.

[5] H Wishik, 'To Question Everything: The Inquiries of Feminist Jurisprudence' (1985) 1 *Berkeley Women's Law Journal* 64 at 77.

Building directly on the critique of liberal legalism discussed in the last chapter, feminists have identified the existence of specific techniques that operate to protect conventional legal method and its outcomes from internal feminist challenge. Processes of boundary definition relegate certain matters as legally irrelevant (because they are political, moral, social, etc), without recognising the constructed and fluctuating nature of those boundaries and without acknowledging the fundamentally political and partisan choices that inform their construction. Meanwhile, doctrines of precedent and techniques of case analysis generate a self-perpetuating and self-justifying maintenance of the status quo, which renders recognition of new approaches both difficult and exceptional. As a result, it is argued by some critics that legal method is ultimately impervious to feminist challenge and that this should have 'concrete consequences for the design of strategies for achieving legal equality.'[6]

More specifically, it has been suggested that feminists must de-centre law, since there is a real and perpetual danger that feminist theory which seeks to engage with the law as an insider will ultimately find itself being co-opted by this powerful discourse.[7] Fineman, for example, has argued that feminist activism should set its target in the domain outside of law. She notes that law, as a system, has engrained techniques that limit and contain feminist criticisms and, as such, it is ill-equipped, or disinclined, or both, to bring about the kind of social transformation that is sought. As a result, while 'law can and should be the *object* of feminist inquiry,' she argues that law reform should not be positioned as the *objective*, since that would 'risk having incompletely developed feminist innovations distorted and appropriated by the institutionalised and intractable dictates of the "law"'.[8]

Importantly, then, Fineman does not altogether reject the relevance of law—she acknowledges that law, whilst not a catalyst for enduring change, can provide a mirror through which to see the social transformations that have been brought about through other ideological institutions[9]—but she argues that feminist scholarship should be about law only in the broadest sense of its role as a manifestation of power in society. What's more, she suggests that feminists should be mindful of the reality that, contrary to conventional and formalist understandings:

---

[6] M Mossman, 'Feminism and Legal Method: The Difference It Makes' in M Fineman and N Thomadsen (eds) *At the Boundaries of Law: Feminism and Legal Theory* (London & New York, Routledge, 1991) at 297.

[7] 'Feminism may enter as the challenger, but the tools inevitably employed are those of the androphite master'—M Fineman, Introduction in M Fineman and N Thomadsen (ed), *At The Boundaries of Law*, ibid at xii—xiii. Echoed in M Fineman, 'Challenging Law, Establishing Differences: The Future of Feminist Legal Scholarship' (1990) 42 *Florida Law Review* 25 at 30.

[8] M Fineman, 'Challenging Law, Establishing Differences: The Future of Feminist Legal Scholarship', *ibid* at 43.

[9] M Fineman, 'Challenging Law, Establishing Differences: The Future of Feminist Legal Scholarship', *ibid* at 33.

On Reform and Reforming Rights

law is not found only in courts and cases, and legislatures and statutes, but in implementing institutions, such as social work and law enforcement, as well.[10]

Indeed, law is pervasive—it is found in our everyday discourses, as well as in the beliefs we hold about the world, and in the norms and values we are committed to.

It is clear that a number of these ideas also animate the scholarship of Smart.[11] Taking seriously the claims that law is pervasive in social life, that feminists are attracted to it as a powerful discourse, and that this attraction may ultimately be ill-advised, Smart draws heavily upon the work of Foucault to develop her analysis.[12] Although himself never specifically interested in law, or feminism, Foucault's analysis of the micro-politics of modern power and of the ways in which claims to knowledge are constructed instances of power relations, have had a profound influence on much feminist work. The merits and demerits of this will be examined in detail in Chapter four. For current purposes, however, it is enough to grasp the central distinction in Foucault's account between what he refers to as 'juridical' and 'disciplinary' power.

While juridical power is bound up with the notions of command, sanction and sovereignty, disciplinary power secures compliance through techniques of surveillance, normalisation and self-regulation. Many commentators, arguably wrongly, have interpreted Foucault as equating law with juridical power.[13] Thus, the upshot of his account for law, so it is argued, is a withering away of its importance as a form of social power and its gradual replacement with more infiltrating and subtle regimes of discipline. But while Smart appears to accept this as an accurate interpretation of Foucault's position on law, she disagrees with the essence of this substantive claim.[14] For Smart, modern society is one in which the role of law is not diminishing but changing; more specifically, law is diversifying into techniques of discipline and governance. As a result, while the juridical model of command and sanc-

---

[10] M Fineman, 'Challenging Law, Establishing Differences: The Future of Feminist Legal Scholarship', *ibid* at 34.

[11] C Smart, *Feminism and the Power of Law* (London & New York, Routledge, 1989).

[12] M Foucault, *The Archaeology of Knowledge* (trans A Sheridan) (New York, Harper Colophon, 1972) & *The History of Sexuality, Volume I* (London, Penguin, 1976) & *Power/Knowledge—Selected Interviews and Other Writings 1972–77* (ed C Gordon) (New York, Pantheon, 1980).

[13] A Hunt & G Wickam, *Foucault and Law—Towards a Sociology of Law as Governance* (London, Pluto Press, 1994). See also A Hunt, *Explorations in Law and Society: Towards a Constitutive Theory of Law* (London & New York, Routledge, 1993). For a different perspective on this interpretation of Foucault, however, see F Ewald, 'Norms, Discipline and the Law' in R Post (ed) *Law and the Order of Culture* (Berkeley, University of California Press, 1991); V Tadros, 'Between Governance and Discipline—The Law and Michel Foucault' (1998) 18 *Oxford Journal of Legal Studies* 75.

[14] For further discussion of Smart's position in this debate, see V Munro, 'Legal Feminism and Foucault—A Critique of the Expulsion of Law' (2001) 28 (4) *Journal of Law and Society* 546.

tion may be less evident, the force and power of law in modern society remains highly significant. More specifically, she argues that law sees itself (and is seen by others) as having the methods to establish the 'truth' of events based on the processes taught to law's agents through specific legal education. Thus, modern law exercises power not just in its material effects, but also in its ability to disqualify other experiences as of lesser value. Non-legal knowledge becomes secondary and non-legal experiences have to be translated into other forms to render them intelligible.[15]

On the basis of this descriptive analysis of the operation of law in modern society, Smart develops a prescriptive thesis which effectively eschews the potential for reform within feminist jurisprudence and calls for a de-centering of law and legal method from feminist analysis. Asserting that:

> feminist legal theory is immobilised in the face of the failure of feminism to affect law and the failure of law to transform the quality of women's lives,

Smart suggests that the feminist tendency to turn to law as the first, last and inevitable point of assistance has inappropriately ceded more power to legal discourse.[16] As a result, she argues that feminists have been trapped in a cycle of being seduced by law's claim to provide a solution, and so accepting as a consequence of pursuing this solution the parameters and constraints defined in advance by legal method and discourse, only to give up thereby the very prospect of seriously engaging the solution that is promised. For Smart, as for Fineman, this realisation entails that, in the future, feminists should 'resist the move towards more law and the creeping hegemony of the legal order.'[17] More specifically, it requires that feminists discourage an automatic resort to law, invest engagement in legal reform with a scepticism regarding the likelihood of its success, and make concerted efforts to invoke, wherever possible, non-legal strategies for securing gender equality.

Importantly, moreover, Smart is at pains to point out that the prescriptive model that she puts forward here demands not just fleeting criticism of law, but its immanent critique. In particular, she laments the fact that even those feminists who have been critical of the law's claims to truth and justice have ended up resorting to its useage in the pragmatic but misguided hope that they can thereby create new, or better, law through its channels.[18] The difficulty with this, as she explains, is that 'while some law reforms may indeed benefit some women, it is certain that all law reform empowers law.'[19] Thus, though she accepts that there may be some circumstances in which this turn to law may be worth the risk, she suggests that feminists

---

[15] C Smart, *Feminism and the Power of Law*, above n 11 at 4.
[16] C Smart, *Feminism and the Power of Law*, above n 11 at 5.
[17] C Smart, *Feminism and the Power of Law*, above n 11 at 5.
[18] C Smart, *Feminism and the Power of Law*, above n 11 at 160.
[19] C Smart, *Feminism and the Power of Law*, above n 11 at 161.

have been too quick to assume this to be the case and have failed to fully acknowledge the implications of this risk in terms of securing longer-term feminist goals. As a result, she argues, feminists who do not challenge the law's centrality and power are almost invariably engaged in a short-sighted and futile project. And in her concluding remarks in *Feminism and the Power of Law*, Smart admonishes such strategies based on legal reform for their 'complicity' with patriarchy and 'irrelevance' for women.[20]

An Evaluation of the 'De-Centering' Thesis

While this analysis of the operation of law's power in modern society has undoubtedly had a significant impact on subsequent feminist thought, critics have highlighted the existence of an important disjunction between Smart's descriptive and prescriptive theses. In her descriptive analysis, as discussed above, Smart emphasises the constructive aspects of legal power and its impact on micro levels of personal and communal experience. This implies an increasingly disciplinary operation of legal power, as it infiltrates social living at intimate levels, constructing and constraining our behaviour through techniques of surveillance and normalisation rather than direct command. Yet, in her prescriptive thesis, in which she calls for a de-centering of law, Smart appears to revert to a more one-dimensional understanding of law as a monolithic entity. As a result, it is argued, she fails to pay attention in her prescriptive thesis to the fact that a logical corollary to the disciplinary operation of legal power she identifies in her descriptive thesis is an increasingly dispersed, fluid and productive agenda for legal reform.[21] Her call to de-centre law, in other words, while backed by recognition of law's plurality, is still dependent on a 'concept of law's power as derived solely from its self-confirming claim to singularity and unity.'[22]

This is problematic, however, not just in terms of the internal consistency of Smart's analysis, but also in terms of the value of her prescriptive agenda itself. Despite having emphasised the role of law as an important site of power struggles in modernity, Smart's reluctance to employ legal mechanisms of reform in her prescriptive thesis forecloses the possibility of transformative attack. Critics point out that this underestimates the importance of law as a process that condenses and aggregates a variety of discursive power strategies within a centralised site. Smart seems to insist here that 'the substance of the law is irrelevant, or not worth bothering with'[23] since

---

[20] R Sandland, 'Between Truth and Difference: Poststructuralism, Law and the Power of Feminism' (1995) 3 *Feminist Legal Studies* 2 at 13.

[21] V Munro, 'Legal Feminism and Foucault—A Critique of the Expulsion of Law', above n 14.

[22] E Kingdom, *What's Wrong with Rights?: Problems for Feminist Politics of Law* (Edinburgh, Edinburgh University Press, 1991) at 6.

[23] R Sandand, 'Between Truth and Difference: Poststructuralism, Law and the Power of Feminism', above n 20 at 16.

Feminist Critique & Legal Reform

engagement with it on its own terms is inevitably counter-productive. But as Sandland has argued, this leads her into:

> an unwarranted nihilism which fails to recognise the strategic potential of a feminism informed by poststructuralist thought to pursue a deconstructivist agenda within legal arenas and discourses.[24]

Smart's theory may indeed provide powerful arguments about the limitations of law as a feminist strategy. But in the final analysis, therefore, critics suggest that she fails to give a full and proper account of why, if law can be powerful in entrenching, expressing and maintaining women's oppression, legal critique and reform cannot hold out at least 'some prospect of progress for women, even if not a panacea?'[25]

In addition, and crucially, it has been emphasised that the 'hands off' approach to legal reform that she and Fineman have advocated fails to acknowledge the extent to which it is the *not* becoming, rather than the becoming, involved in feminist politics of law that may cede ground to antifeminist institutions and practices.[26] As MacKinnon explains, for example, 'one result of this turning away, however realistic its reasons, is that male power continues to own law unopposed.'[27] Particularly in situations in which the relevant problem is already entrenched in the legal domain, the mandate to seek out non-legal strategies for its reform is of limited assistance. While Smart accepts that there are some issues, for example rape, which are 'already in the legal domain' and so 'must be addressed on that terrain,' she continues to point to the futility of feminist demands for legal reform in these arenas and argues that feminist victories secured through the law on sexual assault may ultimately be 'pyhrric'.[28] Not only has this rendered feminists ill-equipped to accord centrality to the peculiarly legal characteristics of rape, it has also significantly undermined the political and symbolic importance of those legal reforms that have been secured (the abolition of the marital rape exemption and the shift from a test of honest to reasonable belief in consent, for example), both to society in general and to particular women and victims.

At a more general level, moreover, the effective paralysis which is encouraged by this insistence on the deconstruction of legal truths without their reformulation, can be seen to have played a key role in contributing to the growing, and often lamented, chasm between contemporary feminist theory

---

[24] R Sandand, 'Between Truth and Difference: Poststructuralism, Law and the Power of Feminism', above n 20 at 14.

[25] N Lacey, 'Closure and Critique in Feminist Jurisprudence: Transcending the Dichotomy or a Foot in Both Camps?' in *Unspeakable Subjects*, above n 1 at 178.

[26] E Kingdom, *What's Wrong with Rights?*, above n 22 at 148.

[27] C MacKinnon, 'The Power to Change' in *Women's Lives, Men's Laws* (Cambridge, Harvard University Press, 2005) at 107.

[28] C Smart, *Feminism and the Power of Law*, above n 11 at 49.

and politics. As Lacey has pointed out, for example, given the political impetus of feminism, it is very unlikely, whatever is dictated by theoretical prescriptive agendas, that 'feminist lawyers will give up hope of the possibility of modest progress through legal change.'[29] Thus, while Smart and Fineman are undoubtedly right in their insistence that, as legal power becomes increasingly dispersed and productive, we cannot rely exclusively on legislative reform campaigns to secure the elimination of gender inequality, their assumption that legal reform has no fruitful role to play in challenging juridical or disciplinary forms of patriarchal power may prove to be misguided. Smart's oft-quoted assertion that 'in accepting law's terms in order to challenge the law, feminism always concedes too much'[30] fails to pay enough attention to her own descriptive recognition of the increasingly diverse, multifaceted and interdisciplinary nature of legal power. What's more, it denies a middle ground between the expulsion of legal reform and the insertion of legal imperialism through its failure to recognise the context-specific nature of the relationship between law and the forms of power than transverse and populate other linguistic and institutional fields. Not all legal reformist strategies are equally flawed, after all, so what feminism needs:

> is not an abandonment of the legal and political project, but rather the development of more sophisticated understandings of legal practices, their strengths as well as their evident and important limitations.[31]

Approaching Reform in the Third Way?

Building on these theoretical and practical concerns over the abandonment of legal reform strategies, a number of feminist commentators have argued for an ongoing, albeit strategic and selective, reliance on law and internal legal challenge. While these feminists acknowledge the seductiveness of law and are alert to the risk of ceding more power to the law in return for superficial victories, they also emphasise the importance of feminist engagement with law, both as a site of social control and as a system of power/knowledge. This approach sees law as both potentially productive *and* dangerous, adopting a contextual analysis towards the utility of legal strategies which maintains a permanently unclosed perspective on their benefits and burdens.

Driving this approach in particular is a fundamental belief in the importance of law in modern society and unease at the suggestion that the best way to respond to its power is simply to ignore it. Just as 'we do not imagine giving up speaking or writing just because our language is deeply

---

[29] N Lacey, 'Closure and Critique in Feminist Jurisprudence: Transcending the Dichotomy or a Foot in Both Camps?' in *Unspeakable Subjects*, above n 1 at 180.

[30] C Smart, *Feminism and the Power of Law*, above n 11 at 5.

[31] N Lacey, 'Closure and Critique in Feminist Jurisprudence: Transcending the Dichotomy or a Foot in Both Camps?' in *Unspeakable Subjects*, above n 1 at 180.

Feminist Critique & Legal Reform

androcentric,' nor, it is argued, should feminists automatically give up legal reform because its methods and assumptions bear the hallmarks of patriarchy.[32] Granted, the fact of this influence gives good grounds for suspicion of the law and mistrust of its promise of an easy solution. But feminists are often forced to engage with realms they do not necessarily trust (medicine, theology, technology, etc).[33] This is not to say that such engagement comes without costs or is always productive, but it is to say that those who have called for the wholesale de-centering of law (including Smart) have failed to pay full attention to the costs of their own strategy. As Cornell explains, 'to put women before the law is a dangerous undertaking' which risks 'reauthorizing a legal system whose authority is ultimately self-legitimating' but feminists cannot ignore the reality that women have inevitably already been entered into the 'preservational economy' of law and thus that the power that law wields in modern society is 'reason enough to challenge it from within.'[34]

This more contextual and cautious approach to the utility of legal reform strategies in feminist analysis has the potential to avoid the double-binds of futile legal reform and constructive paralysis that have plagued previous uncritical or dismissive alternatives. What's more, it also has the benefit of reconciling what might otherwise appear to be an odd contradiction in the work of certain feminist commentators, most notably perhaps MacKinnon. As discussed in preceding chapters, MacKinnon has insisted that the liberal state and its laws are constructed on a patriarchal foundation that legitimises, perpetuates and protects the social practice of male domination over women. But at the same time, and despite this fundamentally pessimistic view of the role of law in modern society, which suggests a deterministic vision within which change can only come via a revolution in gender relations, MacKinnon's practical work—in particular her campaigning with Andrea Dworkin on anti-pornography ordinances and her recent litigation of genocidal rape at the International Criminal Tribunal for the Former Yugoslavia (ICTY)- has also engaged the law, presumably driven by an optimism about the prospect of change therefrom.[35]

---

[32] S Harding, *The Science Question in Feminism* (New York, Cornell University Press, 1986) at 10.

[33] C MacKinnon, *Feminism Unmodified: Discourses on Life and Law* (Cambridge, Harvard University Press, 1987) at 228.

[34] D Cornell, *The Imaginary Domain—Abortion, Pornography and Sexual Harassment* (London, Routledge, 1995) at 235.

[35] In the 1980s, MacKinnon and Dworkin drafted an anti-pornography ordinance which provided a civil remedy to women who could establish that they had been harmed by its existence. The ordinance was adopted in Indianapolis but was ultimately found to be in violation of the First Amendment guarantee of free speech—*American Booksellers Association v Mayor of Indianapolis* 598 F Supp 1316 (SD Ind, 1984; 777 F 2d 323. For further discussion of this approach to pornography, see C MacKinnon, 'Pornography, Civil Rights and Speech' (1985) 20 *Harvard Civil Rights—Civil Liberties Law Review* 1; C MacKinnon, *Only Words*

Now, at first sight, this disjunction between MacKinnon's theory and method might be thought to be opportunistic, confused, or both. Yet, as Naffine has pointed out, MacKinnon is 'not operating at a superficial level' and there is reason to suspect that she is in fact 'well aware of the apparent paradoxes thrown up.'[36] Certainly, in her earlier work, MacKinnon was content to note the precariousness of her position—in *Toward a Feminist Jurisprudence*, she argued that the methodological expression of women's situation under patriarchy was one in which there was:

> no outside to stand on or gaze at, no inside to escape to, too much urgency to wait, no place else to go, and nothing to use but the twisted tools that have been shoved down our throats.[37]

What's more, it is clear that in her later work, she has expanded on the positive dimensions of this position and on the scope which remains for meaningful change even via the twisted tools of law reform. Thus, she comments, for example, that law, while a form of force:

> is also an avenue for demand, a vector of access, an area for contention other than the physical, a forum for voice, a mechanism for accountability, a vehicle of authority, and an expression of norms.[38]

Similarly, noting that it can be a wall, as well as a tool for taking down walls, MacKinnon talks of feminists having made the law into a door; and without displacing her critique of patriarchy, she emphasises that:

> while legal change may not always make social change, sometimes it helps and law *un*changed can make social change impossible.[39]

Read through the lens of this third approach, then, the apparent inconsistency in MacKinnon's work begins to resolve itself. Indeed, her practical engagement with the law emerges as neither a betrayal of her radical theory nor a strategic resignation to law's inevitability. On the contrary, it can be seen to form part of a coherent analysis that refuses to let law 'off the hook' where it fails women, while retaining a cautious optimism about the potential for change offered by legal reform in specific contexts.

(Cambridge, Harvard University Press, 1993); C MacKinnon & A Dworkin (eds) *In Harm's Way: The Pornography Civil Rights Hearings* (Cambridge, Harvard University Press, 1997). For discussion of MacKinnon's recent involvement with rape and genocide at the ICTY, see C MacKinnon, *Women's Lives, Men's Laws*, above n 27; C MacKinnon, *Are Women Human?: And Other International Dialogues* (Cambridge, Harvard University Press, 2006).

[36] N Naffine, 'In Praise of Legal Feminism' (2002) 22(1) *Legal Studies* 71 at 82.

[37] C MacKinnon, 'Feminism, Marxism, Method and the State: Toward a Feminist Jurisprudence' (1983) 8 (2) *Signs* 635 at 637.

[38] C MacKinnon, 'The Power to Change' in *Women's Lives, Men's Laws*, above n 27 at 103.

[39] C MacKinnon, 'The Power to Change' in *Women's Lives, Men's Laws*, above n 27 at 103.

Whether committed to a radical analysis of the systematic oppression of women by men (through law and beyond) or to a postmodern analysis of power relations that construct and normalise (through law and beyond) both men and women, it seems, therefore, that there is scope to preserve a role for legal reform strategies and for the internal challenge to law on its own terms. Importantly, this does not entail that law should be the only, or even the main, focus of feminist attention. Indeed, the wisdom of the insistence that feminists should consider alternative strategies for change rather than defaulting to law is widely acknowledged. That said, however, the value of legal reform in some settings and at some times can and should remain unaffected. As Lacey emphasises, this is crucial, since the political impetus of feminism requires both the development of 'alternative, resistant discourses' *and* an engagement 'with currently powerful discourses and institutions' reflected in modern law.[40] While this 'third way' may be challenged by some for securing a middle ground primarily by postponing difficult questions about which particular contexts will benefit from legal reform activity, it is submitted here that its value lies precisely in the fact that in so doing, it encourages feminists to focus attention not on whether using law is good or bad in the abstract, but rather on whether law reform in this specific time and context will or will not be productive. As Bottomley reminds us, this is vital since there is a:

> role for feminist work which struggles with immediate engagement with law and issues of reform, not only because it is so necessary not to stand aside but because it is where we tease out so much of our thinking. . . . Neither 'law' nor 'theory' will deliver grand plans for great change—the point is to keep on struggling to open issues, keep them open and to keep on seeking and questioning possibilities and potentials.[41]

Feminist Reform and Women's Rights

Perhaps, then, the central theme that emerges out of these debates over the law's potential as a mechanism for feminist reform is that of the duplicity of law. Clearly, the perception of law as an 'unmitigated evil' that animates Smart's call for its de-centering can be argued to be over-generalised and as untenable as any competing perception of it as an innocent pawn of patriarchy.[42] Thus, just as discussion in the previous chapter highlighted the duplicity of liberalism, so too discussion here has illustrated the extent to which, despite its patriarchal methods and discourses, the law can hold out the prospect for meaningful feminist reform, at least in some contexts.

---

[40] N Lacey, 'Closure and Critique in Feminist Jurisprudence: Transceding the Dichotomy or a Foot in Both Camps?' in *Unspeakable Subjects*, above n 1 at 186.

[41] A Bottomley, 'Shock to Thought: An Encounter (of a Third Kind) with Legal Feminism' (2004) 12 *Feminist Legal Studies* 29 at 63–4.

[42] V Kerruish, *Jurisprudence as Ideology* (London, Routledge, 1991) at 3.

On Reform and Reforming Rights

But, of course, accepting the potentiality of law in this way raises in turn a number of further questions. In particular, how should that law reform, where it is rightly embarked upon, best be pursued in order to secure feminist successes? In a context in which law reform claims could be grounded variously in rights, needs or responsibility, it is clear that the dominant liberal approach has tended to prioritise rights analysis, and more specifically, has privileged a particular conception of rights and rights-holders. By turning attention in the remainder of this chapter to the feminist engagement with, and critique of, rights-based claims, this discussion will not only provide a concrete instance of law reform through which to trace the concerns outlined in the previous sections, but, to the extent that rights have often served as an emblem of contemporary liberal ideology, it will also provide a testing ground for the broader critique and reconstruction of liberalism engaged with in the previous chapter.

The Feminist Challenge to Rights

The ability of rights analysis to politicise contentious issues and to provide protection to the individual against state intervention has been illustrated repeatedly in liberal legal history and can barely be disputed. The discriminatory application of the averred hallmarks of the liberal system, namely tolerance and equality, has frequently been uncovered and apparently remedied through the invocation of rights-based strategies. Such strategies were central, for example, to the historical successes enjoyed by the Black civil rights movement and the Suffragette movement, and they continue to be a crucial aspect of the legal armoury of contemporary political lobbyists, who operate in a context within which national legislation and international conventions increasingly invoke the rhetoric of 'basic human rights' to protect particular choices and practices.

However, many critical commentators have voiced concerns regarding the extent to which the liberal tendency to uncritically assume the applicability of dominant rights analysis in all contexts represents a dangerous conceptual move.[43] Such commentators have, for example, highlighted the pitfalls of assuming that conferral of rights will automatically bring about attendant social or economic change and have highlighted the extent to which the history of the women's movement fails to bear this out.[44] While acknowledging the merits of rights discourse as a tool of political dialogue, such commentators emphasise the need to maintain a critical awareness of the biases inherent in the ascription of rights and in the determination of

---

[43] D Rhode, 'Feminist Perspectives on Legal Ideology' in J Mitchell & A Oakley (eds) *What is Feminism?* (Oxford, Blackwell, 1986) & E Kingdom, 'Body Politics and Rights' in J Bridgeman & S Millns (eds) *Law and Body Politics—Regulating the Female Body* (Aldershot, Dartmouth, 1995).

[44] E Kingdom, *What's Wrong with Rights?*, above n 22 at 47.

rights-based claims.[45] Such commentators have argued that even under regimes of rights, the disingenuous social exclusion of particular groups (including, but not restricted to, women) has been maintained[46] and have illustrated the ways in which an appeal to a right can too easily 'be transformed into a general right, and its significance for women lost in the process.'[47] In addition, commentators like Smart have lamented the focus on rights, which, they argue, has 'generated more centralised knowledge about sexual relationships, marriage relationships, child care organisation, and so on' and created thereby the possibility for greater surveillance and discipline through the law.[48]

Alongside these warnings about the dangers of automatically or uncritically relying on rights analysis, moreover, a number of commentators have also challenged certain key assumptions informing the very notion of a right itself. Thus, Glendon, for example, while generally positive about the dominance of rights-based claims within western legal culture, concedes that these rights are often inappropriately conceived as being necessarily property based, autonomous, and protective, rather than potentially also contingent, interconnected and dependent. As she expresses it:

> our rights talk, in its absoluteness, promotes unrealistic expectations, heightens social conflict, and inhibits dialogue that might lead towards consensus, accommodation, or at least the discovery of common ground. . . . In its relentless individualism, it fosters a climate that is inhospitable to society's losers, and that systematically disadvantages caretakers and dependents.[49]

Thus, despite the increasing centrality afforded to rights analysis within liberal legal jurisdictions, considerable scepticism remains regarding the presumptions of individualism and abstraction that underlie this legal strategy.

While these criticisms of the individualism and abstraction in rights analysis clearly reflect the more general criticisms of liberalism, which were discussed in the last chapter, it is important to briefly re-cap on these here in order to fully examine their implications for the use of rights claims as part of a strategy for feminist legal reform.

Rights are too Individualistic

Critics of liberalism have often argued that there is an undue emphasis in prevailing rights analysis on the necessarily individual nature of the rights-bearer

---

[45] M Minow, 'Interpreting Rights—An Essay for Robert Cover' (1987) 96 *Yale Law Journal* 1860.

[46] N Hirschmann & C Di Stefano, 'Revision, Reconstruction and the Challenge of the New' in N Hirschamm & C Di Stefano (eds), *Revisioning the Political—Feminist Reconstructions of Traditional Concepts in Western Political Theory* (Boulder, Westview Press, 1996) at 16.

[47] E Kingdom, *What's Wrong with Rights?*, above n 22 at 79.

[48] C Smart, *Feminism and the Power of Law*, above n 11 at 124.

[49] M Glendon, *Rights Talk: The Impoverishment of Political Discourse* (London, Free Press, 1991) at 14.

and on the relevance of rights as a mechanism for providing boundaries between one's interests and those of another. For these critics, moreover, this individualism is deeply problematic, fostering a drive towards separation and radically dislocated autonomy which denies the complexities of human relationships and identity-formation.[50] Indeed, as Minow puts it, 'rights analysis offers release from hierarchy and subordination' only to those who can match the picture of the abstract, autonomous individual, and this means that for those who do not, or cannot, match that picture, 'the application of rights analysis can be not only unresponsive but also punitive.'[51]

Many commentators have questioned the individualist premises implicit in rights discourse and have challenged the necessarily restricted scope this offers for meaningful resolution of contentious questions.[52] By attaching rights firmly to identifiable individuals, it is argued that rights-based strategies have fostered a strongly separatist agenda that fails to deal adequately with the complexities of connections and relationships between individuals.[53] This separatist agenda assumes the existence of differentiated radically autonomous legal agents with self-centred interests located firmly within the confines of self-contained bodily boundaries.[54] In thus privileging unquestioningly the model of the individual rights-bearer, dominant liberal theories have failed, it is argued, to consider the possibility (and reality) that the self as a rights-bearer and legal person has been profoundly influenced by, and cannot be distinguished from, both social context and personal relationships.[55]

In addition, it is argued that the preoccupation fostered by rights analysis with individual entitlements not only diverts concern away from collective or personal relationships, but also encourages the adoption of a conflict-dominated perception of social interaction. Where the rhetoric of rights encourages a legal environment dominated by demands for individual entitlement, it also engenders an adjudicative function concerned primarily with evaluating competing claims rather than with meaningfully resolving dilemmas (presented under rights analysis as irreconcilable conflicts).[56] To

---

[50] C MacKenzie & N Stoljar, *Relational Autonomy—Feminist Perspectives on Autonomy, Agency and the Social Self* (Oxford, Oxford University Press, 2000).

[51] M Minow, *Making All the Difference—Inclusion, Exclusion and American Law* (Itacha, Cornell University Press, 1990) at 147.

[52] F Olsen, 'Statutory Rape: A Feminist Critique of Rights Analysis' (1984) 63 *Texas Law Review* 387.

[53] D Rhode, 'Feminist Perspectives on Legal Ideology' in J Mitchell & A Oakley (eds) *What is Feminism?*, above n 43 at 151–60.

[54] V Munro, 'Square Pegs in Round Holes: The Dilemma of Conjoined Twins and Individual Rights' (2001) 10(4) *Social and Legal Studies* 459.

[55] M Sandel, *Liberalism and the Limits of Justice* (Cambridge, Cambridge University Press, 1982).

[56] J Bridgeman & S Millns, *Feminist Perspectives on Law—Law's Engagement with the Female Body* (London: Sweet & Maxwell, 1998) at 33.

this extent, it is often argued by feminists that rights tend to be male rather than female in their orientation. As Finley puts it, 'seeing matters as involving conflicts of rights or interests, as contrasted to relational thinking, is male because this way of expressing things is the primary orientation of more men than women.'[57]

Related to this critique, it has also been argued that the tendency to frame rights in negative terms, as protections against state interference or interpersonal encroachment, inappropriately limits their utopian potential, leading to an impoverished framework for social living within which collective responsibility is sidelined. In a context in which ensuring people's well-being may in fact require more, rather than less, intervention from the state, the negativity of rights arguably takes us further away from the blueprint for a good society. Indeed, as West puts it, it creates a puzzling and troubling situation in which states are not only freed from any obligation to ensure the minimal preconditions of a good society, but are in violation of their citizen's rights if they interfere in order to do so. This, it is argued, creates a morally barren world in which citizens have the right to keep the state out of our lives, but have no obligations to help one another or to facilitate communal well-being.[58]

Rights are too Abstract

While the above critiques express concern about the perception of the individual or of the community which is implicated in prevailing rights analysis, other critical theorists have looked to the more pragmatic question of its ability to deal with concrete disputes. More specifically, critics have argued that the project of seeking to frame a claim in terms of rights is futile since rights are inherently indeterminate. Rights, so it is argued, are internally incoherent because they articulate contradictory goals such as 'freedom' and 'security'. Moreover, the invocation of a right by one person can almost always be met with the invocation of a competing right from another person, and there is nothing within rights analysis itself to provide guidance on how such tensions can be resolved, without resort to broader utilitarian calculus.[59]

Related to this is another problem with rights analysis, namely the extent to which talking in terms of rights oversimplifies what are in fact extremely complex power relations. As Rhode comments, rights analysis is incapable of meaningfully resolving complex social issues, since it simply restates the dilemma involved in a more abstract form. But this does nothing to deal

---

[57] L Finley, 'Breaking Women's Silence in Law: The Dilemma of the Gendered Nature of Legal Reasoning' (1989) 64 *Notre Dame Law Review* 886 at 894.

[58] R West, *Re-Imagining Justice: Progressive Interpretations of Formal Equality, Rights and the Rule of Law* (Aldershot: Ashgate, 2003) at 75–6.

[59] For further discussion of the slippage between deontic and utilitarian analysis in the context of the competing right to life claim of conjoined twins, see V Munro, 'Square Pegs in Round Holes: The Dilemma of Conjoined Twins and Individual Rights', above n 54.

with the underlying power issues and obscures the way in which competing interests reflected therein are accommodated.[60] Not only is the ascription of a right thus of limited use in moving towards abiding resolution, it is also dangerous, since this process of abstraction allows decision-makers to mask their preferences under the superficially determinate form of rights-based reasoning. Indeed, as Palmer points out, rights rhetoric, precisely by simplifying complex power relations, assists in a process of legal rationality that ultimately 'fails to overcome existing structural inequalities which are woven into women's daily lives.'[61]

In addition, transposing certain problems into the terrain of rights may be damaging since it defines these problems as amenable to legal solution, even though once thus translated, these problems may be quite different in content or priority from how they were originally conceived or expressed by the individuals involved.[62] Thus, for example, giving the abused wife the right not to be beaten by her husband is not only of little use if the emotional or economic dominance of her husband within the relationship (or indeed the emotional or economic dominance of men within society) is left unaddressed, it may also inappropriately translate her problem into one of how to leave her husband or remove him from the marital home when in fact her problem is one of how to prevent future violence while preserving the integrity of her family unit. As a result of this, Olsen concludes that while the claim to a right can operate on a personal level as a positive way for women to make a seemingly powerful claim, on the deeper, analytical level, the concept that women have rights may in practice be unhelpful since it cannot answer the difficult questions which it inevitably raises.[63]

Rights and Wrong Assumptions

While this feminist critique of rights discourse is well-documented, it is contentious, even amongst feminist commentators themselves. Indeed, many feminists have challenged these allegations of individualism, abstraction and indeterminacy. And just as those feminists who have criticised rights have drawn on the broader critique of liberalism discussed in the previous chapter to support their claims, so those feminists who seek to defend rights, or to highlight their potential for positive reconstruction, have presented arguments that map on to the defences of liberalism lodged by others.

---

[60] D Rhode, 'Feminist Perspectives on Legal Ideology' in J Mitchell & A Oakley (eds) *What is Feminism?*, above n 43 at 151–60. See also M Tushnet, 'An Essay on Rights' (1984) 62 *Texas Law Review* 1375; P Gabel, 'The Phenomenology of Rights-Consciousness and the Pact of the Withdrawn Selves' (1984) 62 *Texas Law Review* 1563.

[61] S Palmer, 'Feminism and the Promise of Human Rights—Possibilities and Paradoxes' in S James & S Palmer (eds.) *Visible Women—Essays on Feminist Legal Theory* (Oxford, Hart Publishing, 2002) at 96.

[62] C Smart, *Feminism and the Power of Law*, above n 11 at 144.

[63] F Olsen, 'Statutory Rape: A Feminist Critique of Rights Analysis', above n 52.

Feminist Reform and Women's Rights

In response to concerns about the individualism of rights analysis, and its attendant promotion of conflict at the expense of collective cooperation, for example, a number of feminists have highlighted the distinction between individualism and self-interest. Rights, it is argued, do not necessarily entail selfishness, although they do entail recognition that each person should be treated as an end in her self. In a context in which women have too often been treated primarily as a means to the ends of others, many feminists have embraced this deontic logic with enthusiasm. Moreover, to the extent that rights focus on autonomy, many feminists have pointed out that their basis lies not in a concern with the isolated individual, but in a concern with the community overall. Indeed, as Minow expresses it:

> even this usual conception of rights, premised on autonomy, relies on a social and communal construction of boundaries among people.[64]

Since these boundaries are invented and reinvented by people in various ways, legal rights are in fact interdependent and mutually defining. Thus, she argues that 'rights can be reconceived as a language for describing and remaking patterns of relationships' and 'can be understood as communally recognised rituals for securing attention in a continuing struggle over boundaries between people.'[65]

Many feminists have built upon this assertion of relationality to argue, moreover, that, contrary to the standard critique, rights do not in fact encourage a conflict-dominated perception of social living, but can facilitate cooperation and connection. As Kiss explains, not only is there nothing alienating about rights to form associations with others, but those political rights (eg to free expression) which enable people to express conflicts can also create a framework for social cooperation. Ascribing rights to someone asserts that their interests, aspirations and vulnerabilities matter enough to impose duties on others. Thus, they imply a moral connection between the right-bearer and others, and in that sense, rights can, and do, 'define a moral community'.[66]

This relates in turn, of course, to the concern expressed by West that rights analysis diverts attention away from the community and from the idea of collective well-being. Community is certainly an important concept in feminist thinking, but Minow has argued that rights can re-confirm rather than undermine it. Indeed, as she explains, although the language of rights, at first glimpse, may say little of community, those who claim rights

---

[64] M Minow, 'Interpreting Rights—An Essay for Robert Cover', above n 45 at 1883. See also M Minow & M Shanley, 'Relational Rights and Responsibilities: Revisioning the Family in Liberal Political Theory and Law' (1996) 11 (1) *Hypatia* 4.

[65] M Minow, *Making All the Difference*, above n 51 at 383.

[66] E Kiss, 'Alchemy or Fool's Gold? Assessing Feminist Doubts about Rights' in M Shanley & U Narayan (eds) *Reconstructing Political Theory: Feminist Perspectives* (Pennsylvania, University of Pennsylvania Press, 1997) at 5.

strengthen their relation to the community in the act of so doing since they 'implicitly agree to abide by the community's response and to accord similar regard to the claims of others.' Thus:

> in a deeper sense, those claiming rights implicitly invest themselves in a larger community, even in the act of seeking to change it.[67]

This realisation is reflected, moreover, in the work of liberal theorists such as Raz who acknowledge that there can be no sharp distinction between rights and the common good, since the origins of rights lie in our commitment to the idea that it is good that people live in a society that protects their individual interests.[68]

In addition, in response to concerns about the abstraction of rights, many feminist commentators have pointed out the potential benefits of this kind of approach. As Kiss argues, for example:

> vulnerable, stigmatised people often have the most to gain from the protection that abstract and impersonal frameworks of rights can provide.[69]

Similarly, while Held accepts that the approach that dominates rights analysis may involve an 'artificial and misleading abstraction' that should not be supposed to provide an adequate approach for morality in general, she notes that 'it may be an abstraction that is useful for some legal and political purposes.'[70] More specifically, a number of feminists have highlighted the strategic potential in the abstraction of rights-based claims.[71] The bluntness of rights as an instrument, while a source of concern to critics, also enables complex issues to be reduced into the kind of simplified form that is most conducive to political lobbying.[72] This, in turn, can have productive effects for the individual parties involved—in the context of domestic violence, for example, the potential for the victim, by relying on an abstract rights-based claim, to transcend curtailing issues of relationship may present a welcome ideological and legal departure. What's more, it may provide a powerful tool in encouraging police forces (still reluctant to

---

[67] M Minow, *Making All the Difference*, above n 51 at 294.

[68] J Raz, 'Rights and Individual Well-Being' in *Ethics in the Public Domain: Essays in the Morality of Law and Politics* (Oxford, Clarendon Press, 1994).

[69] E Kiss, 'Alchemy or Fool's Gold? Assessing Feminist Doubts about Rights' in M Shanley & U Narayan (eds) *Reconstructing Political Theory: Feminist Perspectives*, above n 66 at 6.

[70] V Held, 'Rights', in A Jaggar & I Young (eds), *A Companion to Feminist Philosophy* (Oxford, Blackwell, 2000) at 507.

[71] E Kingdom, 'Body Politics and Rights' in J Bridgeman & S Millns (eds) *Law and Body Politics*, above n 43.

[72] F Beveridge & S Mullaly, 'International Rights and Body Politics' in J Bridgeman & S Millns (eds) *Law and Body Politics*, above n 43.

abstract the violence involved from its contextual and relational background) to intervene in the arena of domestic disputes.[73]

Towards the Reconstruction of Rights

Thus, several commentators have suggested that the feminist critique of liberal rights, while not without merit, has focused too much attention on their limitations and dangers under current circumstances, at the expense of a proper evaluation of their potential. While rights discourse can reinforce alienation and can constrict political debate, it can also, it seems, strengthen links to the community and assist in the development of relational and collective identity.[74] Under the influence of this more positive interpretation, there has been a renewed surge of interest in contemporary feminism, not on criticising rights analysis and trivialising its value for feminist reform, but on emphasising the productive dimension of rights claims and calling, in turn, for a renewed engagement with them as a strategy for political and legal change.

As part of this project, many feminists have paid particular attention to the contexts of care and connection that animate women's lives. While the standard critique would deem these contexts ill-suited to the invocation of (individualist and abstract) rights-based claims, these feminists have sought to illustrate how rights can be reconstructed to recognise and respond effectively to such relational concerns.[75] Without uncritically presuming the value of those relationships to the individuals involved,[76] this reconstruction emphasises that rights are not self-enforcing but dependent on their ability to persuade others and to generate sympathy or solidarity.[77] Remaking, rather than rejecting rights, this approach draws:

> upon an assumption that people are fundamentally connected rather than autonomous, that differences between people are to a significant degree socially constructed and changeable, and that theories of difference reiterate assumptions built into societal institutions that also may be reconstructed.[78]

---

[73] For further discussion, see, eg, R Dobash & R Dobash, *Women, Violence and Social Change* (London & New York, Routledge, 1992); S Grace, *Policing Domestic Violence in the 1990s* (Home Office Research Study 139) (London, HMSO, 1995); S Edwards, *Sex and Gender in the Legal Process* (London: Blackstone Press, 1996); C Hoyle, *Negotiating Domestic Violence: Police, Criminal Justice and Victims* (Oxford, Oxford University Press, 2000); A Finney, *Domestic Violence, Sexual Assault and Stalking: Findings from the 2004/05 British Crime Survey* (London, Home Office, 2006)—available on line at http://www.homeoffice.gov.uk/rds/pdfs06/rdsolr1206.pdf.

[74] E Schneider, 'The Dialectic of Rights and Politics: Perspectives from the Women's Movement' in M Fineman & N Thomadsen (eds), *At the Boundaries of Law*, above n 6 at 303.

[75] M Minow, *Making All the Difference*, above n 51 at 269.

[76] R West, 'Jurisprudence and Gender' (1988) 55 *University of Chicago Law Review* 1.

[77] M Minow, *Making All the Difference*, above n 51 at 296.

[78] M Minow, *Making All the Difference*, above n 51 at 228.

It emphasises that the rationale for rights ultimately lies in a care and concern for others and suggests that:

> the spread of human rights culture may depend less on developing people's capacity to discern universal principles and more on fostering people's sense that the suffering of strangers is a wound to all humanity.[79]

In addition, many feminists have argued that, while rights may have tended in the past to revolve around negative protection from encroachment, there is plenty of scope for rights to be reconstructed in order to accommodate positive entitlements as well. As West points out:

> the notion of a 'positive right' may be disfavoured in contemporary liberal discourse but it is by no means oxymoronic.[80]

Indeed, she argues that the connection between the liberal idea of rights and the constraint of negativity is a contingent, rather than logical, one; and that the contingent connection is not particularly strong, since in other times and other cultures, rights have been understood in more positive terms.[81] In a context in which international human rights jurisprudence is increasingly receptive to the imposition of positive obligations upon states to create structures that ensure individual and communal well-being, it could be argued that this reconstruction is already underway.[82] Certainly, in the specific context of feminism, such a development could enable rights to perform an important function in tackling systemic power imbalances between men and women. Thus, the concept of positive rights could, for example, encourage a more proactive role for the state in securing genuine gender equality in both the public and the private spheres.

Importantly, moreover, feminist commentators who seek to reconstruct rights in this way are not merely pointing to the feasibility of this relational and positive reformulation, but are also presenting a political and pragmatic case for its realisation. While not dismissing the concerns expressed by those who criticise liberal rights, these feminists have emphasised the considerable costs involved in abandoning reliance on rights discourse as a strategy for bringing about change. As West has put it, for example:

> when proponents of the good society turn their backs on rights, they relinquish one way of insisting that moral judgement, moral choice, and moral vision—and not just interests, preferences, votes, power and money—guide political and legal action. They turn their backs on a path ... for transforming those universalistic utopian ideas of the good society into political realities.[83]

---

[79] E Kiss, 'Alchemy or Fool's Gold? Assessing Feminist Doubts about Rights' in M Shanley & U Narayan (eds) *Reconstructing Political Theory: Feminist Perspectives*, above n 66 at 11.

[80] R West, *Re-Imagining Justice*, above n 58 at 83.

[81] R West, *Re-Imagining Justice*, above n 58 at 83.

[82] S Mullally, *Gender, Culture and Human Rights: Reclaiming Universalism* (Oxford, Hart Publishing, 2006).

[83] R West, *Re-Imagining Justice*, above n 58 at 102.

Particularly in the current socio-political climate, the rhetorical value of rights for feminist campaigners should not be dismissed too lightly. Couching a claim in terms of a right represents a major step towards securing recognition of its attendant wrong. Indeed, as Smart explains, to claim that an issue is a matter of rights is to give the claim legitimacy and to make it 'popular', not necessarily in the sense that everyone agrees with it, but in the sense that it becomes accessible.[84] By making the claim thus accessible, talk in terms of rights also has the advantage of permitting feminists to engage with the law on its own terms. And while, as was noted in the discussion above, the law can be a duplicitous friend, there are compelling reasons for continuing to seek out ways to engage with it and to call for it to live up to its potential from within. Thus, Williams, despite her rejection of the tendency to think of rights as ends in themselves, has noted that 'rights rhetoric has been and continues to be an effective form of discourse for blacks.'[85] And Palmer has argued that 'rights rhetoric has played an important part in improving the lives of subordinated groups in society, including women.'[86]

Conclusion: On Rights & Reforming Rights

Discussion in the earlier part of this chapter illustrated the complexity of feminism's relationship to legal reform. In the end, however, it defended the merits of a selective reliance on law, even in the face of measured scepticism about its potential to bring about change in all situations. It is perhaps unsurprising, then, to find that discussion on rights in the latter part of this chapter should yield a similar conclusion. Those who criticise rights for being too individualistic or too abstract undoubtedly have a valid and important point. But in calling for their abandonment, these feminist commentators (like those who call for the rejection of liberalism or the de-centering of law) have failed to subject their own assumptions to critical scrutiny, underestimating the extent to which rights may be reconstructed to carry new meanings and ignoring the existence of contexts in which rights remain potentially productive. As a result, it seems that while feminist doubts about rights reveal 'valuable insights and promising directions of research and political action,' they also betray 'serious problems of overstatement, inconsistency and political naivety.'[87]

[84] C Smart, *Feminism and the Power of Law*, above n 11 at 143.

[85] P Williams, *The Alchemy of Race and Rights—Diary of a Law Professor* (Cambridge, Harvard University Press, 1991) at 149. See also, P Williams, 'Alchemical Notes: Reconstructing Ideals from Deconstructed Rights' (1987) 22 *Harvard Civil Rights—Civil Liberties Law Review* 401.

[86] S Palmer, 'Feminism and the Promise of Human Rights—Possibilities and Paradoxes' in S James & S Palmer (eds) *Visible Women*, above n 61 at 97.

[87] E Kiss, 'Alchemy or Fool's Gold? Assessing Feminist Doubts about Rights' in M Shanley & U Narayan (eds) *Reconstructing Political Theory: Feminist Perspectives*, above n 66 at 2.

On Reform and Reforming Rights

According to Kiss, there are three key lessons that feminists should take from their previous engagement over the issue of rights. Firstly, that feminist political theory needs a more refined model of rights and a fuller understanding of how rights structure relations and institutions. Second, that while rights have more to offer than many feminist critics realise, it is also true that attention to the texture of women's lives can help construct a richer understanding of rights. And third, that although feminists should not turn their backs on rights, there are some aspects of the feminist project which should transcend the realm of rights talk if they are to succeed.

To the extent that the project of reconstructing rights outlined in the previous discussion has created, and continues to create, scope for their relational and positive dimensions to be recognised and developed, it is clear that important steps are already being taken in feminist scholarship to heed the first two of these lessons. In regard to the final lesson, moreover, there is an increasing acceptance (mirroring the 'third way' approach to legal reform discussed above) of the need for a more fluid, contextual and strategic approach to the use of rights analysis. Indeed, in the same way that much feminist scholarship has come to acknowledge that the problem with legal reform strategies is not reliance on law per se but the tendency towards law fetishism, so too it has been increasingly noted that the problem with rights lies primarily in the tendency to automatically assume their value in the contemporary socio-political climate.[88] What feminist theorists and activists really need to avoid is not so much the use of rights but rather the assertion of any blanket position on their utility. Thus, Kingdom has called on feminists to resist 'policy essentialism' over rights, pointing out that 'there can be no single principle in relation to feminist politics of law and the appeal to rights' since there has to be, on each occasion, a 'calculation of specific issues, strategies, tactics and possible outcomes which are important to feminists.'[89]

Relying on law, and more specifically rights analysis, as a means of achieving social change remains a high risk strategy, but it has been suggested in this chapter that it would be riskier still to abandon it to those who are unconcerned with, or opposed to, the goal of gender equality. As Palmer concludes:

> the language of rights has the potential to mobilise movements, to influence political debate, and, perhaps, to contribute to social change.[90]

For feminists, then, 'the challenge lies in giving meaning to rights that are imaginative and responsive to the realities of women's lives' without foreclosing the possibility that there may be other methods of engaging

---

[88] V Kerruish, *Jurisprudence as Ideology*, above n 42 at 174.
[89] E Kingdom, *What's Wrong with Rights?*, above n 22 at 148–9.
[90] S Palmer, 'Feminism and the Promise of Human Rights—Possibilities and Paradoxes' in S James & S Palmer (eds) Visible Women, above n 61 at 115.

Conclusion: On Rights & Reforming Rights

politics and morals that would, in the circumstances, be more fitting or productive.[91]

Central to the kind of context-specific assessment of the productivity of rights (or, more broadly, legal reform) defended in this chapter, of course, is a sensitivity not only to the large-scale distributive and institutional vectors that frame social interaction, but also to the more subtle ways in which relationships between individuals (in their capacity as legal subjects) are invested with multiple power dynamics and constructed by normative expectations that wield concrete effects. In the next chapter, therefore, attention will turn directly to this question of power. Set against a background in which (radical) feminist analysis has arguably struggled to highlight the pervasiveness of male domination without reducing women to passivity, or politics to determinism, it will re-examine the relevance of Foucault's concept of micro-level, disciplinary power. The aim here is to produce a dialogue that transcends the current polarisation of these feminist and Foucaultian positions and that, in so doing, provides a more promising framework for future feminist theory and politics.

---

[91] S Palmer, 'Feminism and the Promise of Human Rights—Possibilities and Paradoxes' in S James & S Palmer (eds) Visible Women, above n 61 at 115.

4
Power, Domination and Patriarchy

In discussion over the previous chapters, it has been argued that MacKinnon's thesis of feminism unmodified, which emerged amidst the feminist debates of the 1980s, brought with it a new breed of so-called 'radical' political and legal theory. This radical approach sought to move beyond the confines of the equality/difference debate and, in so doing, to question the underlying presumption that the relevant benchmark for recognition should be a male one.[1] More specifically, as discussed in Chapter one, it challenged the notion that the subordination of women was a matter of irrational differentiation on the basis of sex. Instead, it drew attention to the phenomenon of male domination, uncovering its role in making gender difference relevant to determining the distribution of benefits, always to the systematic disadvantage of women. Having done so, it argued that feminism must recognise dominance as the central issue, devoting its energy to highlighting the role played by institutional structures in the maintenance of this gendered power relation and to challenging the resultant disparity between men's power and women's subordination.

As has also been previously noted, however, MacKinnon's thesis, and the radical feminism that it represents, have faced mounting challenge, even from those within the feminist community. Stipulating men as the authors of the subjection and victimisation of women and implicating the state as a primary instigator and perpetuator of the patriarchal system, its deterministic and essentialist connotations have provoked sustained criticism.[2] Aside

---

[1] For an overview of this position, see in particular: C MacKinnon, 'Feminism, Marxism, Method and the State: An Agenda for Theory' (1982) 7 (3) *Signs* 515; C MacKinnon, 'Feminism, Marxism, Method and the State: Toward a Feminist Jurisprudence' (1983) 8 (2) *Signs* 635; C MacKinnon, *Feminism Unmodified: Discourses on Life and Law* (Cambridge, Harvard University Press, 1987), C MacKinnon, *Toward A Feminist Theory of State* (Cambridge, Harvard University Press, 1989).

[2] See, eg, L Finley, 'The Nature of Domination and the Nature of Women: Reflections on Feminism Unmodified' (1988) 82 *Northwestern University Law Review* 352; E Jackson, 'Catharine MacKinnon and Feminist Jurisprudence: A Critical Appraisal' (1992) 12 (2) *Journal of Law and Society* 195; K Bartlett, 'MacKinnon's Feminism: Power on Whose Terms?' (1987) 75 *California Law Review* 1559; M Heath, 'Catharine MacKinnon: Towards a Feminist Theory of State' (1997) 9 *Australian Feminist Law Journal* 45; A Harris, 'Race and Essentialism in Feminist Legal Theory' (1990) 42 *Stanford Law Review* 581; M Mahoney, 'Whiteness and Women, In Practice and Theory: A Reply to Catharine MacKinnon' (1993) 5 *Yale Journal of Law and Feminism* 217; D Cornell, *Beyond Accommodation—Ethical Feminism,*

from the difficulties posed by the claim that all women are united by any essential experience (which will be discussed in the next chapter), critics have pointed out that this reification of an ethos of disempowerment makes it difficult to see how women, individually or collectively, can bring about change in the dominant structure. In the specific context of the relationship between power and patriarchy, this has led an increasing number of contemporary feminists to seek alternative theoretical frameworks.[3] Drawing on the work of Foucault,[4] a range of theorists—including Carol Smart,[5] Iris Young,[6] and Judith Butler[7]—have advocated a reconfiguration of feminist analysis to identify a more nuanced understanding of power, which defies simplistic correlation with domination or resource distribution.

There are a number of reasons why, prima facie, Foucault's work, in forwarding a thesis that examines and problematises the relationship between power and sexuality, can be seen to present an attractive conceptual ally to feminism. Equally, though, even a cursory look at Foucault's discussion of this topic makes it clear that he offers a conceptualisation of the operation of power and the instigation of regimes of sexuality that is influenced by, and influential upon, the development of postmodern analysis, and so differs markedly in many regards from that conventionally afforded by radical feminism. Indeed, it is this difference that has been deployed in support of Foucault's work by those contemporary feminist commentators who seek to transcend the essentialism and determinism that they see as implicated in the radical thesis. But at the same time, as was noted in Chapter one, this feminist turn to postmodernism has been far from unanimously welcomed.

Deconstruction and the Law (London & New York, Routledge, 1991); D Cornell, 'Sexual Difference, The Feminine and Equivalency: A Critique of MacKinnon's Toward a Feminist Theory of State' (1991) 100 *Yale Law Review* 2247.

[3] A Allen, *The Power of Feminist Theory: Domination, Resistance, Solidarity* (Oxford, Westview Press, 2001).

[4] M Foucault, *The Archaeology of Knowledge* (trans A Sheridan) (New York, Harper Colophon, 1972); M Foucault, *The History of Sexuality, Volume I* (London, Penguin, 1976); M Foucault, *Power/Knowledge: Selected Interviews and Other Writings 1972–77* (ed C Gordon) (New York, Pantheon, 1980).

[5] C Smart, *Feminism and the Power of Law* (London & New York, Routledge, 1989); C Smart, 'Law's Power, the Sexed Body and Feminist Discourse' (1990) 17 *Journal of Law and Society* 194; C Smart (ed) *Regulating Womanhood: Historical Essays on Marriage, Motherhood and Sexuality* (London & New York, Routledge, 1992); C Smart, *Law, Crime and Sexuality: Essays in Feminism* (London, SAGE, 1995).

[6] I Young, *Justice and The Politics of Difference* (Princeton, Princeton University Press, 1990); I Young, *Intersecting Voices: Dilemmas of Gender, Political Philosophy and Policy* (Princeton, Princeton University Press, 1997); I Young, *Inclusion and Democracy* (Oxford, Oxford University Press, 2000).

[7] J Butler, *Gender Trouble—Feminism and the Subversion of Identity* (London & New York, Routledge, 1990); J Butler, *Bodies that Matter—On the Discursive Limits of Sex* (New York & London Routledge, 1993); J Butler, *The Psychic Life of Power* (Stanford, Stanford University Press, 1997); J Butler, *Excitable Speech: A Politics of the Performative* (New York & London, Routledge, 1997); J Butler, *Undoing Gender* (New York & London, Routlage, 2004).

In particular, concerns have been expressed regarding postmodernism's apparent preoccupation with subversion over progress, and with localised sites of normative construction over structural systems of violence.

Taking MacKinnon's work as a representative example of the radical genre, this chapter will re-evaluate the merits of this contemporary feminist project. Without denying the divergence between them, it will question the cogency of the stark opposition between Foucault and radical feminism that is often produced by highlighting the existence of significant convergence in their respective positions on discourse, embodiment and sexuality. In addition, it will re-evaluate the dominant polarisation of Foucaultian and radical feminist analyses of power relations with reference to Foucault's latter work on domination.[8] This work, while often neglected in commentaries upon Foucault, both in feminist theory and beyond, presents a conceptualisation of power relations that (on first sight at least) seems very different from the accounts of micro-politics and bio-power for which he has become most renowned.[9] Where his earlier work focuses primarily upon the fluidity and omnipresence of power relations, this work re-inserts the importance of asymmetrical power relationships within which the possibility of resistance is extremely limited. In this chapter, the implications of this latter work for feminist analysis will be considered. More specifically, it will be argued that this recognition of domination by Foucault creates an opportunity not only for response to his critics but also for more productive linkages between feminist theorists of radical and postmodern persuasions.

Perspectives on Power—Foucault v MacKinnon?

Concerns pertaining to the distribution and operation of power clearly illuminate the theses of both Foucault and MacKinnon. Recognising the close relationship between the operation of power regimes and the individual's conception of self, both theorists have provided an extensive analysis of the implications of living in a social world fuelled by the dictates of power. What's more, they have both drawn attention to the political significance of discourse and sexuality in the deployment of these dictates. Despite this commonality of concern, however, it is clear that significant points of divergence remain in their respective analytical approaches and that these

---

[8] M Foucault, 'The Ethics of Care for the Self as a Practice of Freedom' in J Bernauer & D Ramussen (ed) *The Final Foucault* (Cambridge, MIT Press, 1994), 1–21. Also published in (1987) 12 *Philosophy and Social Criticism* 6.

[9] Interest in these aspects of Foucault's work does, however, appear to be on the increase, with recent publications on this topic including V Munro, 'On Power and Domination: Feminism and the Final Foucault' (2003) 2 (1) *European Journal of Political Theory* 79; D Taylot & K Vintges (eds) *Feminism and the Final Foucault* (Chicago, University of Illinois Press, 2004); N Widder, 'Foucault and Power Revisited' (2004) 3 (4) *European Journal of Political Theory* 411.

have provided the basis for much contemporary feminist debate and disagreement. In this section, we will examine these points of commonality and difference in more detail.

Most celebrated for his early work on disciplinary power and bio-politics, Foucault does not restrict his model of power to the traditional conception of state regulation of a subservient citizenry, or a general system of domination over groups within the social body.[10] Instead, he draws attention to a network of complex and inter-connected 'disciplinary techniques' through which, he argues, power primarily operates in modern society.[11] These 'disciplinary techniques' operate in myriad ways to instigate regimes of 'truth' and 'normality' that normalise human agents into conformity with prioritised social ideals. In securing the compliance of the agents themselves, they are subtler in their operation than traditional power relations, which have assumed an essentially negative and regulatory function.[12] As Foucault explains, this entails thinking about the mechanisms of power in their 'capillary form of existence', which attends specifically to the myriad ways in which:

> power seeps into the very grain of individuals, reaches right into their bodies, permeates their gestures, their postures, what they say, how they learn to live and work with other people.[13]

Power upon this analysis, then, is not simply an oppressive force imposed systematically from any one source. Rather, it is a positive social presence that operates in all aspects of life and exerts itself in all directions, creating a variety of different relationships other than those within the domination-subordination dynamic of traditional conceptions. Refusing to perpetuate this conception of repression as being paradigmatic, Foucault recognises that it represents only one form among many in the effects generated by the interplay of power relations in society. In so doing, he highlights the oversimplification inherent in alternative attempts to draw a sharp distinction between those wielding power and those subject to it, and illustrates the significance of the failure of such approaches to recognise the important interplay of the 'micro-politics' of power that inevitably operate at this more intimate level.[14]

This conception of power can be sharply contrasted, in many regards, against the perception of power dynamics predominantly advocated by rad-

---

[10] G Gutting, *A Cambridge Companion to Foucault* (Cambridge, Cambridge University Press, 1994).

[11] M Foucault, *The History of Sexuality Volume I*, above n 4 at 92.

[12] This understanding of the operation of power is most clearly reflected in the work of J Austin, *The Province of Jurisprudence Determined* (London, George Weidenfeld & Nicholson Ltd, 1954).

[13] M Foucault in A Sheridan, *Michel Foucault—The Will to Truth* (London & New York, Tavistock, 1980) at 217.

[14] M Foucault, *The History of Sexuality, Volume I*, above n 4 at 94.

ical feminist analysis. For one thing, the hypothesis that power is a commodity held in the hands of patriarchy and systematically denied from the ownership of women can be seen to be antithetical to Foucault's assertion that 'power must be analysed as something that circulates . . . never appropriated as a commodity or a piece of wealth.'[15] What's more, MacKinnon's claim that 'male dominance is perhaps the most pervasive and tenacious system of power in history'[16] diametrically opposes his commitment to the avoidance of over-arching frameworks within the field of power dynamics. Thus, while Foucault seeks a fluid notion of power as a force that bears its effects on every social agent, it can be argued that MacKinnon's theory, in conceiving of it as a commodity wielded in the interests of the socially privileged to maintain the derision of the socially subordinate, falls prey to problematic essentialism and determinism.

For contemporary feminists concerned to transcend these deficiencies, it is no accident then that Foucault's analysis of the micro-levels of power has been put forward as presenting the potential for a significant improvement.[17] By encouraging an analysis of the complex disciplinary role of social expectation in the development of identity and experience, it has been argued that it opens space for a pluralist understanding of womanhood that redresses widely held concerns about essentialism. What's more, as the following discussion will illustrate, it can also be seen to offer an alternative conceptualisation of the nature and possibility of resistance to power, which may provide a remedy against the deterministic tendencies of the radical thesis.

Perspectives on Power and the Possibility of Resistance

While both MacKinnon and Foucault approach the issue of power with agendas for political and ideological resistance in mind, there can be little doubt that the manner in which that resistance is to be realised in each instance is markedly different.

For Foucault, resistance and subversion are the natural corollary of disciplinary practices of power.[18] Thus, rather than being located outside of prevailing power structures, the exercise of resistance is in fact implicated within them. As a result, it is manifest not when those people subject to

---

[15] M Foucault, *Power/Knowledge*, above n 4 at 98.
[16] C MacKinnon, *Toward a Feminist Jurisprudence*, above n 1 at 636–7.
[17] S Bartky, 'Foucault, Feminism and the Modernisation of Patriarchal Power' in I Diamond & L Quinby, (eds) *Feminism and Foucault—Reflections on Resistance* (Boston, Northeastern University Press, 1988); S Bartky, *Feminism and Domination: Studies in the Phenomenology of Oppression* (New York, Routledge, 1990).
[18] This aspect of Foucault's theory is most clearly reflected in his discussion of ethics of the self in *The History of Sexuality Vol III—The Care of the Self* (New York, Vintage, 1988). See J Moss (ed) *The Later Foucault: Politics and Philosophy* (London, SAGE, 1998) for more detailed discussion of Foucault's understanding of resistance.

power seek to transcend and overthrow the prevailing network of intricate power strategies, but when they consciously subvert the expectations of those in power, thereby denying consolidation of their identity within expected parameters. Continual subversion of expectation in this way offers a means of producing change and thereby exercising effective resistance.

In contrast, MacKinnon regards the assimilation of patriarchal norms (including the eroticisation of passivity) as the natural consequence of the pervasive power dynamics of gender domination. At the same time, though, despite recognising the centrality of power disparities to the development of subjectivity, she continues to presume the existence of an absolute ground of knowledge beyond power relations within which women can transcend their status as victims and actualise their capacity for resistance. Lamentably, however, as discussed in previous chapters, MacKinnon gives little guidance as to exactly how this transcendence is to be achieved[19] and in her radical vision of the essential disempowerment of all women, it becomes difficult to see *how* any woman, even MacKinnon herself, could break out of this dominant hegemony.

For MacKinnon, the possibility of resistance is therefore difficult to reconcile with her overall theoretical position—indeed, she acknowledges that some day after it has occurred, the question of 'how sisterhood became powerful while women were powerless will take its place among the classic alchemies of political history.'[20] By contrast, however, for Foucault, it seems that the operation of fluid power sources invites inversion and resistance by its very nature. As Butler explains, resistance consists in 'a taking up of the tools where they lie, when the very 'taking up' is enabled by the tools lying there.'[21] Resistance within the Foucaultian thesis becomes an element of power rather than an aberration of it. There is therefore no need to locate a foundation for resistance that is transcendent of power relationships and concerns about the determinism inherent in MacKinnon's understanding dissolve.

While, as discussed in Chapter one, this Foucaultian conception of resistance has been criticised by some theorists for its failure to offer a sufficiently revolutionary and/or utopian vision for feminist reform,[22] it is submitted here that there is much to commend it. While admittedly limited to a more

---

[19] As Jackson notes, 'MacKinnon's work is infused with a paradoxical mix of debilitating pessimism and unfathomable optimism'—see E Jackson, 'Catharine MacKinnon and Feminist Jurisprudence', above n 2 at 211. For further discussion of this in the context of MacKinnon, see also, Ch 3.

[20] C MacKinnon, *Feminism Unmodified*, above n 1 at 3.

[21] J Butler, *Gender Trouble*, above n 7 at 145.

[22] N Harstock, 'Foucault on Power—A Theory for Women' in L Nicholson (ed) *Feminism/Postmodernism* (London and New York, Routledge, 1990) at 164; See also N Fraser, 'Foucault on Modern Power: Empirical Insights and Normative Confusions' (1981) 23 *Praxis International* 272; N Fraser, 'Foucault: A Young Conservative?' (1985) 96 (1) *Ethics* 165 for further critique.

Power—Focault vs MacKinnon?

engaged form of resistance, this postmodern analysis not only remedies the ontological concerns attributable to MacKinnon's thesis but also enables feminists to undertake a more subversive and infiltrating role in the construction and perpetuation of the dictates of power networks. It:

> opens a space for feminists to understand and intervene in the processes through which meaning is produced, disseminated and transformed in relation to the changing configurations of modern power.[23]

And this, in turn, permits an increased recognition of the role played by the deployment of discourse in this modern power regime.

Perspectives on Power and the Role of Discourse

The idea of power as an essentially normalising rather than repressive force lies at the heart of Foucault's assertion that power is a productive phenomenon. Control of the individual in modern society is ensured, not through the direct repression of the individual by the state, but through the employment of more invisible mechanisms of normalisation. Discourse is the medium within which these constructs of power and normativity unite. As Foucault explains, the various relations of power that 'permeate, characterise and constitute the social body' can only be established through 'the production, accumulation, circulation and functioning of a discourse.'[24]

Incorporation of the significance of discourse into an analysis of power along these lines rests particularly well alongside a feminist political project that, having identified the 'crucial role of discourse in its capacity to produce and sustain hegemonic power,'[25] has developed mechanisms such as consciousness-raising and practical reasoning to enable the critical questioning of discursive dictates.[26]

Like Foucault, MacKinnon has paid specific attention to the relevance and role of discourse as an integral element in the construction and perpetuation of power relationships.[27] However, in maintaining her thesis that those power relationships are hierarchically imposed upon a dynamic of oppressor-oppressed, she presents a conception of discourse that differs from Foucault's in key respects. In particular, her implicit assumption that the power of patriarchal discourse is absolute is contra-indicated by Foucault's commitment to analysis of the micro-levels of power and to the attendant conception of discourse as necessarily plurivocal and fluctuating.[28]

---

[23] L McNay, *Foucault and Feminism* (Cambridge, Polity Press, 1992) at 115.

[24] M Foucault, quoted in T Kelly (ed) *Critique and Power—Recasting the Foucault/Habermas Debate* (Cambridge, MIT Press, 1994) at 31.

[25] I Diamond & L Quinby, *Feminism and Foucault*, above n 17 at Intro X.

[26] K Bartlett, 'Feminist Legal Methods' (1990) 103 *Harvard Law Review* 829.

[27] C MacKinnon, *Only Words* (Cambridge, Harvard University Press, 1993).

[28] J Sawicki, *Disciplining Foucault: Feminism, Power and the Body* (London and New York, Routledge, 1991) at 1.

Thus challenging the radical oppressor-oppressed dichotomy, the Foucaultian conception offers contemporary feminist theorists a more complex analysis of the deployment of discourse as an integral element in the modern power regime.[29] The attendant recognition of the operation of microcosmic power forces in structuring the intimate levels of individual experience offers a strong basis for the long-standing feminist assertion that the 'personal' is also the 'political' and provides helpful analytical tools for those feminists engaged in uncovering the 'micropolitics' of 'private' life.[30] What's more, the recognition of 'bio-power'—a peculiarly modern form of disciplinary power, instigated through the proliferation of quasi-scientific discourses and directed towards the human body—can be aligned alongside the feminist interest in the political and legal relevance of embodiment and sexuality.[31]

Perspectives on Power and the Deployment of Sexuality

Both Foucault and MacKinnon have identified the constructed nature of categories of sexuality. Tracing the impact of the deployment of medical discourse from the nineteenth century, Foucault has noted the tendency to analyse, qualify and disqualify the feminine body 'as being thoroughly saturated with sexuality'[32] and to construct an ideology of sexuality as being comprised of overwhelming urges and uncontrollable natural needs. Hence, Foucault conceives of 'sexuality' as an historically imbued system of discourse which has produced the notion of 'sex' as part of its strategy to conceal and thereby to perpetuate power relations.[33] As Foucault explains:

> sexuality must not be thought of as a kind of natural given which power tries to hold in check or as an obscure domain which knowledge tries gradually to uncover.

Rather, sexuality must be recognised as an historical construct:

> a network in which the stimulation of bodies, the intensification of pleasures, the incitement to discourse, the formation of special knowledges, the strengthening of controls and resistance, are linked to one another in accordance with a few major strategies of knowledge and power.[34]

---

[29] C Smart, 'Law's Power, the Sexed Body and Feminist Discourse,' above note 5.

[30] J Sawicki, 'Feminism, Foucault and 'Subjects' of Power and Freedom' in S Hekman (ed) *Feminist Interpretations of Michel Foucault* (Pennsylvania, University of Pennsylvania Press, 1996) at 160.

[31] See, eg, K Davis, *Embodied Practices—Feminist Perspectives on the Body* (London, SAGE, 1997); R Diprose, *The Bodies of Women—Ethics, Embodiment and Sexual Difference* (London and New York, Routledge, 1994); M McLaren, *Feminism, Foucault and Embodied Subjectivity* (Albany, State University of New York Press, 2002); L McNay, 'The Foucaultian Body and the Exclusion of Experience' (1991) 6 *Hypatia* 125; L McWhorter, *Bodies and Pleasures: Foucault and the Politics of Sexual Normalisation* (Bloomington, Indiana University Press, 1999).

[32] M Foucault, *The History of Sexuality Volume I*, above n 4 at 104.

[33] J Butler, *Gender Trouble*, above n 7 at 95.

[34] M Foucault, *The History of Sexuality Volume I*, above n 4 at 105–6.

This idea of the constructed and imposed nature of categories of sexuality is echoed throughout feminist theory. In *Feminism Unmodified*, for example, MacKinnon states that sexuality is a social construct of whatever the given society eroticises at the time. Considering sexuality to be the 'lynch pin' of gender inequality, she holds it up as a fundamentally social and relational construction, which has men as its authors. Hence:

> feminism is a theory of how the erotization of dominance and submission creates gender, creates woman and man in the social form in which we know them.[35]

Contending that it is through a specific location of the regulation of sexuality within discursive practices such as law and medicine that control over human behaviour is secured, Foucault encourages us to think of our bodies as elements in the articulation of power. This perception of sexuality as not only a group of statements, prohibitions and regulations, but also as a question of power, has been re-iterated by MacKinnon. Coupling this theoretical insight with her radical hypothesis regarding the operation of structures of patriarchal ideology, she argues, for example, that:

> sexual objectification is the primary process of the subjection of women. It unites act with word, construction with expression, perception with enforcement, myth with reality.[36]

There is therefore substantial convergence of opinion between Foucault and MacKinnon on the political significance attributable to sexuality and upon the challenge this offers to a liberal ethos that professes that the domain of sexuality, being exclusively reserved for the private sphere, is without political or legal relevance. It is, however, in regard to the deployment of the construction of sexuality that divergence between the two theorists can be located. Not only does MacKinnon establish the constructed nature of sexuality, she adds alongside this her thesis that it has been designed to meet the normative fashionings attributable to men under prevailing patriarchal conditions. This radical feminist conception is, however, contraindicated by Foucault's assertions against presupposing gendered identities. MacKinnon's classically radical analysis tends to take the category of sex (and the binary restriction on gender) as its point of departure. In contrast, the Foucaultian project demands a more critical inquiry into *how* that very category of 'sex' is constructed within prevailing discourse as a necessary feature of bodily identity.[37]

MacKinnon's theory, in seeking an 'authentic' female voice that exists beneath the pervasive layers of gender oppression, assumes the existence of an inherently united, if historically repressed, female sexual identity that will

---

[35] C MacKinnon, *Feminism Unmodified*, above n 1 at 50.
[36] C MacKinnon, 'Feminism, Marxism, Method and the State: An Agenda for Theory,' above n 1 at 541.
[37] J Butler, *Gender Trouble*, above n 7 at 96.

rise from the ashes of patriarchy once defeated. By contrast, Foucault suggests that attempts to give voice to our supposed identity as 'gendered beings' in pursuit of liberation are futile. They are futile primarily because they ignore our own history as arbitrarily gendered beings, subject to prevailing deployments of sexuality, and fail to question the underlying assumptions that have constructed male and female sexuality as oppositional. In consequence, Foucault is reluctant to affirm such essentialist claims regarding the existence of a gender-specific, pre-social identity. Questioning whether the call to 'liberate our sexuality' has any meaning, Foucault argues that the problem is one not of liberation but of deciphering and working with the practices of freedom through which we determine what constitutes sexual pleasure. From this perspective, as he explains:

> this ethical problem of the definition of freedom is more important than the affirmation (and repetitious at that) that sexuality or desire must be freed.[38]

By drawing upon this Foucaultian analysis, contemporary feminist theorists have been able to conceive of the female body, less as the primary site for the operation of masculinist power, and more as a cultural statement about the context of gender/power relations.[39] The problematic radical preoccupation with commonality in women's bodily experiences has been replaced by a focus on the multiplicity of cultural meanings that can be attributed to the female body. In turn, this has enabled contemporary feminist theorists to shift focus away from a primary concern with overarching systems of domination towards the introduction of dialectical power relations, agency and subversion,[40] and towards a necessary recognition of the role played by women themselves in the perpetuation of gender discrimination.[41]

Perspectives on Domination—Foucault *and* MacKinnon?

Thus far, this chapter has indicated some of the potential benefits offered by employing Foucault in order to move contemporary feminist theorising away from its primary concern with meta-narratives of gender-based domination towards a more fluid analysis of power and a more localised analysis of resistance. At the same time, however, there can be no question that the turn to this kind of approach has not been unanimously welcomed. Indeed, despite ongoing criticism of the apparent essentialism and determinism in the radical thesis, many commentators have expressed concern

---

[38] M Foucault, 'The Ethics of Care of the Self as a Practice of Freedom', above n 8 at 3.
[39] See, eg, L McNay, *Foucault and Feminism*, above n 23; M McLaren, 'Foucault and the Subject of Feminism' (1997) 23 (1) *Social Theory and Practice* 109.
[40] D Smith, *Texts, Facts and Femininity—Exploring the Relations of Ruling* (London, Routledge, 1990).
[41] K Abrams, 'Ideology and Women's Choices' (1990) 24 *Georgia Law Review* 761 at 775.

that the postmodern rejection of transformation in favour of destabilisation that animates Foucault's account robs feminists of elements of theory and practice that are indispensable to their goals.[42] As a result, many contemporary feminist theorists, while accepting the above polarisation of Foucaultian and radical perspectives on power, have been reluctant to affirm the Foucaultian alternative as preferable.[43] West, for example, has argued that women's experiences of patriarchal power—'as intensely nondiscursive, as utterly unimaginative, as profoundly negating and, in short, as frightening and pervasively violent'—bear no resemblance to anything imagined in Foucault's philosophy, which is then of little use to feminism.[44]

What's more, even those feminist theorists who have displayed pro-Foucaultian sympathies have expressed serious reservations regarding his alleged tendency to prioritise analysis of the operation of power at the micro level over analysis of more large-scale frameworks and power regimes. Fraser, for example, has criticised Foucault's thesis on the omnipresence of power for perpetuating an agnostic theory within which power, by virtue of its productive and ineliminable status, becomes normatively neutral.[45] The danger of this, from a feminist perspective, lies in its inability to distinguish between good and bad social practices in any meaningful way[46] and therefore to differentiate between those practices which are imposed upon us more heavily by prevailing power regimes than others. As McNay explains, in other words, it fails to distinguish between those practices that are merely 'suggested' and those that are more or less 'imposed' on the individual via the force of the heavily laden cultural or social sanctions that inform the consequences of non-compliance.[47]

---

[42] N Harstock, 'Foucault on Power—A Theory for Women', above n 22 at 164.

[43] C Ramazanoglu (ed) *Up Against Foucault—Explorations of Some Tensions Between Foucault and Feminism* (London and New York, Routledge, 1993).

[44] R West, *Caring for Justice* (New York, New York University Press, 1997) at 261.

[45] 'Foucault calls too many different sorts of things power and simply leaves it at that. Granted, all cultural practices involve constraints—but these constraints are of a variety of different kinds and thus demand a variety of different normative responses. Granted, there can be no social practices without power—but it does not follow that all forms of power are normatively equivalent nor that any social practices are as good as any other'—N Fraser, *Unruly Practices—Power, Discourse and Gender in Contemporary Theory* (Cambridge, Polity Press, 1989) at 32. For some commentators, the reason behind Foucault's position on this can be traced to the fact that he, as a man, 'writes from the perspective of the dominator' which makes him less able see systematically unequal gender power relations—N Harstock, 'Community/Sexuality/Power—Rethinking Power' in N Hirschmann & C Di Stefano (eds), *Revisioning the Political: Feminist Reconstructions of Traditional Concepts in Western Political Theory* (Boulder, Westview Press, 1996) at 38.

[46] M Deveaux, 'Feminism and Empowerment—A Critical Reading of Foucault' (1994) 20 (2) *Feminist Studies* 223. Reprinted in S Hekman (ed) *Feminist Interpretations of Michel Foucault*, above n 30 at 221.

[47] L McNay, *Foucault and Feminism*, above n 23 at 74.

This alleged tendency within Foucault's work to focus upon the micro over the macro level has also raised concerns regarding his understanding of resistance. As noted above, conceiving of resistance as a necessarily localised phenomenon heralds the potential to move beyond the determinism located within MacKinnon's radical feminist thesis of resistance as unaccounted for transcendence and revolution. However, it also runs the risk of re-inserting the dangers of determinism in its implication that as soon as resistance receives official recognition, it becomes caught up in a network of controlling power relations. This suggests that in order to be effective, resistance to power can only operate at the particular level. In so doing, it appears to deny the exercise of power at the macro level and the imposition of power upon women as a gendered collective that forms the basis of feminist politics. The shortcomings of this oversight are, of course, particularly lamentable to feminist theorists, who:

> must continue to address the personal costs of patriarchal domination, through attention to developing empowering practices of self-creation, while at the same time avoiding the tendency to reduce politics to personal transformation.[48]

According to Fraser and Nicholson, an analysis of the structures of domination involves:

> the identification and critique of macrostructures of inequality and injustice which cut across the boundaries separating relatively discrete practices and institutions.[49]

The predominant charge against Foucault (and more generally against postmodernism) encapsulated in this sceptical commentary is that he has failed to accommodate the phenomenon of domination in his analysis of power, and that therefore his theory falls short for feminist and critical purposes. More specifically, Harstock has argued, for example, that understandings of power which seek to move away from a focus on domination pose three key difficulties—first, they refuse to deal with the problem of the possibility of doing harm to another by one's actions; secondly, they over-emphasise the productive aspects of power's enabling functions; and thirdly, they fail to address the gender dynamics implicated in power relations.[50]

While it is certainly true that the legacy attributed to Foucault most commonly relates to his earlier writings on disciplinary techniques, bio-power and micro-politics, it is not in fact the case that Foucault was ignorant of the significance of domination. In the following section, the emergence of the issue of domination within a series of Foucault's later, and less cele-

---

[48] J Sawicki, 'Foucault, Feminism and Questions of Identity' in G Gutting (ed), *The Cambridge Companion to Foucault*, above n 10 at 308.

[49] N Fraser & L Nicholson, 'Social Criticism Without Philosophy: An Encounter Between Feminism and Postmodernism' in L Nicholson (ed) *Feminism/Postmodernism*, above n 22 at 23.

[50] N Harstock, 'Community/Sexuality/Power—Rethinking Power,' above n 45 at 37–8.

brated, works will be traced and its impact on his earlier discussion of micro-politics and localised resistance will be highlighted. In so doing, the extent to which Foucault is capable of refuting the concerns expressed above regarding his over-emphasis upon the micro level will be considered. In addition, the sharp contrast asserted in much contemporary analysis between the radical feminist and Foucaultian approaches to power and sexuality will be re-evaluated, with a view to re-establishing the relevance of domination within feminist theory and activism.

The Final Foucault and Domination

Without denying the significance of the differences between them, the above discussion posits the existence of certain important parallels in the theoretical positions of both Foucault and MacKinnon. Not only have both highlighted the role played by relationships of power in the construction of identity, they have both also drawn attention to the impact of discourse as a medium of normalisation, and to the political importance of the deployment of sexuality. Despite the significance of these areas of convergence, however, contemporary feminist theorists who seek to replace the radical hypothesis with a Foucaultian influence continue to emphasise the divergence between the two approaches. Focusing specifically upon Foucault's work on domination, this section challenges the cogency of such a categorical distinction.

In a series of lectures and writings conducted towards the end of his life, Foucault returns to the issue of power relations that he addressed so famously in his early works in an attempt to supplement and develop his analysis. Whilst continuing to stand by his previous assertions regarding the fluid, dispersed, and productive nature of modern power, Foucault meets the concerns of his critics regarding his apparent over-emphasis upon the micro level by explicitly initiating a subtle and penetrating analysis of the phenomenon of domination. Throughout this analysis, however, Foucault is keen to emphasise its role as developing and re-affirming, rather than contradicting, his foregoing theoretical claims. In particular, as he emphasises:

> we must distinguish the relationships of power as strategic games between liberties—strategic games that result in the fact that some people try to determine the conduct of others—and the states of domination, which are what we ordinarily call power.[51]

Domination, on Foucault's understanding, is a highly distinct and specific form of power relation. While capable of existing and operating at both the micro and the macro level, a state of domination occurs when the relations of power in question are fixed in such a way that they are 'perpetually

---

[51] M Foucault, 'The Ethics of Care of the Self as a Practice of Freedom', above n 8 at 19.

Power, Domination and Patriarchy

asymmetrical and the margin of liberty is extremely limited.'[52] In such a state of domination, the possibility of effective resistance (deemed immanent to power in Foucault's earlier discussion) is heavily constrained. Thus, the relationship involved is transformed from one involving a free-flowing and reciprocal exchange of manifestations of power to one involving a one-sided ability to unilaterally alter the behaviour of another.[53] Foucault explains the imposition and maintenance of such a state of domination in the following terms:

> a relationship of confrontation reaches its term, its final moment (and the victory of one of the two adversaries) when stable mechanisms replace the free play of antagonistic reactions. Through such mechanisms one can direct, in a fairly constant manner and with reasonable certainty, the conduct of others.[54]

This understanding of domination recognises the existence of specific contexts in which the ordinarily free-flowing and (arguably) normatively neutral power forces of modern society become stagnated. Within this stagnant state, significant benefits are conferred upon the power-holder at the expense of the powerless and the power relationship in question becomes conceivable as a kind of commodity in the manner outlined by radical feminist theory.

While Foucault thus joins with radical feminism in recognising the possibility of domination and identifying the stagnant and oppressive nature of its operation, he continues to question the legitimacy of the mono-causal gender-based explanations for its existence that are often forwarded from this perspective. In contrast to MacKinnon's thesis within which domination is simply a pre-legal and pre-political fact of patriarchal society, Foucault's understanding does not conceive of any overarching or complete system. Rather, a state of domination arises as a result of the ways in which the:

> infinitesimal mechanisms of power . . . have been—and continue to be—invested, colonized, utilised, involuted, transformed, displaced, extended, etc. by ever more general mechanisms and by forms of global domination.[55]

---

[52] M Foucault, 'The Ethics of Care of the Self as a Practice of Freedom', above n 8 at 12. Discussed in D Ivison, 'The Disciplinary Moment: Foucault, Law and the Reinscription of Rights' in J Moss (ed) *The Later Foucault*, above n 18 at 139.

[53] P Patton, 'Foucault's Subject of Power' in J Moss (ed) *The Later Foucault*, above n 18 at 68.

[54] M Foucault, 'Subject and Power', Afterword in Dreyfus & Rabinow (ed) *Michel Foucault—Beyond Structuralism and Hermeneutics* (Hemel Hempstead, Harvester Wheatsheaf, 1982) at 225.

[55] M Foucault, *Introduction to Herculin Barbib: Being the Recently Discovered Memoirs of a 19th Century French Hermaphrodite* (New York, Pantheon, 1980) at 122.

According to Foucault, then, these ever more general mechanisms:

> represent the level at which the local, micro-level power relations have been integrated into patterns of power that cut across temporal, institutional and contextual barriers.[56]

Thus, while recognising the existence of larger-scale patterns of power in the development of domination, Foucault refuses to speak solely in terms of these patterns. While 'Foucault is not the first to identify domination with stable and asymmetrical systems of power relations,' he does:

> make it clear that such systems are always secondary results, achieved within or imposed upon a primary field of relations between subjects of power.[57]

In thus naming and defining the phenomenon of domination, Foucault makes explicit many of the assumptions that have underlain his earlier writings on power relations. Rather than having sought to deny the existence of general schema of domination, it is apparent that Foucault's analysis of micro-politics and disciplinary power, when re-read in light of his latter contributions, was intended to offer a technique for the identification and deconstruction of stagnated and solidified social relations. In this sense, contemporary feminist theorists who have turned to Foucault for answers to whether or not domination exists in a given society have been asking the wrong question of his work. Foucault was in fact rarely concerned with this issue. Instead his focus was on conducting meticulous analysis at the micro-level of power relations to establish how such states would in fact arise, and could in fact be dismantled without seeking utopian transcendence.[58] In this light, it becomes apparent, then, that the results of this project were intended to operate as a methodological tool for the analysis of certain social relations and, contrary to popular interpretations, never to preclude the possibility of understanding those social relations in terms of domination.

---

[56] A Allen, 'Foucault on Power—A Theory for Feminists' in S Hekman (ed) *Feminist Interpretations of Foucault*, above n 30 at 276.

[57] P Patton, 'Foucault's Subject of Power' in J Moss (ed) *The Later Foucault*, above n 18 at 68.

[58] This analysis of Foucault's work is paralleled, moreover, in Alan Hunt's examination of the relationship between Marx (on whose work MacKinnon's thesis is based) and Foucault. As Hunt explains, while there are shared interests in explaining and promoting social change, 'the major conflict between Foucault and Marx is about the possibility of causal explanations. In its simplest form, their difference can be stated as a contest between 'why questions' . . . and 'how questions'. . . . Foucault views 'why questions' as necessarily being searches for origins that bring with them the idea of some causal chain . . . and this, in turn, leads to the intellectual sin of functionalism whose error is that it assigns some fixed role to each social practice or institution.'—A Hunt, 'Getting Marx and Foucault into Bed Together!' (2004) 31 (4) *Journal of Law and Society* 592 at 604.

Power, Domination and Patriarchy

The Final Foucault and Resistance

Within a state of domination, as conceived by Foucault, the possibilities for resistance become substantially reduced, with the range of options for subversion available to the dominated subject being limited. Importantly, however, while resistance becomes more difficult, the possibility of its realisation is never completely obliterated. Although resistance is not implicated in the asymmetrical structure of domination per se, it continues to be immanent in the power relationships that have stagnated and congealed to form this structure. In a state of domination, as in any power relationship, the parties involved retain an at least limited freedom to exercise power and resistance. As Foucault puts it:

> if one or other were completely at the disposition of the other, and became his thing, an object on which he can exercise an infinite and unlimited violence, there could not be a relation of power.'

The reason for this, as he explains, is that:

> in order to exercise a relation of power, there must be on both sides at least a certain form of liberty

which is reflected in the perpetual possibility of resistance, ruse or reaction to that power relation.[59] A state of domination is not, therefore, produced immediately in its totality. Rather, the inherently fluid and pluri-potential nature of the formative power relations involved means that it is in the continual process of being repeatedly produced. According to Foucault, it is the very necessity of such repetition that denies any rigid consolidation of the domination dynamic and proliferates techniques through which the dominated can engineer infinite disjunctions between the dictates of the dominator and the resultant outcome.

What distinguishes a state of domination and characterises its stagnant quality is the inability of the dominated party to exercise a power over the power relationship itself. Within the confines of such domination, regimes of resistance premised upon the invocation of transcendent Enlightenment-esque agendas for unbounded freedom and autonomy are futile. What is required instead is a subversive, infiltrating form of resistance that frustrates further solidification of the power dynamics involved. Particularly in his second and third volumes of *The History of Sexuality*, Foucault indicates (in a somewhat tangential way) that such resistance can be achieved through the deployment of what he refers to as 'techniques of the self'. In real terms, this demands a commitment to 'disruptive excess', i.e. to strategies of subversion which challenge the pretension to domination of our constitutive machinery by rejecting its sustenance through the solidification and mundane repetition of power relations.

---

[59] M Foucault, 'The Ethics of Care of the Self as a Practice of Freedom', above n 8 at 12.

It is in this sense that Foucault maintains an agenda for relative agency and resistance in the face of all-encompassing power relations. Paraphrasing Butler's postmodern analysis, the paradox of the exercise and possibility of resistance is precisely, therefore, that it is enabled, if not produced, by the very power relations against which it struggles. While this constitutive constraint does not necessarily foreclose the possibility of resistance to power, nor to domination, it does locate that resistance as a practice immanent to power, and not as a relation of external opposition to it.[60]

While Foucault's earlier account appears to undermine the radical feminist conception of resistance to domination as an unfeasible normative ideal,[61] there are, therefore, indications in his latter discussion that suggest the possibility of resurrecting agendas for resistance premised upon the dissolution of asymmetrical power. Without offering a model of resistance as transcendence of power, Foucault's understanding of domination re-establishes the possibility of its transformation. More specifically, he emphasises that he does not believe there can be a society without relations of power (that is, relations by which individuals try to influence and determine the conduct of others). Thus, for him the problem is not one of trying to dissolve power relations 'in the utopia of a perfectly transparent communication' but of arming oneself with the techniques to allow the power games be played 'with a minimum of domination.'[62]

Whilst this account of resistance may bear little resemblance to the notion of utopian transcendence promoted by the radical feminist approach of MacKinnon, it successfully offers a potentially transformative rather than merely subversive agenda. In so doing, it challenges foregoing concerns regarding the utility of Foucault for feminist legal strategies. What's more, Foucault's implicit denunciation of states of domination suggests that, while his analytics of power may well be agnostic, his understanding of domination is not normatively neutral. On the contrary, domination represents a static and hierarchical state of power relations to be condemned and challenged because it operates to deny the pluri-potentiality and fluidity inherent in power relationships.[63] Indeed, in *'The Ethics of Care of the Self as a Practice of Freedom'*, Foucault takes this condemnation of domination one step further, echoing the fundamental premise of many critical movements, including feminism, by insisting that the central function of philosophy and politics:

> is precisely the challenging of all phenomena of domination at whatever level or under whatever form they present themselves—political, economic, sexual, institutional and so on.[64]

[60] J Butler, *Gender Trouble*, above n 7 at 15.
[61] B Hindess, 'Politics and Liberation' in J Moss (ed) *The Later Foucault*, above n 18 at 45.
[62] M Foucault, 'The Ethic of Care of the Self as a Practice of Freedom', above n 8 at 18.
[63] B Hindess, *Discourses of Power: From Hobbes to Foucault* (Oxford, Blackwell, 2001) at 104.
[64] M Foucault, 'The Ethics of Care of the Self as a Practice of Freedom', above n 8 at 20.

Power, Domination and Patriarchy

The Final Foucault and Feminism

This return to domination and to the examination of asymmetrical power relationships at both micro and macro level thus successfully counters many of the concerns expressed by feminist commentators. By highlighting the extent to which the true meaning of Foucault's earlier work can only be realised when read in conjunction with his later contributions, it challenges the legitimacy of the dichotomy between radical and postmodern theory that has dominated contemporary feminist analysis. What's more, it re-instates many of the claims made by radical feminist theory in its analysis of power. In particular, it re-instates the radical feminist understanding of asymmetrical relationships within which access to power is monopolised by one partner. It also re-establishes the normative component of feminist theorising (lacking in early Foucaultian analysis) which enables a condemnation of the stifling effect of domination, albeit that the subject of the stifling has become the power relationship itself rather than some primordial female identity. Where popular interpretations of Foucault's earlier work have set him firmly against much radical feminist theorising, it seems, therefore, that analysis of his latter work marks the potential for a re-alignment of aspects of his analysis with specific aspects of that reformist project.

Furthermore, Foucault's latter work not only presents the possibility of potential reconciliation with radical feminism at the abstract level of theorising concepts such as power and resistance, it also provides some concrete support for the more specific focus of feminist critique. In particular, Foucault's reification of the traditional family relationship of the eighteenth and nineteenth centuries as the paradigmatic instance of domination legitimises the radical feminist protestation that male-female relationships represent a potential foundation for domination. In '*The Ethics of Care for the Self as a Practice of Freedom*', Foucault recognises the existence of a various contexts within which:

> the relations of power, instead of being variable and allowing different partners a strategy which alters them, find themselves firmly set and congealed.[65]

However, he chooses the specific example of the eighteenth and nineteenth century marriage to provide his most poignant illustration. Suggesting that the fixed and asymmetrical power relations characteristic of such a marriage meant that the wife was 'subject to a state of domination,' Foucault shows the subtleties and complexities of this relationship itself by identifying the persistence of that domination in the face of her limited access to power. According to Foucault, the husband remained dominant in the relationship despite his wife's theoretical *ability* to be unfaithful or to steal his money

---

[65] M Foucault, '*The Ethics of Care for the Self as a Practice of Freedom*', above n 8 at 3.

because the subversive tactics available to her were 'no more than a certain number of tricks which never brought about a reversal of the situation.'[66]

While Foucault remains reluctant to understand gender relationships primarily or exclusively in terms of domination, his latter works therefore suggest a willingness and ability to recognise domination where it does exist within particular relationships. Importantly, however, the juxtaposition of his understanding of domination and his earlier analysis of power relations is such that simplistic, grand-scale and mono-causal gender-based explanations for the domination dynamic are expelled. Despite Foucault's latter recognition of particular sites of domination, the radical feminist hypothesis of essential victimisation fails to find accommodation within his framework. As mentioned above, while resistance in a state of domination is heavily curtailed, and therefore different in kind from the free-flowing subversion implicated in other power relations, it is never completely obliterated. The implications of this recognition upon the development of future feminist projects are significant. Indeed, in the light of Foucault's cumulative work on both power and domination, it is clear that it is not that:

> the network of power relations in which women find ourselves is congealed, so that women are incapable of exercising power; instead, this network is constricted, so that women's range of options for the exercise of power is limited.[67]

In turn, this questions the affirmation of women as essentially powerless that informs radical feminist theorising and provides a justification for the utility of feminist reform premised upon opening the range of alternatives available. More specifically, it permits the ongoing deployment of a number of techniques that have proven highly successful in securing feminist political challenge, namely the methods of 'asking the woman question', 'practical reasoning' and 'consciousness-raising'.[68] Without identifying and labelling these particular feminist techniques, Foucault provides his own definitions and alludes to their ongoing utility in the more generic context of political challenge. Indeed, as he puts it in his latter work:

> we could criticise politics—beginning for example with the effects of the state of domination—but we could only do this by playing a certain game of truth, showing what were the effects, showing that there were other rational possibilities, teaching people what they ignore about their own situation, on their conditions of work, on their exploitation.[69]

The incorporation of these aspects of Foucault's analysis has the benefit, therefore, of highlighting and challenging domination without thereby

---

[66] M Foucault, 'The Ethics of Care of the Self as a Practice of Freedom', above n 8 at 12.
[67] A Allen, 'Foucault on Power—A Theory for Feminists' in S Hekman (ed) *Feminist Interpretations of Foucault*, above n 30 at 277.
[68] K Bartlett, 'Feminist Legal Methods', above n 26.
[69] M Foucault, 'The Ethic of Care of the Self as a Practice of Freedom', above n 8 at 15.

positing universal structures in which women are without access to power or agency. In conceiving of domination as a pathological example rather than an archetype of power relations, the Foucaultian thesis offers an agenda for resistance within which the primary concern is the dilution of congealed power relations rather than radical transcendence of over-arching power regimes. Alongside a more complex analysis of the intricacies and operation of intimate power relationships, it establishes an epistemological ground for the resistance to domination that radical feminism seeks but is denied by its unmodified understanding. As a result, it offers ongoing maintenance of the political opportunities and rhetoric traditionally associated with radical feminism alongside the sensitivity to context and power disparities requested by more contemporary feminist scholarship.

Conclusion

Contemporary feminist commentary on Foucault has been divided over the merits and demerits of his analysis of power vis-à-vis that of radical feminism. While some theorists have welcomed his focus upon micro-politics and the productive aspects of power, others have expressed serious concerns regarding the effectiveness of Foucaultian, or more generally postmodern, strategies for feminist legal and political purposes. Seeking to defend Foucault from such scepticism, some feminist contributions have begun to question the contemporary understanding of his work as exclusively concerned with the micro level of power regimes. Allen has noted that 'Foucault does more than expose the various ways in which power operates at the micro-level,' since he also examines the circulation of power through cultural discourses and broader institutional contexts and practices, which provides some ways of thinking about power at the macro-level that are also useful for feminist purposes.[70]

While this is certainly true, it has been submitted in this chapter that there is an ongoing tendency to underestimate the importance of Foucault's work on domination in developing a theory of power at the macro level. Further development of this analysis is crucial, however, not least because it challenges the assumption that the Foucaultian position on power can be sharply contrasted against its radical feminist counterpart. In addition, of course, this development is also important on its own terms, for as Allen notes 'the micro level is only *analytically* distinct from the macro level' and can therefore 'only be fully understood in conjunction with the latter.'[71]

---

[70] A Allen, 'Foucault on Power—A Theory for Feminists' in S Hekman (ed) *Feminist Interpretations of Michel Foucault*, above n 30 at 272. This understanding of Foucault is developed in more detail by Allen in her recent book, *The Power of Feminist Theory*, above n 3.

[71] A Allen, 'Foucault on Power—A Theory for Feminists' in S Hekman (ed) *Foucault*, above n 30 at 272.

Conclusion

Foucault's later work portrays an understanding of power that can be differentiated from its predecessor by its ability to explicitly re-instate the phenomenon of domination and to set it up as a legitimate object of critique and challenge. Not only does this recast the relevance of domination within the Foucaultian critical landscape, it also re-asserts its relevance within contemporary feminist critique. As discussed in Chapter one, whilst the postmodern turn in contemporary feminism towards micro-politics and productive, reciprocal accounts of power relationships has enabled a welcome transcendence of the essentialism of radical feminism, it has also tended to promote localised forms of resistance that in their turn have undermined the solidarity required for group allegiance and political action. In consequence, theory has become increasingly disengaged from politics and practice, and well-respected voices within the feminist academy have expressed growing disillusionment.[72] By opening up the possibility of re-deploying analyses of domination within the Foucaultian landscape, Foucault's latter works offer a means of redressing at least some of these concerns.

At the same time, though, some lingering concerns remain. More specifically, to the extent that this approach has emphasised the diversity of the power relations that operate to construct our individual identities, it might be seen to sit uncomfortably alongside a traditional feminist insistence on the legitimacy of seeing women as a collective with a shared position or perspective. To the extent that this apparent tension also goes to the heart of the relationship between feminist theory and feminist politics, it will be examined in detail in the next chapter, with a view to developing an approach that will retain a basis for talking about women as a group without denying their differences and the myriad positions that they inhabit in the networks of power.

---

[72] J Conaghan, 'Reassessing the Feminist Theoretical Project in Law' (2000) 27 (3) *Journal of Law and Society* 351.

5
Womanhood, Essentialism and Identity

One central point of contention that cuts across many of the debates and disagreements in feminist theory that have been examined in previous chapters relates to the existence of a collective female identity. The question of whether women share a common experience or identity, and if they do, of what has generated and framed its content, is one that has animated much contemporary feminist theorising. On the one hand, efforts to posit this kind of collective identity have tended to be criticised for being 'essentialist' and for arbitrarily reifying some women's experiences as paradigmatic whilst ignoring the experiences of others. On the other hand, many feminist activists have, despite these criticisms, continued to talk in terms of collective gender identity and have criticised theoretical approaches that place their emphasis on the differences between, rather than commonalities amongst, women. As Higgins explains, therefore, 'woman is a troublesome term, in feminism and in law' since although the category is not consistently or coherently constituted, the framework through which women have secured improvements in their legal, economic and social status have often depended on ascribing meaning to the term.[1]

Over the course of the following sections, this chapter will set out in more detail the parameters of this debate—within which, Naffine argues, the very integrity of the concept of women has been questioned and the subject matter of feminism threatened with implosion[2]—and will examine its implications particularly for the ongoing relationship between feminist theory and feminist politics. Having done so, it will go on to evaluate the suggestions put forward by some contemporary feminist theorists seeking to mediate this dispute by retaining a basis for group cohesion and political action in the face of internal diversity. More specifically, it will discuss the notion of strategic essentialism, associated with the work of Gayatari Spivak[3] and Diana Fuss,[4] as well as the idea of gender as seriality put forward by Iris

---

[1] T Higgins, 'By Reason Of Their Sex: Feminist Theory, Postmodernism and Justice' (1995) 80 Cornell Law Review 1536 at 1537.
[2] N Naffine, 'In Praise of Legal Feminism' (2002) 22(1) *Legal Studies* 71 at 72.
[3] G Spivak, *In Other Worlds: Essays in Cultural Politics* (New York, Methuen, 1987).
[4] D Fuss, *Essentially Speaking: Feminism, Nature and Difference* (New York, Routledge, 1989).

Womanhood, Essentialism and Identity

Marion Young.[5] Concluding that each of these approaches, despite their respective merits, ultimately fails to offer a compelling basis for explaining gender collectivity, the latter part of this chapter will put forward an alternative approach, which builds on Ludwig Wittgenstein's concept of 'family resemblances'.[6] It will be argued that this approach has the potential to generate not only a new way of conceptualising women's commonality, but also a way of doing so that provides both a normatively attractive account of gender identity and a coherent basis for group political and legal action.

While much of this discussion will take us beyond an exclusive focus on legal commentary, its relevance for this arena should not be underestimated. In a context in which reluctance to invoke monochrome visions of femininity has increasingly impeded collective engagement and proliferated localised forms of resistance, the sphere of the legal has too often been left untouched by feminist activity. Adept in policing the boundaries of its own intelligibility to ensure that those who do not speak its language (a language that eschews particularity and heterogeneity) may not engage, the law has found itself less and less in confrontation, or even conversation, with contemporary feminism. But this is problematic, since as discussed in Chapter three, law is not only a site of social control in which patriarchal privilege remains but also a site for reform in which previous (at least partial) victories have been secured. Thus, the prospect of finding a way beyond these debates, while important for those in various disciplines, holds particular relevance for feminist *legal* thinkers.

Setting the Scene: Essentialism and Difference

On the face of it, the difficulty inherent in identifying a common foundation of female experience or identity was either not acknowledged, or at least not a source of great concern, to early feminist legal thinking. Indeed, as Katherine Bartlett points out, the methods developed by feminist theorists throughout the 1970s and 1980s necessarily entailed reliance on such a foundation.[7] Techniques such as 'asking the woman question' and 'consciousness-raising', which were central to the politics, theory and practice of many feminist legal campaigners, were premised on the existence of a coherent and uniform category of womanhood, which could then be used as a measuring rod against which to show the law's abuse and/or exclusion of women.

---

[5] I Young, 'Gender as Seriality: Thinking about Woman as a Social Collective' (1994) 19 (3) *Signs* 713, reproduced in I Young, *Intersecting Voices: Dilemmas of Gender, Political Philosophy and Policy* (Princeton, Princeton University Press, 1997), 12–37.

[6] L Wittgenstein, *The Philosophical Investigations* (trans G Anscombe) (Oxford, Blackwell, 2000).

[7] K Bartlett, 'Feminist Legal Methods' (1990) 103 *Harvard University Law Review* 829.

Essentailism and Difference

Nowhere was reliance on such techniques more evident than in the work of Catharine MacKinnon.[8] As noted in previous chapters, MacKinnon's work pioneered a theory of feminism unmodified in which attending to women's experiences revealed a picture of collective oppression at the hands of men. For MacKinnon, the feminist view of women's situation indicated without question that:

> across time and space, there is too much variance in women's status, role and treatment for it to be biological, and too little variance for it to be individual.[9]

Thus, while there was a common experience that united all women, it was not based in anything biological or natural, but rather located in the socially constructed relations of domination and submission that characterised the interaction between the genders. The core meaning of womanhood, under conditions of patriarchy, was one of disempowerment, and women's voice, whatever it might sound like or say, had never been heard, other than through the refraction of male definitions. What's more, the law, despite its rhetoric of neutrality and objectivity, played a central role in perpetuating these oppressive relations.

In identifying an experience of womanhood grounded in oppression, MacKinnon's theory shifted the feminist theoretical emphasis towards self-definition and away from male-defined conceptions of women's sameness to or difference from men as the benchmark for entitlement. Unfortunately, however, as discussed in Chapter one, the experience that MacKinnon identified painted a very pessimistic and deterministic picture of relations between the sexes.[10] The extent to which this accorded with women's own definitions was debatable. What's more, it obscured the question of whether all women are subordinate to men in the same way or to the same degree. Thus, it risked purchasing powerful rhetoric and conceptual neatness at the cost of recognising intersectionality between gender and other axes of social stratification.

By contrast, contemporary feminist thinking, influenced by postmodern scepticism of mono-causal explanations of social phenomenon, has increasingly drawn attention to the plurality of experiences available to different women and to the range of factors that cut across gender in creating individual experiences of womanhood. Angela Harris, for example, has criticised MacKinnon for promoting an 'essentialist' account within which her vision of what it means to be female is not only pessimistic, but purportedly

---

[8] See in particular, C MacKinnon, *Feminism Unmodified—Discourses on Life and Law* (Cambridge, Harvard University Press, 1987); *Toward a Feminist Theory of State* (Cambridge, Harvard University Press, 1989).

[9] C MacKinnon, *Feminism* Unmodified, *ibid* at 25.

[10] See, eg, L Finley, 'The Nature of Domination and the Nature of Women: Reflections on Feminism Unmodified' (1988) 82 *Northwestern University Law Review* 352–86; D Cornell, *Beyond Accommodation: Ethical Feminism, Deconstruction and the Law* (London & New York, Routledge, 1991).

capable of being described independently from what it means to be black, white, poor, rich, heterosexual, lesbian, and so on.[11] This monochrome vision, Harris argues, distorts the complexity of the ways in which multiple and intersecting identities are experienced by individual women. This silences the voices of those women for whom their race, class or sexual orientation not only matter, but make a material difference to the way in which they experience their gender identity. In addition, it renders us blind to the ways in which legal norms can write qualitatively as well as quantitatively different scripts, depending on the interaction of gender with other socio-demographic categories. Thus, it threatens to replicate *between* women the patterns of exclusion that feminists contest when they arise between the genders.[12]

Concerned to avoid these shortcomings, a number of contemporary feminists have rejected altogether the project of identifying a common experience or characteristic of womanhood. They have concluded that there is no essence of female identity, located in biology or social context, and that techniques in feminist method that suggest otherwise are counter-productive since they either exclude the voices of non-conforming women or inappropriately stagnate gender identity under the law. Thus, theorists like Carol Smart,[13] Judith Butler[14] and Elizabeth Spelman[15] call, in their different ways, for the development of post-essentialist feminism. This would abandon efforts to locate a unique experience or identity that unites all women, instead celebrating women's differences from one another and developing a theory that acknowledges that (gender) identity is constructed, fluctuating and relational. It would avoid the temptation:

> to take what I understand to be true of me as a woman for some golden nugget of womanness all women have as women

and would ensure that the participation of other women, with different perspectives, were essential to the production of the story, or more aptly stories, of 'woman.'[16] Such an approach would also demand that we recognise that the groups in which we find ourselves are not monolithic but comprised

---

[11] A Harris, 'Race and Essentialism in Feminist Legal Theory' (1990) 42 *Stanford Law Review* 581.

[12] MacKinnon herself has consistently denied these charges of essentialism—see, eg, C MacKinnon, 'From Practice to Theory: Or, What is a White Woman Anyway?' and 'Keeping it Real: On Anti-Essentialism' in C MacKinnon, *Women's Lives, Men's Laws* (Cambridge, Harvard University Press, 2005), 22–31 and 84–90 respectively. In this discussion, MacKinnon emphasises that the basis for women's shared experience on her account is socially construction and thus far from essential.

[13] C Smart, *Feminism and the Power of Law* (London & New York, Routledge, 1989).

[14] J Butler, *Gender Trouble—Feminism and the Subversion of Identity* (London & New York, Routledge, 1990).

[15] E Spelman, *Inessential Woman: Problems of Exclusion in Feminist Thought* (London, Women's Press, 1990).

[16] E Spelman, *Inessential* Woman, *ibid* at 159.

Essentailism and Difference

of members with diverse and conflicting identities—and that we see this not as a threat to group solidarity but as a valuable opportunity for increasing our mutual understanding, as well as for building coalition-based politics.[17]

Of course, engaging with the myriad complexities of intersectionality in this way renders it increasingly difficult, and some would argue impossible or futile, to determine who or what 'woman' as a standalone category is for the purposes of feminist legal or political critique. While this is in keeping with the anti-essentialist spirit of postmodernism, it brings with it a number of potentially unwelcome implications for the feminist movement. For one thing, as Nancy Harstock points out, this sits uncomfortably alongside a feminist politics, that has traditionally found its motivation and justification in the existence of precisely such a united female experience.[18] Indeed, a number of commentators have expressed concern that too close an allegiance to postmodernism may threaten to remove the very platform from which feminism speaks, since it will subject the commonality that lies at the heart of collective campaigns to imminent critique. Making this point with characteristic boldness, MacKinnon warns that postmodernism, as a 'wholly abstract theory', is incapable of grasping the realities of the social world and fundamentally incompatible with a meaningful practice of women's rights, let alone a women's movement.[19]

To the extent that this identifies a tension between the nature of postmodern theory and the focus of feminist legal analysis on gender based disparity and disempowerment, it also ties into a broader concern about the relationship between theory and politics in contemporary legal feminism. As Harstock has argued, postmodernism poses the threat of political paralysis by encouraging feminists to reject the banner of a women's movement, and its calls for grand-scale legal change, in preference for localised and thus fragmented reform agendas. Certainly, as Ann Barron points out, there is:

> a palpable reluctance on the part of (contemporary) feminists to formulate political programmes or proposals for legal reform that purport to articulate the interests and needs of women in general.[20]

According to Joanne Conaghan, this can be attributed, at least in part, to the postmodern focus on difference and on the ways in which legal discourses construct narratives, which has directed feminist attention away from concrete, empirically-based research, and toward abstract theoretical

---

[17] K Crenshaw, 'Intersectionality and Identity Politics: Learning from Violence Against Women of Colour' in M Shanley and U Narayan (eds) *Reconstructing Political Theory: Feminist Perspectives* (Pennsylvania, University of Pennsylvania Press, 1997) at 180.

[18] N Harstock, 'Foucault on Power—A Theory for Women' in L Nicholson (ed) *Feminism/Postmodernism* (New York & London, Routledge, 1990), 157–175.

[19] C MacKinnon, 'Symposium on Unfinished Feminist Business: Some Points Against Postmodernism' (2000) 75 *Chicago-Kent Law Review* 687.

[20] A Barron, 'Feminism, Aestheticism and the Limits of Law' (2000) 8 *Feminist Legal Studies* 275 at 276.

encounters with gendered cultural and legal representations.[21] This shift has been lamented by Nancy Fraser, who argues that the preoccupation with 'cultural' over 'material' considerations,[22] in problematising constructions of gender identity to an extent that renders it impossible to talk about women as a group, has led contemporary feminists to become inappropriately reluctant to engage with the reality of women's daily lives—a reality within which, she argues, women as women continue to face considerable material inequality.[23]

These, then, are the contours of one of the biggest dilemmas facing contemporary feminist legal theory. It is a dilemma frequently posed in terms of essentialism or difference, that is, between isolating or abandoning the search for what identifies women as women under the law.[24] But it is also a dilemma that implicates further debate about the relationship between feminist theory and practice, and more specifically about whether political cohesion should or need be sacrificed to ensure theoretical legitimacy. The internal schism which the existence of these debates within feminism has generated has been acutely felt by many commentators. What's more, it is widely accepted that the way in which these debates are resolved or reconciled will prove crucial to the future direction of feminist theory and activism. It is perhaps no surprise then that a number of attempts have been made by feminists in recent years to navigate a safe passage out of this double-bind of essentialism and political paralysis. Over the following sections, this chapter will examine some of the most prominent of these attempts in more detail, evaluating the extent to which they ultimately succeed in securing a basis for collective identity politics that does not ignore the dynamics of women's experiential and epistemological diversity.

Strategic Essentialism

Introduced by Gayatari Spivak in her work on subaltern studies,[25] the notion of strategic essentialism has been deployed enthusiastically by a

[21] J Conaghan, 'Reassessing the Feminist Theoretical Project in Law' (2000) 27(3) *Journal of Law and Society* 351.

[22] The validity and utility of this distinction has itself, however, been much debated—see N Fraser, 'Recognition or Redistribution?: A Critique of Iris Young's Justice and the Politics of Difference' (1995) 3(2) *Journal of Political Philosophy* 166; I Young, 'Unruly Categories: A Critique of Nancy Fraser's Dual Systems Theory' (1997) 222 *New Left Review* 147; M Yar, 'Beyond Nancy Fraser's Perspective Dualism' (2001) 30(3) *Economy and Society* 288.

[23] N Fraser, *Unruly Practices: Power, Discourse and Gender in Contemporary Theory* (Cambridge, Polity, 1989); *Justice Interruptus: Critical Reflections on the 'Post-Socialist' Condition* (New York & London, Routledge, 1997).

[24] D Cornell, 'The Doubly-Prized World: Myth, Allegory and the Feminine' (1990) 75 *Cornell Law Review* 644 at 644. For further and useful discussion of this debate more generally, see E Spelman, *Inessential Woman*, above n 15.

[25] G Spivak, 'Subaltern Studies: Deconstructing Historiography' in R Guha and G Spivak (eds) *Selected Subaltern Studies* (Oxford, Oxford University Press, 1988). It is arguable that

Strategic Essentialism

number of feminist theorists seeking to mediate the tension between recognising women's diversity and securing a basis for collective feminist action. According to strategic essentialism, feminism should accept the reality that the difference in women's lives renders any claim to commonality at best artificial and at worst misleading. That said, however, they should not reject the rhetoric and ideology of essentialism altogether. On the contrary, despite acknowledging its descriptive falsity, they should continue to act *as if* essentialism were true, that is *as if* there is a stable female experience or identity, in order to encourage the kind of shared identification among women that is required for engaging in collective action. In a context in which the social and legal world often treats women as if they are a unified group, this approach seeks to harness the political effectiveness of playing into that fiction, whilst simultaneously avoiding any commitment to the belief that this female commonality does in fact exist.

Thus, this approach involves not so much a dismissal as a mimicking of essentialism. There is little point in trying, as other feminists have done, to avoid essentialism, since, in one form or another, it is inevitable. Instead, we should focus on identifying the essentialist categories which we have no choice *but* to use in our political engagements and on deploying those categories strategically in pursuit of selected goals. This shifts the focus away from the fact of essentialism and towards the basis for its deployment since the value of essentialism can only be determined by the agenda of those who practice it. In the hands of a hegemonic group, it may continue to be a powerful tool of ideological domination, but in the hands of others, its deliberate mimicking of dominant modes of thinking can represent a reformist weapon.[26] What's more, as Butler argues, 'without the compulsory expectation that feminist actions must be instituted from some stable, unified, and agreed-upon identity,' it is possible that this form of politics may be more efficient, easier to instigate and better received by those for whom the meaning of the category 'women' is permanently moot.[27]

At this level, the idea of strategic essentialism is engaging and provocative, not least since it moves us beyond the inherent limitations of 'the blackmail of essentialism',[28] according to which one must either be 'for' or 'against' essentialism. What's more, it does prima facie achieve its stated

---

Spivak revises/refines her position in later work, calling less for strategic deployment of essentialism and more for a consideration of how we are all essentialist in different ways—G Spivak, 'In a Word: Interview' in N Schor and E Week (eds) *The Essential Difference* (Bloomington, Indiana University Press, 1994).

[26] G Spivak, *In Other Worlds*, above n 3.

[27] J Butler, 'Subjects of Sex/Gender/Desire' in A Phillips (ed), *Feminism and Politics* (Oxford, Oxford University Press, 1998) at 288.

[28] The use of this term is intended to parallel the concept of the 'blackmail of the Enlightenment' that Foucault identifies in his discussion of Kant's work—M Foucault, 'What is Enlightenment?' in P Rabinow (ed) *The Foucault Reader* (New York, Pantheon, 1984).

Womanhood, Essentialism and Identity

purpose of acknowledging women's internal diversity whilst still affording the possibility for collective action as a common group. When we press this approach more carefully, however, it emerges as increasingly problematic. For one thing, it appears to leave wholly unaddressed fundamental questions about *who* would be strategically deploying essentialism in feminist legal and political activism and, equally importantly, about *how* this would come about.

In her 'Manifesto for Cyborgs', Donna Haraway produces a conceptualisation of political coalition formation that might assist us in these regards.[29] She posits a politics based in coalition through affinity rather than through identity, that is, through mutual empathy rather than strict experiential congruence. Such a politics, she argues, is uniquely suited to embracing the partial, contradictory, and permanently unclosed constructions of personal and collective identity that pertain in the context of feminism, without sacrificing efficiency or integrity. While this may well be true, it does rather beg the question of where this pre-political affinity comes from, if not from the existence of some shared experience that bonds women as a group. Of course, it might be argued that since society and its laws tend to (wrongly) assume a commonality amongst women, this affinity comes simply from the shared female experience of being treated as part of an ill-fitting collective. But does this not in itself suggest a shared experience; a commonality that exists and so can be drawn upon rather than fictionalised as the basis for collective action? The political effectiveness of the strategic approach depends, after all, on the existence of a homogenous set of assumptions about women which can be mimicked. Once these assumptions are acknowledged, however, it is not clear why they could not in themselves bring about precisely the kind of real and shared influence on women's lives that MacKinnon and others have isolated. To the extent that this is so, Alison Stone has argued that attempts to deploy essentialism in a solely strategic form are inevitably flawed, since they are always premised on an unacknowledged debt to descriptive essentialism.[30]

Seeking to avoid these difficulties, Diana Fuss proposes an inversion of Haraway's model.[31] For Fuss, the affinity that brings women together into a coalition can never be pre-political, since it is only ever grounded in and created through political activity. It is feminist politics which *creates* a female affinity shared by a coalition of diverse women dispersed across the world, and 'it is politics which feminism cannot do without, politics that is essen-

---

[29] D Haraway, 'A Cyborg Manifesto: Science, Technology, and Socialist-Feminism in the Late Twentieth Century' (1985) 80 *Socialist Review* 65. Re-printed in D Haraway, *Simians, Cyborgs and Women: The Reinvention of Nature* (New York & London, Routledge, 1991).

[30] A Stone, 'Essentialism and Anti-Essentialism in Feminist Philosophy' (2004) 1 (2) *Journal of Moral Philosophy* 135.

[31] D Fuss, *Essentially Speaking*, above n 4.

tial to feminism's many self-definitions.'[32] This approach is, of course, useful to the extent that it re-affirms that the very perception of a common female identity is itself mediated by social processes which bring women together around a specific purpose. But on closer inspection, Fuss' model also continues to pose some problematic questions about the basis of this mobilisation. Indeed, if Fuss is right that the idea of women's commonality can only emerge as a construction of feminist politics; if, in other words, there is nothing pre-existing those politics that can determine the membership of a coalition, or the terms of its reference, then does the emergence of a unique feminist politics not in itself become accidental, opportunistic, or arbitrary? In addition, since building commonality on the basis of political coalition will almost inevitably exclude those women who do not see themselves as feminist or who are not exercised by the concerns of feminist politics, does this approach not perpetuate the kind of marginalisation that has been criticised elsewhere? To the extent that this is so, this variant of strategic essentialism threatens to privilege some (politicised) norms or experiences of womanhood, in the name of female commonality. And while this can be redressed by the invocation of some conception of women as a group prior to self-conscious feminist politics, this leads us back to a reliance on descriptive essentialism and to the kind of model Fuss rejects.

Clearly, then, dominant models of strategic essentialism have been undermined by their inability to provide an explanation for the galvinising of individual women into political collectives that does not rely on some notion of shared affinity or experience. Beyond this, however, there are a number of additional concerns that might legitimately be voiced regarding the desirability of this approach to feminist legal theory and politics. For one thing, strategic essentialism poses the perpetual risk of instrumentalising theory, since it renders political affiliation and deployment one strategy among many in the struggle for women's empowerment. This, of course, reflects the position, derived from Lyotard's work, that knowledge in contemporary society is legitimised by its utility more than by its truth,[33] and is affirmed (to some extent) by a Foucaultian perspective that conceives of all reformist agendas as mere strategies in an omnipresent struggle for power.[34] Despite

---

[32] D Fuss, *Essentially Speaking*, above n 4 at 37.

[33] 'The relationship of the suppliers and users of knowledge to the knowledge they supply and use is now tending, and will increasingly tend, to assume the form already taken by the relationship of commodity producers and consumers to the commodities they produce and consume'—J Lyotard, *The Postmodern Condition* (Manchester, Manchester University Press, 1979) at 4.

[34] M Foucault, *Power/Knowledge: Selected Interviews and Other Writings 1972–77* (ed C Gordon) (New York, Pantheon, 1980); M. Foucault, *Discipline and Punish—The Birth of The Prison* (trans A Sheridan) (New York, Vintage, 1979). Of course, it should be borne in mind here that the understanding of (micro) power reflected in Foucault's work is highly distinctive, and while potentially productive for feminist analysis, it is not unproblematically so. For further discussion, see Ch 4.

this, however, it might well be argued (as it has been in the context of the turn to anti-foundationalism more generally) that feminist legal analysis loses something valuable by talking solely in terms of strategy, pretence and mimic, rather than reform, legitimacy and representation. Most obviously, it is these latter forms of terminology that have been the staple dialect of liberal law, and while feminist analysis has never accepted them uncritically, it has often acknowledged the importance of being able to engage in and with law's terms. Indeed, many feminists have questioned whether this reduction of politics to a series of strategies for subversion undermines the transformative agendas of feminism, by denying it the conceptual tools necessary to realise its utopia.[35] As Cornell reminds us, after all:

> the affirmation of the feminine . . . is not simply strategic, or goal-oriented, but also utopian in that it tries to keep alive an 'elsewhere' beyond our current conceptions of the political as an instrumental struggle for power.[36]

In the final analysis, then, strategic essentialism is valuable for its candour in seeking to transcend the 'blackmail of essentialism'. But when its foundations are probed, it appears to leave much to be desired—either collapsing into a descriptive essentialism that belies its strategic pretensions or failing to provide a compelling account of the origins of the coalitions that enter its strategic game. In addition, it might be questioned whether this is an appropriate technique to be deployed in the legal arena, and we might wonder whether the politicised and instrumentalised account of collective gender identity that it proposes adequately represents women's own narratives and experiences of relating to and with other (diverse) women.

Iris Marion Young: Gender as Seriality

Recognising many of the difficulties thus associated with the deployment of strategic essentialism, Iris Marion Young seeks to develop an alternative way out of this feminist dilemma of describing women as a group without falling prey to essentialism.[37] She does so primarily by appropriating the concept of a social series developed by Jean Paul Sartre in his *Critique of Dialectical Reason*[38] to argue that, although women do not share a deep

---

[35] Although this critique of subversion has most often been raised in the context of Foucaultian theory, its claims have significance also for the strategising of politics inherent in the present approach—see, eg, N Harstock, 'Foucault on Power—A Theory for Women,' in L Nicholson (ed), *Feminism/Postmodernism*, above n 18; S Benhabib, 'Feminism and Postmodernism—An Uneasy Alliance?' in S Benhabib, J Butler, D Cornell & N Fraser (eds) *Feminist Contentions—A Philosophical Exchange* (London & New York, Routledge, 1995).

[36] D Cornell, *Beyond Accommodation*, above n 10 at 182.

[37] I Young, 'Gender as Seriality: Thinking about Woman as a Social Collective,' above n 5.

[38] J Sartre, *Critique of Dialectical Reason I. Theory of Practical Ensembles* (trans A Sheridan-Smith) (London, New Left Books, 1976).

communal affiliation, they nonetheless share a loose connection, on the basis of which stronger group bonds can be developed.

In order to understand Young's argument, it is necessary first to understand the Sartrean conceptualisation of the forms of social collectivity upon which she draws. According to Sartre, a social group involves a collection of people who recognise themselves as unified with others in pursuit of a common project. By contrast, a social series involves a collection of people who are unified passively by the objects upon which their actions are targeted, without any self-conscious mutual identification or the establishment of any common project in relation to those actions. In a social series, therefore, members pursue their own individual ends, but they are united loosely with one another since the objects in regard to which they pursue those ends are the same, having been conditioned and created by the same external structures.

To illustrate this more clearly, Young deploys Sartre's example that people waiting at a bus stop would constitute a social series. These people form a social collective in that they are minimally related to one another by the fact that they each target their own action to the same end of waiting for a bus, and do so in a context in which the conditions bearing upon that end (queuing, tickets and timetables) are subject to the same externally imposed constraints. But, significantly, these commuters have nothing necessarily in common in terms of their experiences or characteristics. In particular, they do not identify with one another and do not see themselves as involved in any collective project targeted to the achievement of a specific goal.

There are of course myriad such social series in existence at any time, and people will find themselves floating in and out of them at regular intervals. What is significant about these series, however, is that their minimal collective nature always entails a latent potential for stronger affiliation. Indeed, as Young explains, it is always possible for a series to transform itself into a group—if the bus does not arrive, for example, members of the series might come to mutually identify as hard-done-by commuters, perhaps forging a common project of sharing a taxi, and thereby coming to bear the hallmarks of a more conscious and integrated group. And yet, just as quickly as a series transforms into a group, it can revert to being nothing more than a series when the project has been completed. What is significant here is not just the fluidity of the distinction between series and groups, but also that what causes these groups to emerge can be located within the parameters of the serialised context itself. It is, after all, only as a reaction to the conditions under which series members wait for the bus (an unreliable transport system) that the group emerges and mobilises itself.

Applying these ideas in the context of gender, Young argues that women can best be seen as constituting a particular example of a social series. This, she argues, has the benefit of acknowledging a minimal level of social connection with other women, emerging in a context in which actions are similarly socially structured and targeted towards particular ends. Yet, at the same time, it avoids any need for self-reflective identification with other women or for affiliation through the pursuit of common goals. As she explains, 'there is a unity to the series "women" but it is a passive unity',[39] it does not arise from the individuals themselves, but from the structural relations and conditions in which they are positioned. In the specific context of gender, the structural relations and conditions of particular relevance are those relating to enforced heterosexuality and the sexual division of labour. Thus, the unity of women does not come from any shared attribute, but rather from the fact that being female enables us to predict something about the general constraints an individual woman will face, albeit that it tells us nothing about how she will deal with them.

According to Young, thinking of gender, as well as of other structures like race and class, as instances of social seriality is useful, since it permits talking in collective terms without assuming a shared identity or a common attribute. Any given woman will belong to a number of series, and can choose to make none or only some of these memberships important to her sense of identity. What's more, she can choose to vary her assessment of the relative importance of series memberships depending on her context or current priorities. A black, working-class woman, for example, will always exist as a member of the series of women, and so will find herself passively sharing with white, hispanic, or asian women the structural constraints that set the context within which she exists and functions. But equally, she will share a similar bond with black men of whatever class, and with working class men of whatever race, and she may choose to value these affiliations more highly throughout her life, or at particular instances in which she experiences, for example, the negative impact of a white woman's racism on a black man. In so doing, however, she does not leave the series of women; on the contrary, her membership in the collective remains intact and so too, therefore, does the possibility of identifying and talking in terms of an inclusive affiliation of diverse and non-mutually identifying individual women.

Clearly, then, this aspect of series membership permits recognition of the intersectionality between axes of social stratification in a way arguably denied by many other feminist analyses. At the same time, however, it renders some reference to women as a broad social collective legitimate even in the face of considerable internal differences. What's more, this seriality approach has a considerable advantage over the strategic essentialist approach since it can properly explain the background against which women might consciously elevate their social series to the level of a social

---

[39] I Young, 'Gender as Seriality: Thinking about Women as a Social Collective', above n 5 at 32.

group, ie as a reaction to the structural conditions in which they pursue their individual goals. When women's politics emerge, members of the social series have come together to forge a group, taking something about the serial conditions of women as the explicit and shared aim of their actions. Thus there remains a constant, albeit differently constituted, link between feminist groups and the series collective of women to which they at least implicitly refer—feminism does not emerge as articulating the voice of all womanhood, but *feminisms* emerge as groups of women reacting to and building upon their serialised unity in a self-conscious and targeted way.

While there are thus many advantages to Young's analysis, it remains open to criticism on at least two counts. Firstly, according to Stone, for those feminist theorists who are committed to the anti-essentialist project, Young's defence of women's collective status in a series may be seen as disappointing since it tacitly re-inscribes the essentialism that she claims to successfully avoid.[40] Although Young denies that women within a social series share a common experience or identity, she nonetheless insists that all women's lives are oriented, despite their diversity, around the same or similarly structured objects and realities, namely expectations of normative heterosexuality and of a sexual division of labour. This begs the question, however, of whether Young's claim that all women share certain structural conditions is really that different, or indeed that much less problematic, normalising or essentialist, than the much-disputed claim that all women share certain attributes or experiences. It is striking, for example, that the notion of 'gendered life', which is based, like Young's theory, on the premise that women share:

> the potential for experiencing a variety of situations, statuses, and ideological and political impositions in which gender is culturally relevant,

leads Martha Fineman to conclude, (cf Young) that a deep affiliation between women does in fact exist, grounded precisely in the unifying potential of these culturally stereotyped impositions.[41] At its core, Young's claim is that although women have no common features, there are nonetheless common features which organise the social realities constraining all women's

---

[40] A Stone, 'Essentialism and Anti-Essentialism in Feminist Philosophy', above n 30.
[41] M Fineman, 'Feminist Theory and Law' (1995) 18 *Harvard Journal of Law and Public Policy* 349 at 359. According to Fineman, while 'there are some difference among women that may, in some instances, be more significant than are the gendered life differences between men and women,' in the aggregate 'women's shared or collective gendered experiences, both actual and potential, differ significantly from men's.' Like Young, she does not argue that all women react the same way or reach identical conclusions about issues in our society but she argues that 'uniformity in interpretation and experiences is not necessary to the concept of gendered life. Individual experiences may differ from the socially constructed and culturally defined nexus, but they are still affected by them'—M Fineman, 'Challenging Law, Establishing Differences: The Future of Feminist Legal Scholarship' (1990) 42 *Florida Law Review* 25 at 36–8.

lives. But, as Stone has argued, this may well prove to be a distinction without a difference, in which case Young's analysis fails on its own terms by remaining fundamentally tied to some form of descriptive essentialism.

We should, however, exercise some caution here. After all, it may be that some form of essentialism is inevitable. What's more, as Conaghan has noted, pursuing anti-essentialism too single-mindedly can itself constitute a form of essentialism.[42] If Young's approach provides a credible and viable conception of the relationship between women, then the simple fact of its lingering essentialism may be of limited, if any, relevance. Lamentably, however, it is submitted that this is not the case. Indeed, contrary to what was argued above, it might be thought that the shortcomings of this approach lie less in a failure to reject essentialism than in a failure to provide a compelling account of the basis of women's commonality.

The collectivity of women presented in Young's theory is one that takes the form of a social series, grounded in a passive unity without mutual identification, collective ends, common experiences or shared attributes. But when we reflect on this more closely, a number of problems emerge with applying this model to gender. More specifically, it becomes clear that despite her recognition that the series women is more complex than the series bus passengers, Young fails to consider whether those complexities do, or should, render her analogy unsustainable. The basis that unites women as a collective may indeed be variable and illusive, perhaps even passive, but it is surely not of the same largely contingent and hollow form as that which unites the paradigmatic series of bus passengers. The fact of being a woman, while its significance and implications may vary considerably depending on context, wields the *potential* for influence across whole swathes of our daily interactions in a way that the fact of being a bus passenger simply does not. What's more, the extent to which we are able to choose to enter and to remain within these differing collectives is markedly different. In addition, moreover, the structural constraints operating on women as a collective are themselves fundamentally different in kind, and arguably more resistant to change, than those operating in the central case. For one thing, the demands imposed by normative heterosexuality and the sexual division of labour are more complex in structure and more multidimensional than the demands imposed by bus timetables or ticket-buying. They are also more oppressive: non-conformance carries serious and weighty social, personal and relational consequences of the sort that are not produced by jumping the bus queue. Furthermore, and perhaps most significantly for feminist purposes, it might be argued that the constraints operating on women have been constructed to reflect the interests of one definitionally external series (men) rather than the interests of society as a whole (cf the case of the commuters).

---

[42] J Conaghan, 'Reassessing the Feminist Theoretical Project in Law', above n 21 at 373.

These differences in structural constraint are in themselves significant, but they also highlight the way in which different series might be led, through operating within those constraints, to develop bonds amongst their membership of differing depths. Experiencing constraints constructed to the advantage of others, imposed with strong social normative force and wielding heavy consequences for non-compliance is likely to generate bonds of a deeper and more enduring nature than those that unite the series of bus passengers, even where there remains no conscious self-identification or mobilisation of the sort typifying the transition to a group. In denying this reality, Young's account threatens to sidestep complexity, and to inappropriately equate the constraints upon, and the bonds between, members of the series of women on the one hand, and members of the series of bus commuters on the other. This in turn threatens to offer a reductive vision of women's collectivity, which affords no middle ground between the largely contingent and minimalist unity of a social series and the strong mutual identification and shared endeavour involved in a group. This is particularly lamentable since many women, if asked about the nature of their relationship to other women, would doubtless seek to place themselves squarely within this terrain.

Despite this, however, it should be noted that there are a number of valuable insights in Young's work, in particular her recognition that, in order to resolve the feminist dilemma over maintaining collectivity in the face of difference, we must think more imaginatively about the *nature* rather than the *content* of women's bonds of commonality. This is something that also infuses the work of Haraway, who from a different perspective, emphasises that:

> the permanent partiality of feminist points of view has consequences for our expectations of forms of political organisation and participation.[43]

It will be argued in the following section that the work of Ludwig Wittgenstein, especially his idea of 'family resemblances', may prove particularly helpful in assisting contemporary feminist theorists to work through these ideas.

Back to the Rough Ground: Wittgenstein

The writings of Ludwig Wittgenstein are complex and wide-ranging, and this chapter is not an appropriate forum in which to engage with all the questions that continue to be raised by his work. In what follows, therefore, a restricted focus will be adopted in which those components of his analysis that may prove useful to our project of theorising gender identity will be

---

[43] D Haraway, 'A Manifesto for Cyborgs: Science, Technology and Socialist Feminism in the 1980s' in L Nicholson (ed) *Feminism/ Postmodernism*, above n 18 at 215.

selectively appropriated. In particular, this section will focus on his idea of 'family resemblances' and on the potential this offers for maintaining a meaningful conception of collectivity in the face of internal diversity.

In marked contrast to his earlier writings in *The Tractatus*,[44] Wittgenstein aims in *The Philosophical Investigations* to set his readers free from a philosophical picture, according to which we can understand terms of language and forms of life only by uncovering their 'essence'.[45] Although this approach has 'held us captive', Wittgenstein argues that it is flawed by its tendency to sublimate logic as abstracted from experience, and its attendant failure to see that the two are indistinguishable. For Wittgenstein, logic absent its empirical foundations becomes hollow—it leads us:

> on to slippery ice where there is no friction and so in a certain sense the conditions are ideal, but also, just because of that, we are unable to walk.'[46]

Since we want and need to walk, Wittgenstein advises that we resist the pull to essentialism, retreating instead to the 'rough ground'. Thus, his latter project focuses on examining that which is already open to view—ie the way in which language is deployed in our everyday communications—rather than excavating for shared characteristics attributable to all instances of a given concept.

In rejecting philosophical efforts to secure conceptual coherence through the discovery of a shared essence, and asserting instead that we identify the content and parameters of concepts through concrete analysis, the approach of *The Philosophical Investigations* is a bold one. Its rejection of abstract theorising is, of course, echoed in much contemporary feminist work. In addition, its attentiveness to the particularity of experiences in the 'rough ground' can be seen to parallel the efforts of feminist theorists (most notably perhaps Carol Gilligan)[47] to listen to the concrete moral voices of women.[48] To this extent, and despite the fact that his own views on women may have left much to be desired,[49] there may therefore be scope for some useful

---

[44] L Wittgenstein, *Tractatus Logico-Philosophicus* (trans D Pears and B McGuiness) (London & New York, Routledge, 1961).

[45] L Wittgenstein, *The Philosophical Investigations*, above n 6.

[46] L Wittgenstein, *The Philosophical Investigations*, above n 6 at s 107. Note that the use of the term 'empirical' in this context is not intended to place Wittgenstein alongside Hume and others in their philosophical challenge to the 'idealists'. Wittgenstein's call is to look at practices as they are in life, without reducing them either to innate ideas or to only what is empirically verifiable.

[47] C Gilligan, *In a Different Voice—Psychological Theory and Women's Development* (re-issued ed) (Cambridge, Harvard University Press, 1993).

[48] S Hekman, 'The Moral Language Game' in N Scheman and P O'Connor (eds) *Feminist Interpretations of Ludwig Wittgenstein* (Pennsylvania, Pennsylvania State University Press, 2002) at 169. See also S Hekman, *Moral Voices, Moral Selves: Carol Gilligan and Feminist Moral Theory* (Cambridge, Polity Press, 1995).

[49] P Rooney, 'Philosophy, Language and Wizardry' in N Scheman and P O'Connor (eds) *Feminist Interpretations of Ludwig Wittgenstein*, ibid at 26.

engagement between feminism and Wittgenstein. But it is in his notion of 'family resemblances' and its application to the specific context of the feminist dilemma over essentialism/difference that it will be argued that there is the most fertile ground.

Through his investigation of our actual use of linguistic categories, Wittgenstein learns that, rather than using language to *represent* the essence of a concept, we use it refer to a range of instances connected to one another in various ways, despite their internal differences. As he expresses it:

> instead of producing something common to all that we call language, ... these phenomena have no one thing in common which makes us use the same word for all,—but that they are related to one another in many different ways.[50]

Wittgenstein explains the nature of this relation through the use of the concept of 'games': there is no single characteristic shared by all the myriad things that we refer to as 'games' (board games, card games, Olympic games, ball games and so on), but there is a complex network of overlapping and intersecting similarities that can be discerned between the individual members.[51] These similarities he characterises as 'family resemblances' since they parallel the way in which resemblances between family members (build, eye colour, temperament and so on) overlap and criss-cross within and between generations:[52] just because a family portrait does not reveal a common feature that unites all members, this does not mean that those portrayed are not rightly referred to as a family by virtue of the similarities they share as a collective.

At first blush, the structure that Wittgenstein identifies through the idea of family resemblances may seem ill-conceived. For one thing, as Rundle points out, it defends an intuitively difficult notion of unity according to which two items could conceivably and legitimately fall under the same concept despite having no features whatsoever in common.[53] But in reality this need not be problematic. As Mulhall explains, this is only troubling to our understanding of conceptual unity if we fail to take account of the way in which such items are in fact linked together by a chain of overlapping resemblances that pass from one to the other via intermediate cases.[54] Mulhall uses the example of the concept of a 'picture' to try to illustrate this point. We use this term to refer both to an abstract painting by Pollock and to the latest Hollywood blockbuster. Looked at in isolation and on their own terms, it may well be true that there is no single feature shared by these two

---

[50] L Wittgenstein, *The Philosophical Investigations*, above n 6 at s 65.
[51] L Wittgenstein, *The Philosophical Investigations*, above n 6 at s 66.
[52] L Wittgenstein, *The Philosophical Investigations*, above n 6 at s 67.
[53] B Rundle, *Wittgenstein and Contemporary Philosophy of Language* (Oxford, Blackwell, 1990) at 49–50.
[54] S Mulhall, *Inheritance and Originality: Wittgenstein, Heidegger, Kierkegaard* (Oxford, Clarendon Press, 2003) at 84–6.

instances of a 'picture'. But it may still be appropriate for them to be regarded as a 'picture' since, when each instance is situated in its social context, and the development over time from artwork to film depiction is understood, it becomes apparent that they are in fact linked together by a series of interim connections mediated via other pictorial forms.

In thus providing a new way of understanding conceptual unity and its structure, Wittgenstein's notion of 'family resemblances' is rich on its own terms. What's more, for current feminist purposes, it offers a potentially promising route out of the dilemma of asserting commonality in the face of diversity. Indeed, once it is acknowledged that the bonds of commonality uniting members of a collective can be complex, inter-connected, and grounded in relative rather than strict similarity, new ways of conceptualising women's unity emerge. A Wittgensteinian analysis allows us to recognise the existence of a meaningful interconnection between women (that is neither mimicked nor minimalist) without trivialising the difficulties that feminists have encountered in 'uncovering' the 'essence' of womanhood. Equally, though, under the emerging model, there is no requirement for a strict sense of shared identity, and recognition of internal difference presents no threat to coherence.

Thus, while our retreat to the 'rough ground' provokes an approach cognisant of myriad diversity and intersectionality, it is not one that entails the problematic consequences of postmodernism, since there is no assumption that difference precludes collectivity. On the contrary, the existence of diversity demands a re-imagining of what constitutes commonality, and of what structures are required to sustain unity. Accepting that there is no one characteristic that all women hold in common does not entail abandoning talk of women as a collective any more than it entails abandoning projects based on group action. As Heyes puts it, this:

> provides an alternative ontology that sidesteps the view that there is an essential womanness, separable from class, race, and other contexts . . . (but allows us to) use the term *women*, make generalisations about women, and engage in feminist politics.[55]

Of course, this begs the central question of whether, and on what basis, it would be legitimate to claim that women do in fact share this family resemblance structure. Looking, as Wittgenstein directs, to the ways in which the concept of women is used in everyday language, it is clear is that it does have a fairly constant meaning and that it is used, often wholly unproblematically, in communication to refer to a range of individuals who, despite their diversity, are acknowledged (by themselves and others) as sharing a common bond. Now, when we try to isolate and identify the

---

[55] C Heyes, 'Back to the Rough Ground!: Wittgenstein, Essentialism and Feminist Methods' in N Scheman and P O'Connor (eds) *Feminist Interpretations of Ludwig Wittgenstein*, above n 48 at 203.

nature of that bond by finding an essence central to all the uses of the term 'women', we, like many feminists before us, will become tongue-tied. But as Wittgenstein points out, this does not mean that the concept lacks meaning. On the contrary, it indicates that its meaning resides in the complex pattern of similarities that can be discerned across the various instances in which the concept is meaningfully invoked: bisexual women, like heterosexual women, may form sexual relationships with men, but unlike heterosexual women, may also form sexual relationships with women;[56] white women, like black women, may experience sexual objectification, but unlike black women, may not endure a legacy of slavery that prejudices perceptions of their sexual availability; middle-class women, like working-class women, may be mothers, but unlike working-class women, may not struggle with the competing demands of work and childcare. These are examples plucked largely at random, but what they illustrate is the multidimensional nature of the relationships and similarities that cut across the diverse ways in which we (sensibly) use the concept 'women'. Each of these takes its place in a network of resemblances that unites members with one another in some regards but with few, if any, in all.

The collective concept of women that emerges through this process is, clearly, quite different from that which previous feminist theories have proposed or searched for. Most notably, this is a concept without pretence to rigid limits. For Wittgenstein, however, there is no reason to suspect that a blurred concept cannot still be a useful one. Indeed, such blurring is, in his view, inevitable, since 'if a concept depends on a pattern of life, then there must be some indefiniteness to it.'[57] Granted, then, we cannot explain the parameters of such concepts in categorical terms, but we can give examples of specific instances and add that other instances which are 'similar' will be included. Clearly this lack of rigidity sacrifices a measure of theoretical closure by acknowledging the existence of penumbral vagueness, but it purchases considerable flexibility and attention to concrete experience. In addition, since determinations of what counts as similar, and thus of what is included within a conceptual category, are determined, according to Wittgenstein, with specific purposes in mind, this positions at the centre of our thinking the critical realisation that categories are delimited as a consequence of political strategy rather than ontological necessity.[58]

---

[56] This example is cited by C Heyes, 'Back to the Rough Ground!: Wittgenstein, Essentialism and Feminist Methods', in N Scheman and P O'Connor (eds) *Feminist Interpretations of Ludwig Wittgenstein*, above n 48 at 196.

[57] L Wittgenstein, *Remarks on the Philosophy of Psychology Volume II*, (trans GH von Wright and H Nyman) (Oxford, Blackwell, 1980) at s 652.

[58] C Heyes, 'Back to the Rough Ground!: Wittgenstein, Essentialism and Feminist Methods', in N Scheman and P O'Connor (eds) *Feminist Interpretations of Ludwig Wittgenstein*, above n 48 at 200.

This, of course, is particularly significant in the context of feminist theorising, since it frees up feminist campaigners to seek redefinition of the boundaries of 'womanhood', explicitly acknowledging that in so doing they are involved in a political enterprise. Thus, the precise boundaries and the deployment of the collective category of *women* remain strategic, and this is important since it acknowledges both the political imperative in feminism and the artificiality of membership premised on shared essence. Significantly, however, the nature of the strategy involved is somewhat different from that which animates the agenda of coalition politics or the theories of Spivak and Fuss. Strategy interjects here only at the point of drawing boundaries to determine which similarities (resemblances) are relevant for a given purpose—as such, unlike strategic essentialism, it works on the premise that similarities do exist, do have normative significance, and need not be artificially constructed or imposed on political actors to make sense of their collectivity.

Thus, it appears that deploying Wittgenstein's concept of 'family resemblances' in the specific context of gender identity may prove particularly productive, providing the opportunity for feminist theorists to devise woman-defined understandings of femininity that defy the imputations of patriarchal stereotyping. There is no pretence here to strict similarity or sameness, either as a purely political ploy or as a background structural constraint, and so the descriptive essentialism that has proven so tenacious elsewhere is avoided. Equally, however, a unity to the collective concept 'women' remains, since the network of relative similarities amongst individual women is recognised. This is important, not only because it permits collective action under the banner of a women's movement, but also because, in contrast to strategic essentialism and gender as seriality, the basis on which this arises reflects an experience of complex, multi-faceted, but very real, affinity amongst women as women. While there is no one strand of shared experience or attribute that runs through all women, there is nonetheless an overlapping of many different strands, which come together to form a thread of considerable strength: as Wittgenstein explains, this 'is not a something, but not a nothing either.'[59]

Conclusion: 'False Prison' Breaks & Feminist Legal Theory

Wittgenstein's latter writings display a marked contrast against his earlier work, not only in terms of their substance, but also in terms of their style. *The Philosophical Investigations* is replete with the use of analogy and metaphor, which results in the production of a number of teasing, but rarely fully developed, insights. The notion of 'family resemblance' provides a particularly clear example of this tendency. And while at one level this might

---

[59] L Wittgenstein, *The Philosophical Investigations*, above n 6 at s 304.

be frustrating, at another level, it is precisely this which affords the opportunity for such useful appropriation by contemporary feminists.

In the specific context of feminist *legal* analysis, the possibility of charting a path beyond the dilemma of essentialism/difference, afforded by the Wittgensteinian model, has particularly significant consequences. As noted above, feminist disillusionment with the possibility of locating, or the legitimacy of asserting, a collective gender identity has diverted contemporary attention away from grand-scale legal reform agendas that purport to articulate, represent or improve the rights of women as a group. While this shift is motivated by honourable intentions—to attend to the diversity of each woman's life, to the intersectionality of axes of social stratification, and to the need to produce tailored change which reflects this—its unfortunate consequence has been the reduction of collective legal and political engagement to strategies for localised reform or personal transformation: because each women is unique, she is on her own as a legal subject, or so it would seem.

This is particularly lamentable in the legal context, since it has often been argued (by feminists and others) that the law is stubbornly impervious to critique that is not framed by its own dialect or points of reference. Drakopoulou, for example, argues that while 'elsewhere, questions of subjectivity are easily accepted as a source of fruitful debate,' in law 'they destabilise our project and undermine its political and ethical legitimacy.'[60] Law, both as a site of power/knowledge and as a system for social control, tends to produce a discourse that operates most comfortably at the macro-level. It makes pretences to universality and abstraction, whilst resisting particularity and context. Of course, this is not to say that the law ignores the individual; far from it. But the individual is brought before the law not so much as an entity in its own right, but as a member of some larger collective (as a human being, as a worker, as a mother, etc) and it is on the basis of this membership that the law assigns that individual her rights and entitlements. Thus, by encouraging a radical deconstruction of the collective category of women, the postmodern influence in contemporary feminism has not only deprived the women's movement of the kind of critical mass most conducive to political leverage, it has also deprived feminist legal reformers of a path by which to engage meaningfully with the law and law-makers.

Localised reform strategies have become the staple basis for contemporary feminist activity. Yet, they have increasingly taken place in areas of social life traditionally thought of as outside the law, where there can be a clearer emphasis on subversion of cultural practices, stereotypes and non-juridical forms of normalisation. While the extension of feminist activism

---

[60] M Drakopoulou, 'The Ethic of Care, Female Subjectivity and Feminist Legal Scholarship' (2000) 8 *Feminist Legal Studies* 199 at 210.

into these forums is welcome, it is lamentable that it has occurred at the exclusion of, rather than as a complement to, ongoing efforts for large-scale legal reform. As discussed in Chapter three, without placing undue faith in the 'healing power of law', it is clear that law can offer the potential for important changes in women's lives. While the analysis of power and domination discussed in the last chapter enabled contemporary feminists to attend to the macro-level without thereby undermining their commitment to Foucaultian analyses of the fluidity, productivity and omnipresence of power, it was noted that, to be compelling, feminist politics would need to establish a stronger basis for its claim to women's collectivity. It has been argued here that Wittgeinstein's theory, which enables us to see the concept of 'women' as having a unity sustained through family resemblances, may be best placed to assist contemporary feminism in this regard. In particular, this analysis navigates a course between radical deconstruction of collective gender identity on the one hand and rigid descriptive essentialism on the other, thereby absolving the need for any choice to be made between recognition of women's internal diversity and political engagement grounded in a real and meaningful sense of female collectivity.

Discussion in the next chapter draws together the strands of analysis that have animated the previous discussion, moving on to consider their implications for the concept of equality that has been so central to feminist theory and politics. More specifically, in a world in which, according to MacKinnon:

> feminism's search for a group is a search for the truth of all women's collectivity in the face of the enforced lie that all women are the same,[61]

it will re-examine the relationship between equality and respect, with a view to developing a revised agenda for feminist reform.

---

[61] C MacKinnon, *Toward a Feminist Theory of State*, above n 8 at 38.

6
Equality, Respect and Feminist Futures

In the opening line of *Sovereign Virtue*, Ronald Dworkin asserts that 'equality is the endangered species of political ideals.'[1] In a context in which he suggests that liberal politicians have increasingly rejected equality, Dworkin calls for a return to an ethos of egalitarianism, reiterating his basic position that:

> no government is legitimate that does not show equal concern for the fate of all those citizens over whom it claims dominion and from whom it claims allegiance.[2]

At the same time, however, a number of other commentators and theorists have welcomed this apparent rejection of the equality paradigm, drawing particular attention to what they see as the concept's inherent inability to move beyond the comparative, or to answer crucial questions regarding exactly *what* it is that people should be equal to one another in relation to.[3]

To the extent that considerable energy continues to be devoted to analysing the concept of equality in political theory, it may well be that both of these positions have over-stated the extent of egalitarianism's contemporary demise in mainstream (or more aptly perhaps 'malestream') political discourse.[4] Certainly, it can barely be disputed that, whatever the difficulties

---

[1] R Dworkin, *Sovereign Virtue: The Theory and Practice of Equality* (Cambridge, Harvard University Press, 2000) at 1.

[2] R Dworkin, *Sovereign Virtue, ibid* at 1.

[3] For an overview of the debates on the currency of egalitarianism, see, for example, R Dworkin, *Sovereign Virtue, ibid*; G Cohen, 'On the Currency of Egalitarian Justice' (1989) 99 *Ethics* 906; A Sen, *Inequality Re-Examined* (Oxford, Oxford University Press, 1992). For critical discussion of the role and value of equality as a moral ideal, see P Westen, 'The Empty Idea of Equality' (1982) 95 (3) *Harvard Law Review* 537; P Westen, *Speaking of Equality: An Analysis of the Rhetorical Force of Equality in Moral and Legal Discourse* (Princeton, Princeton University Press, 1990); D Parfitt, 'Equality and Priority' in A Mason (ed) *Ideals of Equality* (Oxford, Blackwells, 1998); C Peters, 'Equality Revisited' (1997) 110 *Harvard Law Review* 1210; C Peters, 'Outcomes, Reasons and Equality' (2000) 80 *Boston University Law Review* 1095; H Frankfurt, 'Equality as a Moral Ideal' (1987) 98 (1) *Ethics* 21. I am indebted both to Timothy Macklem and to the Jurisprudence students we taught together for their lively discussion of many of the issues raised in this literature.

[4] Contemporary debates about the concept of equality, in part sparked by Dworkin's work, certainly may appear to suggest otherwise—see, eg, E Anderson, 'What is the Point of Equality?' (1999) 109 *Ethics* 287; S Scheffler, 'What is Egalitarianism?' (2003) 31(1) *Philosophy and Public Affairs* 5; R Dworkin, 'Equality, Luck and Hierarchy' (2003) 31(2) *Philosophy and Public Affairs* 190; S Scheffler, 'Equality as the Virtue of Sovereigns' (2003) 31(2) *Philosophy and Public Affairs* 199.

Equality, Respect and Feminist Futures

and disappointments that have been attributed to the equality paradigm more broadly, it continues to be one that has captured the imagination of many feminists. In particular, despite its myriad complexity and the much lamented failure of formal equality mandates to fully deliver in practice what they have promised in theory, which was discussed in Chapter one, many feminist theorists and activists remain committed to refining or reformulating this concept and its demands in order to deploy them more effectively in the service of gender politics.

Building on the more nuanced understanding of power relations and patriarchal domination discussed in Chapter four, and acknowledging the potential outlined in Chapter five for an ongoing engagement with women as a (familial) collective concept, discussion in this chapter will return to the issue of equality that has been so central to feminist discourse, theorising and politics. In particular, it will critically examine some of the ways in which the concept of equality has been re-deployed within contemporary feminist work, reflecting on the extent to which it has succeeded in moving the concept beyond the limitations of its early, more simplistic and formal, manifestations. In so doing, discussion here will also draw on the fundamental challenges that have been lodged to the concept of equality from within analytical jurisprudence and/or political theory, in order to question the ultimate value of this essentially comparative, and arguably 'empty', normative ideal.[5] Having done so, this chapter will suggest that despite the many benefits that may be offered by reformulating equality, feminists would be well-advised to avoid seeing equality as their ultimate goal. More specifically, it will be argued here that equality is best understood by feminists, in both their theory and their activism, not as an end in itself but rather as a means to an end, with the end in question being one of respect. In the final sections of this chapter, therefore, the case for respect as the goal of feminist engagement will be considered, and the role played by equality in providing a vital precondition to the operation of genuine respect, will be elucidated and explained.

The Trouble(s) with Formal Equality

As discussed in Chapter one, feminism has long been motivated by a shared sense of frustration at the unequal treatment afforded to women vis-à-vis men. In particular, the exclusion of women from social, economic, political or legal spheres, rationalised on the basis of their 'special' gender characteristics, has been approached with suspicion and has provided a focus for sustained challenge. As part of this project, the concept of formal equality, demanding as it does that like be treated alike, has provided a useful means of holding social and political institutions to account. It has placed the onus

---

[5] P Westen, 'The Empty Idea of Equality', above n 3.

The Trouble(s) with Formal Equality

on those who seek to exclude women from male-dominated spheres to establish the legitimacy of the gender differences on which they purport to rely. Whether those exclusions are grounded in innocent mistakes, illegitimate stereotypes or malicious misrepresentations about gender characteristics and capabilities, where they cannot be justified in this way, they are untenable; or at least so the theory goes.

There can be no doubt moreover that adopting this call to formally equal treatment has assisted in securing a number of at least prima facie victories for the feminist movement. The extension of the vote to women, the admission of women into higher education, and the development of measures to ensure the recruitment, promotion and remuneration of women on comparable scales with men, for example, have all been fought for and facilitated, if not won, by demands grounded in ideals of equal concern and respect, and of non-discrimination on the grounds of arbitrary sex distinctions. At the same time, however, as was also noted in previous chapters, a number of feminists have questioned to extent to which this understanding of equal treatment has yielded meaningful improvements in women's daily lives. Even in the public realms in which equality logic has secured women hitherto unauthorised access, they often continue to do less well than men, or at least they tend to reap less rewards for their successes. As a result, a number of feminist commentators have come to conclude that, even in modern times, 'equality is valued nearly everywhere but practiced almost nowhere.'[6]

For some, this realisation has simply added vigour, urgency and cogency to their claims that the equal treatment of men and women remains an as yet unachieved goal. For others, however, it has generated a more deep-seated and critical reflection on the value of the formal equality paradigm itself. It has been suggested that this model is fundamentally flawed, from a feminist perspective, since it starts from the dubious premise that society is largely equal, in order to focus its attention on those isolated arenas of social living that, purportedly due to historical anomaly or cultural confusion, have remained the exclusive preserve of men. In this context, it has been uncritically assumed that substantive improvements will be secured simply by removing barriers to participation in situations in which women can establish themselves to be equally as capable as men. While such an approach may be welcomed by those who insist that people pay the 'true social cost' of their choices,[7] critics have pointed out that this fails to recognise the complex ways in which socially constructed norms of 'appropriate' gender roles, as well as pragmatic constraints of material disadvantage or domestic responsibility, impact disproportionately on women's ability to take up the opportunities that are formally on offer to them.[8]

[6] C MacKinnon, 'Toward a New Theory of Equality' in C MacKinnon, *Women's Lives, Men's Laws* (Cambridge, Harvard University Press, 2005) at 44.
[7] R Dworkin, *Sovereign Virtue*, above n 1 at 289.
[8] E Anderson, 'What is the Point of Equality?' above n 4 at 297. See also discussion in Ch 1.

More generally, critics have also argued that this approach tends to disguise the need to engage with the complex power relations and cultural norms that construct gender dynamics, or with the prospect of a more insidious and strategic gender hierarchy. In a context in which others have noted that there is a circularity built into the concept of formal equality—it 'tells us to treat people alike; but when we ask who "like people" are, we are told they are "people who should be treated alike" '[9]—feminist critics have suggested that this approach to gender politics may prove to be not only unhelpful, but also to leave scope for considerable injustice. In particular, by ignoring the social and historical conditions under which distinctions between individuals and/or groups are created, identified as relevant and sustained, these critics argue that it fails to acknowledge, let alone challenge, the use of men's experience as the benchmark for entitlement. It is this which leads MacKinnon to conclude that sex equality is 'a contradiction in terms'[10] (since the former presupposes difference while the latter presupposes sameness) and an ideal that 'cannot touch the situation of most women, where the force of social inequality effectively precludes sex comparisons.'[11]

Re-formulating the Formal/Re-imagining Equality

Significantly, though, it is also clear that these concerns about the concept of equality, as conventionally fashioned, have not necessarily led to its outright rejection by feminists. Mirroring the revisionist mentality outlined in previous chapters in regard to liberalism, as well as to legal reform and rights discourse, Littleton and others have insisted that the mere fact that 'equality is enmeshed in and ensnared by the very gender system that feminists are resisting' does not mean that it is not 'capable of having meaning beyond that system.'[12] On the contrary, these feminists argue that the concept of equality can be reconstructed in order to provide an effective 'means of challenging, rather than legitimating, social institutions created from the phallocentric perspective.'[13] For Littleton, this reconstruction can be achieved by adopting a model of 'equality as acceptance' under which sex difference is not denied, trivialised, nor designated a conceptual embarrassment but instead the focus is placed on the ways in which such difference

---

[9] P Westen, 'The Empty Idea of Equality' above n 3 at 547.

[10] C MacKinnon, *Feminism Unmodified: Discourses on Life and Law* (Cambridge, Harvard University Press, 1987) at 33.

[11] C MacKinnon, 'Reflections on Sex Equality Under Law' in L Kauffman (ed), *American Feminist Thought at Century's End: A Reader* (Oxford, Blackwells, 1993) at 376. Originally printed at (1991) 100 (5) *Yale Law Journal* 1281.

[12] C Littleton, 'Reconstructing Sexual Equality' (1987) 75 *California Law Review* 1279 at 1283.

[13] C Littleton, 'Reconstructing Sexual Equality,'*ibid* at 1283.

is relied upon to justify inequality. The objective here is to illustrate the partiality of the male norm and, rather than seeking to eliminate sex differences in the name of equality, to render them:

> costless relative to each other, so that anyone may follow a . . . lifestyle according to their natural inclination or choice, without being punished for following a female lifestyle or rewarded for following a male one.[14]

In a similar fashion, Rhode, by drawing attention to 'the difference that difference makes,'[15] has also supported the retention of an approach to feminist politics that demands that 'the culturally coded 'male' and 'female' components be equally valued' without dictating 'the coin in which such value must be measured.'[16]

MacKinnon too, despite her typically trenchant criticism, indicates some optimism about this project of reconstructing the equality paradigm and about its potential to secure substantive improvement in women's lives. As she puts it:

> if the social status quo were no longer maintained through the abstract equality model, then equality law could not even be applied without producing social change.[17]

While some commentators have argued that the social change that MacKinnon hopes for here would lead to an androgynous utopia in which all gender difference is eliminated,[18] others have insisted that this would be to misinterpret the spirit of her polemical claim that currently different treatment entails inferior treatment. Indeed, as Réaume convincingly argues, the allegiance to equality that MacKinnon betrays here does not require that all sex difference be obliterated for all time, but rather that any evaluation or accreditation of such difference must be postponed, pending the institution of a genuinely post-patriarchal society in which women are no longer disempowered.[19]

---

[14] C Littleton, 'Reconstructing Sexual Equality' *ibid* at 1297.

[15] D Rhode, *Justice and Gender* (Cambridge, Harvard University Press, 1989). Like Littleton, Rhode emphasises the social construction of what counts as 'different', arguing that 'the issue is not difference per se but the consequences of addressing it in a particular way under particular social and historical circumstances'—D Rhode, 'The Politics of Paradigms: Gender Difference and Gender Disadvantage' in A Phillips (ed) *Feminism and Politics* (Oxford, Oxford University Press, 1998) at 349. Also in G Brock and S James (eds) *Beyond Equality and Difference* (London, Routledge, 1992).

[16] C Littleton, 'Reconstructing Sexual Equality' above n 12 at 1303.

[17] C MacKinnon, 'Reflections on Sex Equality Under Law' in L Kauffman (ed), *American Feminist Thought at Century's End*, above n 11 at 396

[18] T Macklem, *Beyond Comparison: Sex and Discrimination* (Cambridge, Cambridge University Press, 2003).

[19] D Réaume, 'Comparing Theories of Sex Discrimination: The Role of Comparison' (2005) 25(3) *Oxford Journal of Legal Studies* 547.

As such, it is clear that while MacKinnon's approach may be sympathetic to demands for a revised concept of equality which challenges the cultural privileging of typically 'masculine' character traits and lifestyle choices, it also entails a more radical vision which goes beyond merely redistributing value in the name of acceptance to interrogating and deconstructing the (gendered) processes by which value is ascribed in the first place. Thus, the concept of equality that emerges here is one that, perhaps unsurprisingly given MacKinnon's overall thesis, is closely bound up with the concepts of power, domination and empowerment. MacKinnon insists that equality is a test of:

> whether the politics or practice in question integrally contributes to the maintenance of an underclass or a deprived position because of gender status.[20]

Thus, any equality-based strategy, if it is to be substantively useful, must be interested in 'rectifying the legal inequality of groups that are historically unequal in society' rather than in merely according solicitude 'to pure legal artefacts.'[21] While Réaume may be right, therefore, to conclude that this does not entail the elimination of gender difference, it does demand that men and women benefit from equal power, not only in their enjoyment of the opportunities and resources out of which they create a sense of self, but also in terms of having the different choices that may emerge from this process accepted and equivalently evaluated—politically, socially and economically.

Equality as Empowerment?

This call to 'give women equal power in social life'[22] has been taken up and re-examined recently by Davina Cooper. Noting that identities, interests and objectives are themselves shaped by (in)equality, Cooper highlights the difficulties associated with the conventional claim that equality entails valuing people *despite* their social and material differences. In her view, such an approach misses the crucial point that the very existence of 'such inequalities symbolically and materially demonstrate that equal value is not being granted.'[23] As a result, she suggests that equality requires not just ensuring that people, and their choices, are accorded equal concern and respect (as Dworkin would suggest), but also a proactive strategy that makes people's

---

[20] C MacKinnon, *Sexual Harassment of Working Women: A Case of Sex Discrimination* (New Haven, Yale University Press, 1979) at 117.

[21] C MacKinnon, 'Reflections on Sex Equality Under Law' in L Kauffman (ed), *American Feminist Thought at Century's End*, above n 11 at 396.

[22] C MacKinnon, *Feminism Unmodified*, above n 10 at 45.

[23] D Cooper, 'And You Can't Find Me Nowhere: Relocating Identity and Structure Within Equality Jurisprudence' (2000) 27 (2) *Journal of Law and Society* 249 at 252.

Equality as Empowerment?

lives more equal.[24] In addition, she emphasises that the terms in which this equality should be measured are not resources, satisfaction or recognition, but rather power; or more accurately on this account, the ability to exert power as an expression of equal value. As Cooper explains:

> all people should have the same capacity to impact upon their environment whether discursively, by means of resources, or in terms of participation within, recreating or disrupting, institutional structures.[25]

Thus, while this model makes no prescriptions regarding the interests, goals and desires that people will cultivate, it does invoke a participatory vision which demands a parity of involvement and influence in the legal, political and social processes that determine those desires.

At the same time, however, other feminists, in particular Iris Young, have rejected any metaphorical extension of the distributive paradigm to non-material social goods such as power, on the basis that this will inevitably stifle their inherently dynamic nature and inappropriately represent them as static commodities.[26] Expressing a similar concern, albeit from a different perspective, Dworkin has worried that this approach will undermine the hope that, in an egalitarian society, citizens will take part in politics out of a shared concern for justice, since 'when people are fastidious not to have too much influence, or jealous that they do not have enough,' they tend to think of power 'as a discrete resource rather than a collective responsibility.'[27] Unlike Dworkin's account, however, Cooper does not restrict the limits of power's operation to the political realm, and thus her analysis yields a position in which power emerges as a profoundly relational concept. Expressing her indebtedness to the work of Foucault, Cooper questions whether there is anything *necessarily* corrupting to a fluid understanding of power in deploying the extended metaphor of distribution in the pursuit of gender equality.[28] Committed to the idea that power operates in both productive *and* repressive ways and recognising that an individual's position in

---

[24] In this sense, Cooper sees her work as demanding 'equal value taken beyond the liberal terrain of equal concern and respect'—D Cooper, 'And You Can't Find Me Nowhere,' *ibid* at 251. The limits of Dworkin's 'administrative conception of equality' have also been noted, from a somewhat different perspective, by Scheffler, who argues that 'Dworkin's ideal of equality, as applied to questions of distribution, is not itself a model of social or political equality at all. It is perfectly compatible with social hierarchy, inasmuch as it involves one relatively powerful party (the state) choosing how to distribute resources among those with relatively less power'—S Scheffler, 'What is Egalitarianism?' above n 4 at 36.

[25] D Cooper, 'And You Can't Find Me Nowhere,' above n 23 at 255–6.

[26] In fact, Young singles out talk of distributing power as 'a particularly clear case of the misleading and undesirable implications of extending the concept of distribution beyond material goods'—I Young, *Justice and the Politics of Difference* (Princeton, Princeton University Press, 1990) at 30.

[27] R Dworkin, *Sovereign Virtue*, above n 1 at 198.

[28] D Cooper, *Challenging Diversity: Rethinking Equality and the Value of Difference* (Cambridge, Cambridge University Press, 2004) at 78.

Equality, Respect and Feminist Futures

any power relation will be complex, fluctuating and rarely best characterised by an oppressor/oppressed binary,[29] Cooper identifies a number of ways in which applying equality to power might actually help prevent solidification of the distributive paradigm. In particular, although not directly in response to Young, she emphasises that it 'asserts an active, participatory vision' which can be contrasted with 'models of equality which equate satisfaction with consumable products' since it also draws attention to 'technologies' that allow some to generate outcomes denied to others.[30]

To the extent that, as discussed in Chapter four, the fluid and dynamic understanding of power that animates Cooper's theory can be contrasted against the more dyadic and static vision that informs MacKinnon's analysis (and which Young specifically cautions against), it is clear, therefore, that Cooper's approach, though marked by a shared commitment to the equal empowerment of men and women, also represents a departure from this 'unmodified' feminist vision. In particular, this approach emphasises that:

> equality should not stop at the threshold of the collective, but should apply between people regardless of shared or disparate identities.[31]

As Cooper reminds us, this is important for two reasons—first, 'it is not enough for groups to be equal if individuals within groups have unequal power;' and secondly, as the focus on inter-sectionality discussed in the last chapter has established, 'nobody belongs to a single social group.'[32] At the same time, though, conscious of the risk that too individualistic an approach could trivialise inequality or ignore its origins, Cooper also emphasises that the structural analyses that have animated previous accounts must not be abandoned. Practices, identities and norms that are 'knotted to major forms of social asymmetry' continue to be targeted,[33] albeit that the contingency of those patterns and the scope this offers for shifts and resistance is now emphasised.

By both insisting on a more fluid and productive understanding of power and deconstructing collective identities without foreclosing the possibility of their useage, Cooper's demand for an egalitarian distribution of power between the sexes can thus be seen to reformulate the concept of equality in a way that complements the position on domination, resistance and identity that was defended in discussion over previous chapters. At the same time, this approach, by imposing a dual demand for equal enjoyment of personal freedom/self-expression *and* social involvement/influence, also has the potential to reconnect the cultural and the material of women's lives. In a

---

[29] D Cooper, *Challenging Diversity, ibid* at 78–9.
[30] D Cooper, 'And You Can't Find Me Nowhere,' above n 23 at 256.
[31] D Cooper, 'And You Can't Find Me Nowhere,' above n 23 at 250.
[32] D Cooper, 'And You Can't Find Me Nowhere,' above n 23 at 256–7.
[33] D Cooper, 'And You Can't Find Me Nowhere,' above n 23 at 271.

context in which, as noted in previous chapters, the demands of recognition and redistribution have often been viewed as being in competition, and this has generated a marked tension in the respective allegiances of feminist theory and politics, the benefits offered by an approach that facilitates this kind of holistic strategy, whilst still tapping into the rhetorical power of the call to equality, are certainly considerable. However, it will be argued in the remaining sections that inherent shortcomings in the concept of equality mean that even this more nuanced approach can, in the final analysis, only take feminism part of the way towards its ultimate goal.

Equality Beyond Comparison?

These interjections into the vision of sex equality have undoubtedly been useful in taking feminist legal and political thinking beyond the narrow, and increasingly restrictive, confines of the sameness/difference debate and towards a more complex, concrete and productive agenda for reform. At the same time, though, it is clear that the trigger for feminist objection under these models continues to be one grounded in the treatment received by women vis-à-vis men. Despite the diversity in the measure of their analysis—be it opportunity, resources, recognition, freedom or empowerment—these approaches continue to invoke comparative rather than absolute distributive paradigms. It is clear, moreover, that this reliance on the comparative has been difficult for feminists to shake off. Indeed, even those theorists such as Cain[34] and Gross[35] who purport to have rejected equality—precisely because of its grounding in sex comparison—in favour of a focus on female agency and self-determination, continue to find the basic motivation for their arguments in the belief 'that women's interests and experiences should be *equally* as important in shaping social life.'[36]

Granted, MacKinnon may be right to emphasise that the kind of 'substantive comparisons' deployed in these accounts, by recognising both hierarchy and history, 'pose few of the dangers that abstract Aristotelian comparisons do.'[37] But many commentators have remained critical of the limits that this comparative approach imposes, both symbolically and practically, on feminist analysis and reform. What's more, to the extent that these reconstructed equality models have coupled their comparative ignition with a normative platform that condemns inequality as, by definition, wrongful, they have also been challenged by several non-feminist theorists.

---

[34] P Cain, 'Feminism and the Limits of Equality' (1990) 24 *Georgia Law Review* 803.

[35] E Gross, 'What is Feminist Theory?' in C Pateman and E Gross (eds) *Feminist Challenges: Social and Political Theory* (London, Allen & Unwin, 1986) at 193.

[36] W Kymlicka, *Contemporary Political Philosophy: An Introduction* (2nd edn) (Oxford, Oxford University Press, 2002) at 384.

[37] C MacKinnon, 'Reflections on Sex Equality Under Law' in L Kauffman (ed), *American Feminist Thought at Century's End*, above n 11 at 397.

Equality, Respect and Feminist Futures

In particular, Parfitt has argued that this kind of approach, which he refers to as 'telic egalitarianism,' is vulnerable to challenge via the 'levelling down' objection.[38] This arises whenever we ask whether advocates of this approach would be satisfied if the measure in regard to which equality is being sought—be it acceptance, power or influence—was distributed so that men's allocation was simply reduced to the same (lower) level that is currently accorded to women. For those who object to inequality per se and who see equality as the central objective, it would seem, prima facie, that there can be no answer to this other than an affirmative. Yet, critics of this approach have emphasised that this conclusion rests somewhat uncomfortably alongside our basic intuitions about what social justice (pursued through equality) should look like. In addition, from a feminist perspective, it can be argued that this distorts the movement's fundamental ethos, which, as outlined in Chapter one, is not to reduce male power relative to women but to improve the status of women on its own terms. Not only does a strategy of 'levelling down' miss the point of this feminist project, it also has the lamentable effect of re-affirming an oppositional image of feminists as 'anti-men' which, in turn, reduces male sympathy and impedes cross-gender coalition.

According to Parfitt, one way of avoiding this levelling down objection without moving beyond equality, which he sees as a fundamentally comparative concept, would be to accept that equality is not in fact the only value to be pursued. While this runs counter to 'telic egalitarianism', Parfitt identifies a second category—referred to as 'deontic egalitarianism'—which, he argues, would accept that an evaluation of the injustice of inequality always depends on some additional, free-standing reason for its condemnation, over and above the simple fact of discriminatory treatment.[39] Under this model, it is not necessarily bad that some people are worse off than others, since the injustice of inequality must be established by some other measure—eg because it has been deliberately created to ensure someone's subordination or because it has established negative effects on a person's life. As a result, unlike its telic counterpart, this approach can accept that there may be no inherent value in levelling down unequal treatment, unless some additional moral benefit will be yielded in the process.

At the same time, though, this deontic approach produces its own problems. For one thing, it is not clear that it accords any better with our intuitions of justice, since there may well be situations in which we consider inequality to be unjust, even where it is not deliberately produced n or does not have any impact. Moreover, for this account to be compelling, we

---

[38] D Parfitt, 'Equality and Priority' in A Mason (ed) *Ideals of Equality*, above n 3. For further discussion, see L Temkin, 'Equality, Priority or What?' (2003) 19 *Economics and Philosophy* 61; L Temkin, 'Egalitarianism Defended' (2003) 113 *Ethics* 764.

[39] For further discussion, see, eg, T Scanlon, 'The Diversity of Objections to Inequality' in M Clayton & A Williams (eds) *The Ideal of Equality* (Basingstoke, MacMillan Press, 2000).

would need to identify the 'something else' at play in informing our intuitions. But not only does this raise difficult questions about what exactly this free-stranding moral measure is, it also exposes the extremely limited role that the concept of equality continues to play in this context. Indeed, for Westen, equality ultimately emerges under this analysis as an empty vessel with no substantive content of its own: capable of being used to state and analyse any right, he argues that it produces little other than confusion by doing circuitously what could be done directly.[40] What's more, it is not just that the use of equality adds an unnecessary layer to our thinking in a context in which the outcome of our moral deliberation is determined by consideration of an alternative, free-standing measure, but that the tendency amongst egalitarians to assert that equality has a more substantive meaning operates to mystify and 'skew' moral and political discourse. As Westen explains, then:

> although equality is derivative, people do not realise that it is derivative, and not realising it, they allow equality to distort the substance of their decision-making.[41]

For him, as for Parfitt, the solution is to turn away from equality, to realise that our conceptions of justice can function more effectively without it, and to focus instead on the underlying, absolute moral values rather than their comparative veneer.

Respect as an Alternative Moral Ideal

Without necessarily supporting the claim that equality is a wholly empty ideal (not least since it seems credible that there may be *some* moral value in the fraternity that is fostered by living in a community in which everyone is prima facie accorded equal treatment),[42] it will be argued in this section that there may be a number of benefits offered to feminism in thinking beyond the comparative frameworks of egalitarianism. More specifically, drawing on the work of Frankfurt in particular, this section will argue that, so far as feminist theory and activism is concerned, there is indeed 'something else' above and beyond equality that is driving its utopian vision, and that this 'something else' can be located and identified in the concept of respect.

---

[40] P Westen, 'The Empty Idea of Equality', above n 3 at 581. A similar position is also adopted in this regard by Peters who argues that: 'equality can serve only as a descriptive device' which reflects a symptom of the disease of substantive (nonegalitarian) injustice but 'prescriptively, equality is analytically empty. It can do nothing to explain our moral intuitions or to tell us how people should be treated'—C Peters, 'Equality Revisited,' above n 3 at 1257. For a critical response to this, see E Chemerinsky, 'In Defense of Equality: A Reply to Professor Westen' (1983) 81 *Michigan Law Review* 575; K Greenawalt, 'How Empty is the Idea of Equality?' (1983) 83 *Columbia Law Review* 1167.

[41] P Westen, 'The Empty Idea of Equality', above n 3 at 592.

[42] R Dworkin, *Law's Empire* (London, Fontana Press, 1986), especially ch 6.

The rejection of egalitarianism outlined above has led a number of theorists to support instead a 'prioritarian' approach according to which, while the ultimate aim is for everyone for flourish as much as possible, those who are worst off deserve a greater weight in the moral and distributive deliberations of social justice. On first sight, this approach might be thought to resemble precisely the kind of comparative framework that these theorists have previously challenged. But, as Raz points out, the basis for this response is in fact quite different:

> what makes us care about various inequalities is not the inequality but the concern identified by the underlying principle. It is the hunger of the hungry, the need of the needy, the suffering of the ill, and so on.

Granted, Raz accepts that the fact that a person is worse off than another in the respect under question may be relevant. Its relevance, though, is 'not as an independent evil of inequality,' but rather:

> in showing that their hunger is greater, their need more pressing, their suffering more hurtful, and therefore our concern for the hungry, the needy, the suffering, and not our concern for equality, make us give them priority.[43]

Phrased in negative terms, then, under this approach, the injustice that we identify when someone has a bad life does not stem from the comparative fact that someone else has a good life, but rather from the absolute fact that this person has a bad life. For Frankfurt, this translates into a theory of social justice that is grounded in criteria of sufficiency rather than in a concern with sheer equality. Under this approach, what matters is that people have enough of whatever is to be distributed—be it opportunity, resources, power, influence, or recognition—to make their lives go well, and the fact that what they receive may be more than or less than that received by another is of limited moral relevance. As Frankfurt expresses it:

> what is important from the point of view of morality is not that everyone should have *the same*, but that each should have *enough*.[44]

Similarly, Crisp has noted that while we have reason to prioritise one person where their situation warrants our compassion, where people are sufficiently well-catered for, there will no such claim to compassion, even if others have more.[45]

---

[43] J Raz, *The Morality of Freedom* (Oxford, Oxford University Press, 1986) at 240.

[44] H Frankfurt, 'Equality as a Moral Ideal,' above n 3 at 21.

[45] R Crisp, 'Equality, Priority and Compassion' (2003) 113 *Ethics* 745. For discussion of, and challenge to this position, see, eg, Temkin, who argues that: although 'part of the basis for giving priority to the worse off lies in considerations of sufficiency. People below certain absolute levels should have their basic needs met . . . (it also lies in part) in considerations supporting equality, understood as *comparative fairness*'—L Temkin, 'Equality, Priority or What?' above n 38 at 85.

Central to the development of this kind of non-egalitarian response, therefore, is an insistence that, in a context in which the mere fact of different treatment vis-à-vis another is not relevant, people should be treated 'in accordance with the net effect of all the relevant criteria and *only* the relevant criteria.'[46] To the extent that this approach involves close attention to the particular circumstances of each individual, on their own terms, Frankfurt suggests that it is driven by a prescriptive norm of respect. Contrasting the demands of respect to those of equality, Frankfurt notes that it is a more personal value, which demands dealing with a person:

> exclusively on the basis of those aspects of his particular character or circumstances that are actually relevant to the issue at hand.[47]

While someone insisting that she be treated equally will calculate her demands on the basis of how others are treated, the person who insists that she be treated with respect will demand that the realities of her individual condition, interests and needs are responded to.[48] Thus, Frankfurt argues that a concern for respect over equality provides a less alienating vision within which there is a focus on genuine self-definition and self-determination: it attends to people's authentic ambitions that:

> derive from the character of their own lives and not those which are imposed upon them by the conditions in which others happen to live.[49]

Respect, Sufficiency and Feminism

On first sight, this turn to respect—which entails, amongst other things, women's ability to make choices from a relatively unconstrained range of options, in a context in which they have enough opportunity to chart a narrative for their life that they endorse, and an adequate set of resources from which to ensure that their basic needs and interests are catered for—may be promising from a feminist perspective, not least since it is well-suited to the long-standing commitment to specificity, context and particularity. Even in Cooper's egalitarian account, it is acknowledged that it may be 'more helpful' for feminists to:

---

[46] C Peters, 'Equality Revisited,' above n 3 at 1228.

[47] H Frankfurt, 'Equality and Respect' in *Necessity, Volition, and Love* (Cambridge, Cambridge University Press, 1999) at 150.

[48] At first sight, as Armitage points out, this suggestion that egalitarian theorists have failed to pay due attention to respect, and indeed have developed the concept of equality in distinction to it, may seem unconvincing, particularly in the case of Dworkin who talks specifically about the need to treat people with equal concern and *respect*. However, as Armitage goes on to show, there is reason to think that the vision of respect that Dworkin works with is somewhat different in nature, since it is seen 'as a constituent or outcome of the good life, but not as a means to build a good life'—F Armitage, 'Respect and Types of Injustice' (2006) 12 (9) *Res Publica* 9 at 17.

[49] H Frankfurt, 'Equality and Respect' in *Necessity, Volition, and Love*, above n 47 at 153–4.

adopt an approach which reads equality of power through, and in relation to, other social values, such as care, respect and responsibility—values, in certain circumstances, which will trump claims to individual parity.[50]

Moreover, Martha Nussbaum's 'capabilities' approach, which was formulated as part of her reconstruction of liberalism discussed in Chapter two, has specifically called on feminists to shift focus away from the comparative frameworks of egalitarianism and towards absolute considerations of sufficiency in the background conditions, resources and opportunities out of which one renders oneself capable of a good life.[51] Seeking to develop an approach that:

> is respectful of each person's struggle for flourishing, that treats each person as an end and as a source of agency and worth in their own right,[52]

Nussbaum draws on Amartya Sen's work on the notion of capability to provide an account of what respect for human dignity, as a minimum threshold, requires—and to call governments to order in their responses thereto.[53]

At the same time, though, this turn to sufficiency, and more specifically to respect as the driving moral force behind it, can also be seen to present difficulties—both in general, and for feminist theory in particular. Aside from the possibly negative consequences of abandoning a discourse of egalitarianism that has achieved some high profile feminist successes and which continues to have contemporary political currency, the concept of sufficiency that underpins Frankfurt's work remains 'fuzzy.' Critics have argued that his idea that we should have 'enough' of the resources and opportunities available to us as individuals remains 'powerfully obscure,' offering little guidance as to *who* it is that will determine what constitutes an adequate distribution and, equally importantly, as to *how* they will go about doing so.[54] If an individual is greedy by disposition, for example, does treating them with respect require satiating their desire for excess? Conversely, can we claim to be respecting such greedy individuals if we ignore their genuine conviction that they need more than is objectively sufficient of a particular good in order to lead an adequate life?

To some extent, of course, the mere fact that the sufficiency model raises such difficult questions in its concrete translation does not, in and of itself, provide a reason to reject it—especially if the questions that it raises go to

---

[50] D Cooper, *Challenging Diversity*, above n 28 at 82.

[51] M Nussbaum, *Sex and Social Justice* (Oxford, Oxford University Press, 1999).

[52] M Nussbaum, *Women and Human Development: The Capabilities Approach* (Cambridge, Cambridge University Press, 2000) at 69.

[53] M Nussbaum, *Women and Human Development: The Capabilities Approach*, ibid at 12.

[54] R Goodin, 'Egalitarianism, Fetishistic and Otherwise,' (1987) 98 (1) *Ethics* 44 at 49. Similar objections can been lodged at other theories relying on criteria of adequacy, eg Raz on autonomy—in J Raz, *The Morality of Freedom*, above n 43, especially chs 14 and 15.

Respect as an Alternative Moral Ideal

the heart of a proper conception of social justice.[55] At the same time, though, it is clear that a sufficiency-based approach may prove particularly problematic in situations in which, according to feminist analysis, many women, rather than operating with an over-demanding conception of sufficiency, have become accustomed to accepting or expecting less, and so tend to operate with an *under*-developed sense of entitlement. Indeed, in a context in which many feminists have argued that we simply do not and cannot know whether there are any important differences between the sexes that have not been created by the dynamic of domination and subordination, the dangers presented by an exclusive focus on sufficiency are aptly brought forward, as indeed is the tendency in Frankfurt's work to uncritically assume the ability of both men and women to enter and operate within the terrain in which what constitutes a 'good life' is determined.

As discussed in previous chapters, feminist work has clearly highlighted the ways in which women's social role has been constructed as being bound up with caring for others and self-sacrifice. What's more, it has illustrated the various and complex ways in which women's marginalisation and subordination has been masked and maintained within patriarchal structures, with many women accepting uncritically the existing order of things or proactively defending it as a legitimate expression of their agency. In this context, many feminists have emphasised the importance of engaging critically with women's subjective determinations of what counts as a sufficient distribution of social benefits, and relatedly of what qualifies—from their perspective—as a good life. The dilemma that emerges, then, is one of how to be confident, in the currently patriarchal world, that women's self-definitions have not been perverted, distorted or limited in some way by either false consciousness or structural constraint.

Reflecting on this dilemma in the context of Nussbaum's approach, Phillips identifies a tension between her inclination that there are certain structural inequalities (including those based on gender) that undermine self-respect and emotional development so significantly as to count as capability failures, and her postponement of the question of equality pending achievement of a threshold of basic sufficiency.[56] While Nussbaum is aware of the difficulties presented by 'adaptive preferences' in the context of women's development,[57] she resists talking in terms of functioning rather than capabilities and emphasises the importance of respecting the choices

---

[55] In some literature, of course, it is the very impossibility of being able to fully address these questions that fuels the pursuit of justice itself—see J Derrida, 'Force of Law: The Mystical Foundations of Authority' in D Cornell, M Rosenfield and D Carlson (eds) *Deconstruction and the Possibility of Justice* (New York, Routledge, 1992).

[56] M Nussbaum, *Sex and Social Justice*, above n 51 at 43.

[57] M Nussbaum, *Women and Human Development: The Capabilities Approach*, above n 52 at 139.

(including choices not to function) made by individual women.[58] However, according to Phillips, this leads her into a 'curiously illiberal liberalism' in which issues of equality, though acknowledged as important, are no longer on the theoretical or political agenda.[59] Expressing her reluctance to reject comparative frameworks in this way, Phillips emphasises that it is precisely because equality is relational that it can 'direct us more urgently to differential powers and capabilities' and so, crucially, affords the potential to test 'not just whether individuals have the minimum necessary for choice, but whether their position in social hierarchies shapes their choices in unequal ways'.[60]

Thus, Phillips argues that feminists must retain equality as the ultimate political goal, since this approach is both the most productive—in terms of addressing 'the danger of presuming that what people put up with is what they want or need'[61]—and the most intuitive—since women have good cause to feel aggrieved if men 'end up with more time, more money or more power,' even if they have sufficient for them to flourish.[62]

Respect Beyond Equality?

Conscious of the dangers of affirming the characteristics of powerlessness through a call to respect women's perspectives or choices, it is far from surprising that, like Phillips, many feminists have been suspicious of claims to tailored treatment of the sexes, and have tended instead to stubbornly re-iterate demands for equality. But in thinking through the relationship between equality and respect, raised but not necessarily resolved by Nussbaum's capabilities approach, it appears that Frankfurt's work can also be instructive. More specifically, his analysis can be deployed to support the claim, put forward here, that the feminist pursuit of equality re-instated by Phillips is not an end in itself, but rather a precursor or means to the end of respect.

Despite their considerable diversity, Frankfurt acknowledges that there will be certain circumstances under which the requirements of equality and respect will converge. In particular, he suggests that in situations in which there is no (reliable) information about the similarities and differences between people, as will often be the case where the government is involved

---

[58] M Nussbaum, *Sex and Social Justice*, above n 51 at 44; M Nussbaum, *Women and Human Development: The Capabilities Approach*, above n 52 at 88.

[59] A Phillips, 'Feminism and Liberalism: Has Martha Nussbaum Got It Right?' (2001) 8 (2) *Constellations* 249 at 250. This critique is echoed by Mullally who also suggests that Nussbaum's failure to take 'the additional step of identifying equality as a central goal' is problematic—S Mullally, *Gender, Culture and Human Rights: Reclaiming Universalism* (Oxford, Hart Publishing, 2006) at 62.

[60] A Phillips, 'Feminism and Liberalism: Has Martha Nussbaum Got It Right?' *ibid* at 264.

[61] A Phillips, 'Feminism and Liberalism: Has Martha Nussbaum Got It Right?' *ibid* at 265.

[62] A Phillips, 'Feminism and Liberalism: Has Martha Nussbaum Got It Right?' *ibid* at 259.

in large-scale distributive decision-making, it may be appropriate to treat both the same—ie equally.⁶³ In this situation, since the decision-maker has no relevant information about the people under review, it would be arbitrary and disrespectful to treat any one of them differently.⁶⁴ Similarly, feminists might well argue, in a world in which we cannot know what, if any, different choices women would make if they commenced from a platform of empowerment alongside men, there are also good reasons to claim ignorance and revert to equality paradigms.

At the same time, though, Frankfurt is at pains to point out that this should not be construed as a victory for equality over respect. On the contrary, the reason that guides the decision-maker towards equal distribution is not grounded in any prior ideal of equality, but rather in 'the moral importance of respect and hence of impartiality,' which:

> 'constrains us to treat people the same when we know nothing that provides us with a special reason for treating them differently.'⁶⁵

In this light, then, the feminist commitment to equality outlined above can be recognised as contingent rather than inevitable—it is only in a society in which men and women have equal power, in the sense of being equally capable of influencing social institutions and ideologies—that we can be confident about what women (collectively or individually) would wish for, choose, or consider to be sufficient to their pursuit of a good life. While Phillips may be right, therefore, to insist upon the importance of securing equality, it emerges here as only the first step to feminist success, since it is not (or at least not only) the fact of equal treatment that is morally significant, and women's self-determination can only be achieved by moving beyond the comparative to accredit the choices that women make from a position of equal empowerment.

---

⁶³ Indeed, according to Frankfurt, in such situations, there may well be 'good reasons for governments or for individuals to deal with problems . . . in accordance with an egalitarian standard'—H Frankfurt, 'Equality as a Moral Ideal,' above n 3 at 22.

⁶⁴ In a similar vein, Woolf has argued that theories that attempt to exact egalitarian fairness will 'undermine the respect of at least some of its citizens by treating them precisely in the way that is inconsistent with respecting them, or allowing them to retain their self-respect'—J Woolf, 'Fairness, Respect and the Egalitarian Ethos' (1998) 27(2) *Philosophy and Public Affairs* 97 at 107. Support for this idea also comes, of course, from the work of John Rawls who has argued that when individuals are placed in the original position—and so know little of their own or other's needs and interests—they will 'express their respect for one another in the very constitution of their society' in the process of which frameworks premised on equal liberties and the stringent justification of inequality will emerge—J Rawls, *A Theory of Justice* (revised edn) (Oxford, Oxford University Press, 2000) at 156.

⁶⁵ H Frankfurt, 'Equality and Respect' in *Necessity, Volition, and Love*, above n 47 at 151. Similarly, Peters has argued that while treating people *rightly* (in the sense of invoking a nonegalitarian standard of justice) may always, in some sense, involve treating them equally, 'if we treat people equally, we do not necessarily treat them rightly'—C Peters, 'Equality Revisited,' above n 3 at 1213.

Amongst other things, then, the approach outlined here has the benefit of re-casting the dichotomy between equality and respect in a way that absolves the need for feminists to choose between them. It problematises the unjust social relations that impose disproportionate cultural or material constraints on women's lives, without jettisoning thereby the prospect that, at some future time, when power has been equalised between the genders, men and women may make different choices (some of which may conform to current gender roles/norms) and that these should also be respected. This can be seen to complement, on some readings at least, the approach adopted by Drucilla Cornell, who argues for the establishment and protection of an imaginary domain in which women are free to create and re-create their identity, and in which women benefit from a background programme of equivalent rights.[66] While some have criticised Cornell's work for prioritising freedom *over* equality, on closer inspection, her account of freedom (which is bound up with the correlative notion of respect outlined here) emerges as laced with the language and demands of equality as a precursor to the establishment of processes for meaningful self-individuation.[67]

Likewise, as discussed above, there are clearly some parallels between the approach defended here and that adopted in Nussbaum's recent work on capabilities. At the same time, though, it is also clear that there are some important differences. More specifically, while Nussbaum's account is sensitive to the need to ensure that the material preconditions of genuine choice are in place as a basic aspect of securing the capabilities for human flourishing, critics have argued that the key premise informing her approach is one of choice *rather than* (cf as well as, or following from) equality. Certainly, by Nussbaum's own admission, the issue of equality, if not abandoned, has been set aside or postponed in her capabilities account.[68] By contrast, the approach put forward in this chapter affords an explicit role for equality *within* its parameters. The value of Nussbaum's insistence that women 'are not seen as passive recipients of social planning but as dignified beings who shape their own lives' is undeniable,[69] but it is submitted here that respect for women's choices and perspectives (and all that this entails) cannot be secured prior to the achievement of a 'ground-zero'

---

[66] D Cornell, *The Imaginary Domain—Abortion, Pornography and Sexual Harassment* (London and New York, Routledge, 1995).

[67] As Cornell puts it: 'first, we must demand inclusion in the moral community of persons as a matter of right and demand that, as persons, we be given equal and maximum liberty to determine our sexual lives . . .; second, as recognised persons, we must demand a scope of rights, resources and capabilities consistent with our treatment as equals'—D Cornell, *At the Heart of Freedom: Feminism, Sex and Equality* (Princeton, Princeton University Press, 1998) at 67.

[68] A Phillips, 'Feminism and Liberalism: Has Martha Nussbaum Got It Right?' above n 59 at 258.

[69] M Nussbaum, *Sex and Social Justice*, above n 51 at 45.

equalisation of social power between the genders. Egalitarianism (in all its relational and comparative glory) has a crucial role to play in taking women to this point, but in the final analysis, it is ill-equipped to move beyond it; and it is at this juncture that frameworks grounded in sufficiency, freedom and respect must come to the forefront.

Like the approaches of both Cornell and Nussbaum, then, this approach emphasises the inter-dependence of empowerment and opportunity on the one hand, and determination and recognition on the other. At the same time, though, the approach offered here provides a more candid and conscious examination of the relationship between these guiding feminist ideals, as well as of their chronology. While this may require some fresh thinking around feminist politics, and around its tendency to reify equality as the ultimate and enduring aim, the potential it offers in terms of moving feminist analysis forward, not only beyond (comparative) egalitarianism but also beyond debates over construction vs agency, power vs freedom, structure vs context, and resource vs recognition, means that there is a great deal to commend it.

Conclusion: Toward A Respect Agenda

It has been argued that 'equality is at once the most appealing and the most threatening of ideas,' and that while:

> its appeal is the comfort of commonality, the promise of impartiality, the hope of genuine meritocracy, its threat is the same

or, more aptly, 'its threat is too much of *the same*' which risks usurping individuality.[70] In this chapter, it has been suggested that if feminism wishes to move beyond the comparative, and to provide a compelling theoretical basis for a utopia that does not demand constant suspicion of gender difference, then the call to respect outlined above must be an attractive one. The appeal of the concept of equality is clearly strongest in a world in which we know little of relevance about ourselves or one another. Thus, in a world in which, as MacKinnon and others have argued, we cannot be sure about what it means to be a woman, there are good reasons to support this model. At the same time, though, if the final goal of feminism is not only to prepare women for the task of self-definition, but also to take seriously their conclusions and to respond to them sensitively, at some point it needs to move beyond equality, and towards a more particularised version of sufficiency and respect. Amongst other things, such an approach allows feminism to envisage a future in which the choices that women make, in all their diversity, can be valued and expressions of women's agency can be accredited, even where they involve acceptance of traditional roles.

---

[70] C Peters, 'Equality Revisited,' above n 3 at 1211

Equality, Respect and Feminist Futures

At the same time, though, it has been argued here that equality of power remains a vital precondition to this turn to respect, not least since it enables feminists to attend to the dangers of re-affirming women's powerlessness under the guise of respecting either their substantive choices or their subjective assessments of sufficient distribution. While this explains the tenacity of egalitarianism in the mindset of much contemporary feminism, it also generates some fresh thinking about the relationship between gender, equality and social justice. To the extent that equality of power emerges as a means to an end rather than an end in itself, the contingency of the comparative framework is uncovered and scope for gender difference in the post-patriarchal future is created, without jettisoning the egalitarian project of ensuring that women enjoy equal power in a currently less than equal world. This is important, as Rhode reminds us, because 'effective strategies for gender equality require a reassessment of ends as well as means.' There is, after all, a danger in reifying the pursuit of equality into the final objective of gender politics, since what is at issue 'is not simply equality between the sexes, but the quality of life for both of them.'[71]

By accounting for the force and tenacity of the equality paradigm in feminist analysis, without reducing feminist politics to its comparative confines or restricting feminist hopes to the achievement of androgyny, the relationship outlined between egalitarianism and respect in this chapter offers considerable potential for productive development. Without denying the significance of structural asymmetries based on gender, it builds on the Foucaultian analysis outlined in Chapter four to insist that the terrain in which our respective power is measured is a localised one, and that it attends to the complex ways in which our capacity to exert influence in one sphere may have multiple, and unpredictable, effects on our capacity to do so in others. Equality of power on this understanding is not demonstrable in a fixed calculation, and while accepting that strict parity of power at all times and all places may be an unachievable ideal, this approach also recognises the need to de-stagnate solidified structures of domination and to ensure a tolerable equality of engagement in the floating networks of power relations. Moreover, it appreciates that any rush to absolute criteria of respect or sufficiency, in the absence of this preliminary engagement with equality of power, would simply re-affirm and thus reify current distributive patterns. At the same time, though, its insistence on respect as the ultimate goal of feminist analysis, when supported by this background of equality of power, acknowledges both the diversity and the familiarity of women's lives, as discussed in Chapter five. More specifically, it recognises the structural constraints under which choices are made and perspectives are framed, without reducing individual women's choices to those structures, or insisting on a shared female perspective beyond them.

[71] D Rhode, *Justice and Gender*, above n 15 at 320.

Concluding Remarks

Feminist legal and political analysis, for all its successes and achievements, has been confronted in contemporary times with a number of difficult dilemmas, which in their turn have generated significant—partly disruptive, partly productive—internal disagreements. Recent decades of feminist engagement have been marked by a 'hermeneutics of suspicion'[1] within which claims to universalism have been re-cast as disguising the power of a particular group, and the very possibility of talking about women as a collective/potentially unified category has been problematised. Frustration at the failure of liberal ideals of universality, abstraction, and rationality to live up to their promise in terms of securing greater inclusion and empowerment of women has promoted a turn away from the normative and conceptual resources of liberal legalism, including the language of rights, social justice and formal equality. At the same time, the influence of postmodernism has promoted a deconstruction and fragmentation of concepts that were hitherto relied upon in the deployment of feminist critique. A shift in attention from 'structure' to 'discourse,' from 'resources' to 'recognition,' and from 'reform' to 'resistance' has been identified, and increasingly lamented, particularly by those who have emphasised the systematic nature of men's domination over women, the material impact of this inequality on women's daily lives, and the centrality of utopias or faith in progress for collective feminist politics.

Against this backdrop, recent feminist scholarship—in law, political theory and beyond—has experienced, and been called upon to navigate, somewhat of an 'existential crisis'. The project of this book has been to re-examine some of the key debates that have been engaged in this process and to re-evaluate the avenues they offer for moving forwards. At least some of these debates, it has emerged, have been founded on misconceptions that have distracted productive feminist engagement. What's more, while some have shown themselves to be amenable to resolution, others have been acknowledged as providing inevitable and unavoidable points of tension, which can at best only be negotiated and refined on a case-by-case basis. In the final analysis, therefore, this book cannot claim to have dissolved or transcended all the debates that have marked the terrain of contemporary feminist legal and political scholarship. But, then again, it is not clear that it should have sought to do so—as Bartlett reminds us, after all, feminism displays its confidence precisely in its 'self-conscious status as ongoing

---

[1] S Benhabib, 'Sexual Difference and Collective Identity: The New Global Constellation' in S James and S Palmer (eds) *Visible Women: Essays on Feminist Legal Theory and Political Philosophy* (Oxford, Hart Publishing, 2002) at 155.

Concluding Remarks

rather than complete, questioning rather than declarative, and self-critical rather than complacent.'[2] This book has sought to return some of that confidence, depleted by recent criticisms and schisms, to feminism.

To the extent that the arguments presented here have called for a reconsideration, reconstruction and redeployment of selective ideals or methods typically associated with the liberal tradition, they can be seen to lend support to what Benhabib identifies as 'a new awareness' in feminist scholarship—an awareness that recognises the bonds of interdependence that continue to unite women of different classes and races and that betrays a renewed respect for the moral and political legacy of universalism.[3] At the same time, though, this book has been more circumspect than some in its approach—for the emphasis is on what feminism can usefully take from liberalism and not on defending liberalism per se from feminist or critical challenge. It is true that feminist analysis may at times have done a disservice to the diversity and sophistication of some aspects of liberal thinking, or to the work of specific theorists. And it is clear that ideals of impartiality, universality, abstraction and rationality should not be dismissed too lightly, since—when applied with sensitivity to the issues of gender politics—they offer the potential to secure important feminist successes. That said, however, blinkered adherence to liberalism is just as problematic as 'straw-manning' critique, and it has been stressed throughout that the value of these ideals must be constantly kept under review, recognised as both contingent and contextual.

Moreover, this emphasis on contingency has emerged as equally as vital in the context of key ideas in conventional feminist analysis—ie power, womanhood and equality. By conceptualising power as dispersed, productive and omnipresent, postmodernism has questioned conventional (radical) feminist accounts of monolithic male domination and of a collective female condition of disempowerment. While this has generated insightful theoretical nuances, it has also generated considerable disquiet, particularly in terms of the legitimacy of the normative platform from which feminism has historically mobilised its consensus and grounded its calls for progressive change. This book has argued, however, that it is possible both to challenge macro-level, systemic structures of domination where they exist and to identify a shared sense of connection or resemblance amongst individual women, without falling foul of the determinist and essentialist pitfalls that have plagued previous feminist accounts.

Asymmetrical power relationships do exist in society and male-female interaction may well provide a particularly vivid, pervasive and tenacious illustration. But it has been argued here that their emergence represents a secondary, pathological result of the stagnation of otherwise fluid power

---

[2] K Bartlett, 'Anglo-American Law' in A Jaggar and I Young (eds) *A Companion to Feminist Philosophy* (Oxford, Blackwell Publishing, 2000) at 540.

[3] S Benhabib, 'Sexual Difference and Collective Identity: The New Global Constellation' in S James and S Palmer (eds) *Visible* Women, above n 1 at 155.

Concluding Remarks

relations, and that scope to de-solidify them through resistance and subversion, though not without its difficulties, is always, therefore, imminent within them. Similarly, while individual women may exhibit an array of internal differences—in terms of their commitments, preferences and social location—the preceding analysis has insisted that they nonetheless remain connected in their diversity by a resemblance (not a strict similarity) that links one to another. It is this that renders the collective concept of 'women' coherent, while also leaving open its exact parameters to be determined on each and every occasion of its useage.

Such an understanding of power and gender identity, while valuable on its own terms, also helps foster new agendas for feminist politics that are grounded in and developed out of feminist theory, rather than distant or detached therefrom. Applying these insights to the concept of equality, around which there has already been so much feminist and liberal attention, has promoted fresh understandings of its demands and its operation. Formal models of treating like alike have been replaced with a more critical engagement with the processes through which 'likeness' is adjudged and a more sophisticated understanding of the need for equivalent (cf strictly equal) treatment. What's more, the idea that equality represents a precondition of, or means to, the end of respect has also emerged, taking on board the wisdom of the feminist insistence on the material and on the constraining impact of (male-defined) gender norms on women's choices whilst simultaneously acknowledging the imperatives to move beyond sex comparison, pay attention to context and recognise the preferences that women operating in a world of equal empowerment would opt to make their own.

Discussion over the course of the previous chapters has been wide-ranging and has involved the selective and critical appropriation of concepts from a range of sources in legal and political philosophy, some of which prima facie at least have not been particularly sympathetic to the feminist project, or even interested in women's lives. Dialogue that transverses conventional theoretical fault lines in this way is always demanding and rarely uncomplicated, perpetually raising new points of contention and consideration. At the same time, though, it offers feminism the prospect of deeper engagement with alternative frameworks—which, in turn, may yield concepts and methods that can be reconstructed or deployed effectively—and of occupying (when it suits its purpose) conceptual terrain that is no longer restricted to the perimeter.

While it was suggested towards the end of Chapter one that the development of feminist analysis is not necessarily best thought of as linear, it has been emphasised throughout this book that it is nonetheless progressive. In this light, this book's re-engagement with liberal ideals, rights analysis, legal reform strategies, as well as structural concepts of domination, collective notions of gender identity and blueprints for respecting sexual difference, can be seen to represent important steps forward.

Bibliography

Abrams, K 'Ideology and Women's Choices' (1990) 24 *Georgia Law Review* 761.
Alcoff, L 'Cultural Feminism v Poststructuralism: The Identity Crisis in Feminist Theory' (1988) 13 *Signs* 405.
Allen, A *The Power of Feminist Theory: Domination, Resistance, Solidarity* (Oxford, Westview Press, 2001).
Anderson, E 'What is the Point of Equality?' (1999) 109 *Ethics* 287.
Arac, J (ed) *After Foucault: Humanistic Knowledge, Postmodern Challenges* (New Brunswick, Rutgers University Press, 1988).
Armitage, F 'Respect and Types of Injustice' (2006) 12 (6) *Res Publica* 9.
Armstrong, T *Michel Foucault—Philosopher* (London, Harvester Wheatsheaf, 1992).
Assiter, A *Enlightened Women—Modernist Feminism in a Postmodern Age* (London & New York, Routledge, 1996).
Austin, J *The Province of Jurisprudence Determined* (London, George Weidenfeld & Nicholson, 1954).
Baier, A *Moral Prejudices: Essays on Ethics* (Cambridge, Harvard University Press, 1994).
Barrett, M & **Phillips**, A (eds) *Destabilizing Theory: Contemporary Feminist Debates* (Cambridge, Polity Press, 1992).
Barron, A 'Feminism, Aestheticism and the Limits of Law' (2000) 8 *Feminist Legal Studies* 275.
Barry, B *The Liberal Theory of Justice: A Critical Examination of the Principal Doctrines in A Theory of Justice by John Rawls* (Oxford, Clarendon Press, 1973).
—— *Culture and Equality* (Cambridge, Polity Press, 2000).
Bartky, S *Feminism and Domination: Studies in the Phenomenology of Oppression* (New York, Routledge, 1990).
Bartlett, K 'MacKinnon's Feminism: Power on Whose Terms?' (1987) 75 *California Law Review* 1559.
—— 'Feminist Legal Methods' (1990) 103 *Harvard Law Review* 829.
Bell, V *Interrogating Incest—Feminism, Foucault and the Law* (London, Routledge, 1993).
Benhabib, S *Situating the Self: Gender, Community and Postmodernism in Contemporary Ethics* (Cambridge, Polity Press, 1992).
—— *Democracy and Difference: Contesting the Boundaries of the Political* (Princeton, Princeton University Press, 1996).
—— *The Claims of Culture: Equality and Diversity in the Global Era* (Princeton, Princeton University Press, 2002).
Benhabib, S, **Butler**, J, **Cornell**, D & **Fraser**, N (eds) *Feminist Contentions* (London & New York, Routledge, 1995).

Bibliography

Benhabib, S & **Cornell**, D (eds) *Feminism as Critique: On the Politics of Gender* (Minneapolis, University of Minnesota Press, 1987).

Benjamin, J *The Bonds of Love: Psychoanalysis, Feminism and the Problem of Domination* (London, Virago Press, 1990).

Bernauer, J & **Ramussen**, D (eds) *The Final Foucault* (Cambridge, MIT Press, 1994).

Bordo, S *Unbearable Weight: Feminism, Western Culture and the Body* (Berkeley, University of California Press, 1995).

Bottomley, A (ed) *Feminist Perspectives on the Foundational Subjects of Law* (London, Cavendish Publishing, 1996).

—— 'Shock to Thought: An Encounter (of a Third Kind) with Legal Feminism' (2004) 12 *Feminist Legal Studies* 29.

Bottomley, A & **Conaghan**, J (eds) *Feminist Theory and Legal Strategy* (Oxford, Blackwell, 1993).

Braidotti, R *Nomadic Subjects: Embodiment and Sexual Difference in Contemporary Feminist Theory* (New York, Columbia University Press, 1994).

Bridgeman, J & **Milns**, S (eds) *Law and Body Politics: Regulating the Female Body* (Aldershot, Dartmouth, 1995).

—— (eds) *Feminist Perspectives on Law: Law's Engagement with the Female Body* (London, Sweet & Maxwell, 1998).

Brock, G & **James**, S (eds) *Beyond Equality and Difference* (London, Routledge, 1992).

Bronfen, E & **Kavka**, M *Feminist Consequences: Theory for the New Century* (New York, Columbia University Press, 2000).

Brown, W *States of Injury: Power and Freedom in Late Modernity* (Princeton, Princeton University Press, 1995).

Bubek, D *Care, Gender and Justice* (Oxford, Clarendon Press, 1995),

Butler, J *Gender Trouble: Feminism and the Subversion of Identity* (London & New York, Routledge, 1990).

—— *Bodies that Matter: On the Discursive Limits of Sex* (London & New York, Routledge, 1993).

—— *The Psychic Life of Power* (Stanford, Stanford University Press, 1997).

—— *Excitable Speech: A Politics of the Performative* (London & New York, Routledge, 1997).

—— *Undoing Gender* (New York & London, Routledge, 2004).

Butler, J & **Scott**, J (eds) *Feminists Theorize the Political* (London & New York, Routledge, 1992).

Cain, P 'Feminism and the Limits of Equality' (1990) 24 *Georgia Law Review* 803.

Card, C (ed) *On Feminist Ethics and Politics* (Lawrence, University of Kansas Press, 1999).

Carty, A (ed) *Post-modern Law: Enlightenment, Revolution and the Death of Man* (Edinburgh, Edinburgh University Press, 1990).

Charles, N *Gender in Modern Britain* (Oxford, Oxford University Press, 2002).

Chemerinsky, E 'In Defense of Equality: A Reply to Professor Westen' (1983) 81 *Michigan Law Review* 575.

Chodorow, N *The Reproduction of Mothering: Psychoanalysis and the Sociology of Gender* (Berkeley, University of California Press, 1978).

Bibliography

Clayton, M & **Williams**, A (eds) *The Ideal of Equality* (Basingstoke, MacMillan Press, 2000).

Cohen, G 'On the Currency of Egalitarian Justice' (1989) 99 *Ethics* 906.

Conaghan, J 'Reassessing the Feminist Theoretical Project in Law' (2000) 27 (3) *Journal of Law and Society* 351.

Cooper, D 'And You Can't Find Me Nowhere: Relocating Identity and Structure Within Equality Jurisprudence' (2000) 27 (2) *Journal of Law and Society* 249.

—— *Challenging Diversity: Rethinking Equality and the Value of Difference* (Cambridge, Cambridge University Press, 2004).

Corea, G *The Mother Machine* (London, Women's Press, 1988).

Cornell, D 'Beyond Tragedy and Complacency' (1987) *Northwester University Law Review* 81.

—— 'The Doubly-Prized World: Myth, Allegory and the Feminine' (1990) 75 *Cornell Law Review* 644.

—— *Beyond Accommodation: Ethical Feminism, Deconstruction and the Law* (London & New York, Routledge, 1991).

—— 'Sexual Difference, the Feminine and Equivalency: A Critique of MacKinnon's Toward a Feminist Theory of State' (1991) 100 *Yale Law Review* 2247.

—— *The Philosophy of the Limit* (London, Routledge, 1992).

—— *The Imaginary Domain: Abortion, Pornography and Sexual Harassment* (London & New York, Routledge, 1995).

—— *At the Heart of Freedom: Feminism, Sex and Equality* (Princeton, Princeton University Press, 1998).

—— *Just Cause: Freedom, Identity and Rights* (New York, Rowman & Littlefield, 2000).

Cornell, D, **Rosenfield**, M & **Carlson**, D (eds) *Deconstruction and the Possibility of Justice* (New York, Routledge, 1992).

Coward, R *Sacred Cows: Is Feminism Relevant to the New Millenium?* (London, Harper Collins, 2000).

Crenshaw, K 'Race, Reform and Retrenchment: Transformation and Legitimation in Antidiscrimination Law' (1988) 101 *Harvard Law Review* 1331.

—— (ed) *Critical Race Theory* (New York, Free Press, 1995).

Crisp, R 'Equality, Priority and Compassion' (2003) 113 *Ethics* 745.

Dalton, C 'Where We Stand—Observations on the Situation of Feminist Legal Thought' (1987) 3 *Berkeley Women's Law Journal* 1.

Davies, M *Asking the Law Question* (Sydney, Law Book Company, 1994).

—— *Delimiting the Law—Postmodernism and the Politics of Law* (London, Pluto Press, 1996).

Davis, K *Embodied Practices—Feminist Perspectives on the Body* (London, SAGE, 1997).

De Beauvoir, S *The Second Sex* (trans H Parshley) (London, Vintage Press, 1997).

Deveaux, M 'Feminism and Empowerment: A Critical Reading of Foucault' (1994) 20 (2) *Feminist Studies* 223.

Diamond, I & **Quinby**, L (eds) *Feminism and Foucault—Reflections on Resistance* (Boston, Northeastern University Press, 1988).

Diprose, R *The Bodies of Women—Ethics, Embodiment and Sexual Difference* (London & New York, Routledge, 1994).

Bibliography

Dobash, R & **Dobash**, R *Women, Violence and Social Change* (London & New York, Routledge, 1992).

Douzinas, C, **Washington**, R & **McVeigh**, S *Postmodern Jurisprudence—The Law of Text in The Texts of Law* (London & New York, Routledge, 1991).

Drakopoulou, M 'The Ethic of Care, Female Subjectivity and Feminist Legal Scholarship' (2000) 8 *Feminist Legal Studies* 199.

Dreyfus, H & **Rabinow**, P *Michel Foucault—Beyond Structuralism and Hermeneutics* (Hemel Hempstead, Harvester Wheatsheaf, 1982).

Duncan, S 'Disrupting the Surface of Order and Innocence—Towards a Theory of Sexuality and The Law' (1994) 2 (1) *Feminist Legal Studies* 1.

Durkheim, E *The Division of Labour in Society* (trans W Hall) (London, MacMillan, 1948).

Dworkin, A *Life and Death: Unapologetic Writings on the Continuing War Against Women* (London, Virago Press, 1997).

Dworkin, R *Taking Rights Seriously* (London, Duckworth Press, 1977).

—— *Law's Empire* (London, Fontana Press, 1986).

—— *Sovereign Virtue: The Theory and Practice of Equality* (Cambridge, Harvard University Press, 2000).

—— 'Equality, Luck and Hierarchy' (2003) 31 (2) *Philosophy and Public Affairs* 190.

Edwards, S *Policing Domestic Violence* (Manchester, Manchester University Press, 1989).

—— *Sex and Gender in the Legal Process* (London, Blackstones, 1996).

Eichner, M 'On Postmodern Feminist Legal Theory' (2001) 36 *Harvard Civil Rights/Civil Liberties Law Review* 1.

Eisenstein, H & **Jardine**, A (eds) *The Future of Difference* (New Brunswik, Rutgers University Press, 1990).

Eisenstein, Z *Feminism and Sexual Equality: Crisis in Liberal America* (New York, Monthly Review Press, 1984).

English, J 'Justice Between Generations' (1977) 31 *Philosophical Studies* 91.

Estrich, S *Real Rape* (Cambridge, Harvard University Press, 1987).

Evans, M *The Woman Question* (London, SAGE, 1994).

Faludi, S *Backlash—The Undeclared War Against Women* (London, Vintage, 1992).

Faubion, J (ed) *Aesthetics—Essential Works of Michel Foucault 1954–84* (London, Penguin, 1998).

Fegan, E 'Ideology After Discourse: A Reconception of Feminist Analysis of Law' (1996) 23 *Journal of Law and Society* 173.

Ferguson, K *The Feminist Case Against Bureaucracy* (Philadelphia, Temple University Press, 1984).

—— *The Man Question—Visions of Subjectivity in Feminist Theory* (Berkeley, University of California Press, 1993).

Finch, E & **Munro**, V 'Breaking Boundaries: Sexual Consent in the Jury Room' (2006) 26 (3) *Legal Studies* 303.

Fineman, M 'Challenging Law, Establishing Differences: The Future of Feminist Legal Scholarhsip' (1990) 42 *Florida Law Review* 25.

—— *The Illusion of Equality: The Rhetoric and Reality of Divorce Reform* (Chicago, University of Chicago Press, 1991).

—— 'Feminist Theory in Law: The Difference it Makes' (1992) 2 *Columbia Journal of Gender and Law* 1.

Bibliography

—— 'Feminist Theory and Law' (1995) 18 *Harvard Journal of Law and Public Policy* 349.
—— 'Cracking the Foundational Myths: Independence, Autonomy and Self-Sufficiency' (2000) 8 *American University Journal of Gender, Social Policy and the Law* 13.
—— *The Autonomy Myth: A Theory of Dependency* (New York, New Press, 2003).
Fineman, M & **Thomadsen**, N (eds) *At the Boundaries of Law: Feminism and Legal Theory* (London & New York, Routledge, 1991).
Finley, L 'The Nature of Domination and The Nature of Women: Reflections on Feminism Unmodified' (1988) 82 *Northwestern University Law Review* 352.
—— 'Breaking Women's Silence in Law: The Dilemma of the Gendered Nature of Legal Reasoning' (1989) 64 *Notre Dame Law Review* 886.
Finney, A *Domestic Violence, Sexual Assault and Stalking: Findings from the 2004/05 British Crime Survey* (London, Home Office, 2006) available on line at http://www.homeoffice.gov.uk/rds.pdfs06/rdsolr1206.pdf.
Firestone, S *The Dialectics of Sex: The Case for Feminist Revolution* (London, Women's Press, 1979).
Fitzpatrick, P (ed) *Dangerous Supplements: Resistance and Renewal in Jurisprudence* (London, Pluto Press, 1991).
Flax, J *Thinking Fragments: Psychoanalysis, Feminism and Postmodernism in the Contemporary West* (Berkeley, University of California Press, 1990).
Foucault, M *The Archaeology of Knowledge* (trans A Sheridan) (New York, Harper Colophon, 1972).
—— *The History of Sexuality, Volume I* (London, Penguin, 1976).
—— *Discipline and Punish—The Birth of The Prison* (trans A Sheridan) (London, Vintage, 1979).
—— *Introduction to Herculin Barbib: Being the Recently Discovered Memoirs of a 19th Century French Hermaphrodite* (New York, Pantheon, 1980).
—— *Power/Knowledge—Selected Interviews and Other Writings 1972–77* (ed C Gordon) (New York, Pantheon, 1980).
—— *The History of Sexuality Volume II—The Use of Pleasure* (trans R Hurley) (New York, Pantheon, 1985).
—— *The History of Sexuality Volume III—The Care of the Self* (trans R Hurley) (New York, Pantheon, 1986).
—— 'The Ethics of Care for the Self as a Practice of Freedom' (1987) 12 *Philosophy and Social Criticism* 6.
Frankfurt, H 'Equality as a Moral Ideal' (1987) 98 (1) *Ethics* 21.
—— *Necessity, Volition and Love* (Cambridge, Cambridge University Press, 1999).
Fraser, N 'Foucault on Modern Power: Empirical Insights and Normative Confusions' (1981) 23 *Praxis International* 272.
—— 'Foucault: A Young Conservative?' (1985) 96 (1) *Ethics* 165.
—— *Unruly Practices: Power, Discourse and Gender in Contemporary Theory* (Cambridge, Polity Press, 1989).
—— 'Recognition or Redistribution? A Critique of Iris Young's Justice and the Politics of Difference' (1995) 3 (2) *Journal of Political Philosophy* 166.
—— *Justice Interruptus: Critical Reflections on the 'Post-Socialist' Condition* (New York & London, Routledge, 1997).

Bibliography

Fraser, N & **Bartky**, S (1992) *Revaluing French Feminism—Critical Essays on Difference, Agency & Culture* (Bloomington, Indiana University Press).

Frazer, E, **Hornsby** & **Lovibond**, S *Ethics—A Feminist Reader* (Oxford, Blackwell, 1992).

Frazer, E & **Lacey**, N *The Politics of Community—A Feminist Critique of the Liberal-Communitarian Debate* (Hemel Hempstead, Harvester Wheatsheaf, 1993).

Freeman, S (ed) *Collected Papers* (Cambridge, Harvard University Press, 1997)

—— (ed) *The Cambridge Companion to Rawls* (Cambridge, Cambridge University Press, 2003).

Fricker, M & **Hornsby**, J (eds) *The Cambridge Companion to Feminism in Philosophy* (Cambridge, Cambridge University Press, 2000).

Friedman, M 'Feminism and Modern Friendship—Dislocating the Community' (1989) 99 *Ethics* 275.

—— *Autonomy, Gender, Politics* (Oxford, Oxford University Press, 2003).

Frug, M 'A Postmodern Feminist Legal Manifesto (An Unfinished Draft)' (1992) 105 *Harvard Law Review* 1045.

—— *Postmodern Legal Feminism* (London & New York, Routledge, 1992).

Fuss, D *Essentially Speaking: Feminism, Nature and Difference* (New York, Routledge, 1989).

Gabel, P 'The Phenomenology of Rights-Consciousness and the Pact of the Withdrawn Selves' (1984) 62 *Texas Law Review* 1563.

Gardiner, J *Provoking Agents: Gender and Agency in Theory and Practice* (Chicago, University of Illinois Press, 1995).

Gatens, M *Feminism and Philosophy: Perspectives on Difference and Equality* (Bloomington, Indiana University Press, 1991).

Gavison, R 'Feminism and the Public/Private Distinction' (1992) 45 *Stanford Law Review* 1.

Gilligan, C *In a Different Voice: Psychological Theory and Women's Development*, (re-issued edition) (Cambridge, Harvard University Press, 1993).

Glendon, M *Rights Talk: The Impoverishment of Political Discourse* (London, Free Press, 1991).

Glock, H (ed) *Wittgenstein: A Critical Reader* (Oxford, Blackwell, 2001).

Goodin, R 'Egalitarianism, Fetishistic and Otherwise' (1987) 98 (1) *Ethics* 44.

Grace, S *Policing Domestic Violence in the 1990s* (Home Office Research Study 139) (London, HMSO, 1995).

Green, K 'Rawls, Women and the Priority of Liberty' (1986) 64 *Australian Journal of Philosophy* 26.

—— *The Woman of Reason—Feminism, Humanism and Political Thought* (New York, Continuum, 1995).

Greenawalt, K 'How Empty is the Idea of Equality?' (1983) 83 *Columbia Law Review* 1167.

Grimshaw, D & **Rubery**, J *The Gender Pay Gap: A Research Review* (Manchester, Equal Opportunities Commission, 2001)

Guha, R & **Spivak**, G (eds) *Selected Subaltern Studies* (Oxford, Oxford University Press, 1988).

Gutting, G *A Cambridge Companion to Foucault* (Cambridge, Cambridge University Press, 1994).

Halley, J *Split Decisions: How and Why to Take a Break from Feminism* (Princeton, Princeton University Press, 2006).

Haraway, D 'A Manifesto for Cyborgs: Science, Technology, and Socialist-Feminism in the Late Twentieth Century' (1985) 80 *Socialist Review* 65.

—— 'Situated Knowledges: The Science Question in Feminism and the Privilege of Partial Perspective' (1988) 14 *Feminist Studies* 575.

—— *Simians, Cyborgs and Women: The Reinvention of Nature* (London & New York, Routledge, 1991).

Harding, S *The Science Question in Feminism* (New York, Cornell University Press, 1986).

Harris, A 'Race and Essentialism in Feminist Legal Theory' (1990) 42 *Stanford Law Review* 581.

—— 'Building Theory, Building Community' (1998) 8 (3) *Social and Legal Studies* 313.

Hart, H *The Concept of Law* (Oxford, Oxford University Press, 1961).

—— *The Concept of Law* (revised edition) (Oxford, Clarendon Press, 1994).

Heath, M 'Catharine MacKinnon: Towards a Feminist Theory of State' (1997) 9 *Australian Feminist Law Journal* 45.

Hekman, S *Gender and Knowledge: Elements of a Postmodern Feminism* (Cambridge, Polity Press, 1990).

—— *Moral Voices, Moral Selves: Carol Gilligan and Feminist Moral Theory* (Cambridge, Polity Press, 1995).

—— *Feminist Interpretations of Michel Foucault* (Pennsylvania, University of Pennsylvania Press, 1996).

—— (ed) *Feminism, Identity and Difference* (London, Frank Cass, 1999).

—— *The Future of Differences: Truth and Method in Feminist Theory* (Cambridge, Polity Press, 1999).

Held, V *Feminist Morality: Transforming Culture, Society, Politics* (Chicago, University of Chicago Press, 1993).

—— (ed) *Justice and Care: Essential Readings in Feminist Ethics* (Boulder, Westview Press, 1995).

Higgins, T 'By Reason of Their Sex: Feminist Theory, Postmodernism and Justice' (1995) 80 *Cornell Law Review* 1536.

Higgins, T 'Anti-essentialism, Relativism and Human Rights' (1996) 19 *Harvard Women's Law Journal* 89.

—— 'Revisiting the Public-Private Distinction in Feminist Theorising' (2000) 75 *Chicago-Kent Law Review* 847.

Hindness, B *Discourses of Power: From Hobbes to Foucault* (Oxford, Blackwell, 2001).

Hirsch, M & **Keller**, E (eds) *Conflicts in Feminism* (London, Routledge, 1990)

Hirschmann, N & **Di Stefano**, C (eds) *Revisioning the Political: Feminist Reconstructions of Traditional Concepts in Western Political Theory* (Boulder, Westview Press, 1996).

Holmes, O 'The Path of Law' (reprinted) (1996) 110 *Harvard Law Review* 991.

Hoy, D *Foucault: A Critical Reader* (Oxford, Basil Blackwell, 1986).

Hoyle, C *Negotiating Domestic Violence: Police, Criminal Justice and Victims* (Oxford, Oxford University Press, 2000).

Bibliography

Hunt, A *Explorations in Law and Society: Towards a Constitutive Theory of Law* (London & New York, Routledge, 1993).

—— 'Getting Marx and Foucault Into Bed Together!' (2004) 31 (4) *Journal of Law and Society* 592.

Hunt, A & **Wichkam**, G *Foucault and Law—Towards a Sociology of Law as Governance* (London, Pluto Press, 1994).

Hunter, R 'Deconstructing the Subjects of Feminism' (1996) 6 *Australian Feminist Law Journal* 135.

Hutchison, A 'Inessentially Speaking (Is There Politics After Postmodernism?)' (1991) 89 *Michigan Law Review* 1549.

Jackson, E 'Catherine MacKinnon and Feminist Jurisprudence: A Critical Appraisal' (1992) 12 (2) *Journal of Law and Society* 195.

—— 'Contradictions and Coherence in Feminist Responses to Law' (1993) 20 *Journal of Law and Society* 398.

Jaggar, A *Feminist Politics and Human Nature* (Totowa, Rowman & Littlefield, 1983).

Jaggar, A & **Young**, I (eds) *A Companion to Feminist Philosophy* (Oxford, Blackwell, 2000).

James, S & **Palmer**, S (eds) *Visible Women: Essays on Feminist Legal Theory and Political Philosophy* (Oxford, Hart Publishing, 2002).

Kauffman, L (ed) *American Feminist Thought at Century's End: A Reader* (Oxford, Blackwell, 1993).

Kelly, T (ed) *Critique and Power: Recasting the Foucault/Habermas Debate* (Cambridge, MIT Press, 1994).

Kennedy, D *Sexy Dressing, etc.—Essays on The Power and Politics of Cultural Identity* (Cambridge, Harvard University Press, 1993).

—— *A Critique of Adjudication* (Cambridge, Harvard University Press, 1997).

Kerruish, V *Jurisprudence as Ideology* (London, Routledge, 1991).

Kingdom, E *What's Wrong with Rights?: Problems for Feminist Politics of Law* (Edinburgh, Edinburgh University Press, 1991).

Kittay, E *Love's Labour: Essays on Women, Equality and Dependence* (New York, Routledge, 1999).

Kittay, E & **Meyers**, D (eds) *Women and Moral Theory* (Totowa, Rowman & Littlefield, 1987).

Knop, K (ed) *Gender and Human Rights* (Oxford, Oxford University Press, 2006).

Kohlberg, L *The Philosophy of Moral Development* (San Francisco, Harper & Row, 1981).

Kritzman, L (ed) *Michel Foucault—Politics, Philosophy, Culture* (London & New York, Routledge, 1990).

Kymlicka, W *Contemporary Political Philosophy: An Introduction* (2nd edition) (Oxford, Oxford University Press, 2002).

Lacey, N 'Feminist Legal Theory' (1989) *Oxford Journal of Legal Studies* 9.

—— 'Feminist Legal Theory Beyond Neutrality' (1995) *Current Legal Problems* 3.

—— *Unspeakable Subjects: Feminist Essays in Legal and Social Theory* (Oxford, Hart Publishing, 1998).

—— 'Beset by Boundaries: The Home Office Review of Sexual Offences' (2001) *Criminal Law Review* 3.

Bibliography

Landes, J (ed) *Feminism and the Public and the Private* (Oxford, Oxford University Press, 1998).
Larrabee, M (ed) *An Ethic of Care: Feminist and Interdisciplinary Perspectives* (London & New York, Routledge, 1993).
Lees, S *Carnal Knowledge—Rape on Trial* (London, Penguin, 1996).
Littleton, C 'Reconstructing Sexual Equality' (1987) 75 *California Law Review* 1279.
—— 'Feminist Jurisprudence: The Difference Method Makes' (1989) 41 *Stanford Law Review* 751.
Llewellyn, K 'A Realistic Jurisprudence: The Next Step' (1930) 30 *Columbia Law Review* 413.
—— 'Some Realism about Realism' (1931) 44 *Harvard Law Review* 1222.
Lloyd, G *The Man of Reason—Male and Female in Western Philosophy* (London & New York, Routledge, 1993).
Lovell, T *British Feminist Thought* (Oxford, Basil Blackwell, 1990).
Lovibond, S 'Feminism / Postmodernism' (1989) 178 *New Left Review* 22.
—— 'Feminism and the 'Crisis of Rationality'' (1994) 203–8 *New Left Review* 72.
—— 'Meaning What We Say—Feminist Ethics and The Critique of Humanism' (1996) 215–20 *New Left Review* 98.
—— *Ethical Formation* (Cambridge, Harvard University Press, 2002).
Lukes, S *Power: A Radical View* (2nd edition) (Basingstoke, Palgrave MacMillan, 2005).
Lukes, S & **Scull**, A *Durkeim and the Law* (Oxford, Martin Robertson, 1983).
Lyotard, J *The Postmodern Condition: A Report on Knowledge* (Manchester, Manchester University Press, 1979).
MacKenzie, C & **Stoljar**, N *Relational Autonomy: Feminist Perspectives on Autonomy, Agency and The Social Self* (Oxford, Oxford University Press, 2000).
MacKinnon, C *Sexual Harassment of Working Women: A Case of Sex Discrimination* (New Haven, Yale University Press, 1979).
—— 'Feminism, Marxism, Method & The State: An Agenda for Theory' (1982) 7 (3) *Signs* 515.
—— 'Feminism, Marxism, Method & The State: Toward a Feminist Jurisprudence' (1983) 8 (2) *Signs* 635.
—— 'Pornography, Civil Rights and Speech' (1985) 20 *Harvard Civil Rights—Civil Liberties Law Review* 1.
—— *Feminism Unmodified: Discourses on Life and Law* (Cambridge, Harvard University Press, 1987).
—— *Toward a Feminist Theory of State* (Cambridge, Harvard University Press, 1989).
—— 'Reflections on Sex Equality Under Law' (1991) 100 (5) *Yale Law Review* 1281.
—— *Only Words* (Cambridge, Harvard University Press, 1993).
—— 'Symposium on Unfinished Feminist Business: Some Points Against Postmodernism' (2000) 75 *Chicago-Kent Law Review* 687.
—— *Sex Equality* (New York, Foundation Press, 2001).
—— *Women's Lives, Men's Laws* (Cambridge, Harvard University Press, 2005).
—— *Are Women Human? And Other International Dialogues* (Cambridge, Harvard University Press, 2006).

Bibliography

MacKinnon, C & **Dworkin**, A (eds) *In Harm's Way: The Pornography Civil Rights Hearings* (Cambridge, Harvard University Press, 1997).

McClain, L 'Atomistic Man Revisited: Liberalism, Connection and Feminist Jurisprudence' (1992) 65 *Southern California Law Review* 1171.

McColgan, A 'In Defence of Battered Women Who Kill' (1993) 13 *Oxford Journal of Legal Studies* 508.

—— *Women Under the Law: The False Promise of Human Rights* (Harlow, Longman, 2000).

McGinn, M *Wittgenstein and the Philosophical Investigations* (London & New York, Routledge, 1997).

McLaren, M 'Foucault and the Subject of Feminism' (1997) 23 (1) *Social Theory and Practice* 109.

—— *Feminism, Foucault and Embodied Subjectivity* (Albany, State University of New York Press, 2002).

McNay, L 'The Foucauldian Body and the Exclusion of Experience' (1991) 6 *Hypatia* 125.

—— *Foucault and Feminism* (Cambridge, Polity Press, 1992).

—— *Foucault: A Critical Introduction* (Cambridge, Polity Press, 1994).

—— *Gender and Agency: Reconfiguring the Subject in Feminist and Social Theory* (Cambridge, Polity Press, 2000).

McWhorter, L *Bodies and Pleasures: Foucault and the Politics of Sexual Normalisation* (Bloomington, Indiana University Press, 1999).

Macklem, T *Beyond Comparison: Sex and Discrimination* (Cambridge, Cambridge University Press, 2003).

Mahoney, M 'Whiteness and Women, In Practice and Theory: A Reply to Catharine MacKinnon' (1993) 5 *Yale Journal of Law and Feminism* 217.

Marshall, J *Humanity, Freedom and Feminism* (Aldershot, Ashgate Publishing, 2005).

—— Feminist Jurisprudence: Keeping the Subject Alive' (2006) 14 (1) *Feminist Legal Studies* 27.

Martins, J & **Roberts**, C *Women and Employment: A Lifetime Perspective* (London, Department of Employment/OPCS, 1984).

Mason, A (ed) *Ideals of Equality* (Oxford, Blackwell, 1998).

Medina, J 'Identity Trouble: Disidentification and the Problem of Difference' (2003) 29 (6) *Philosophy and Social Criticism* 655.

Merry, S *Human Rights and Gender Violence: Translating International Law into Local Justice* (Chicago, University of Chicago Press, 2006).

Meyers, D *Self, Society and Personal Choice* (New York, Columbia University Press, 1989)

—— (ed) *Feminists Rethink the Self* (Oxford, Westview Press, 1997).

—— *Gender in the Mirror: Cultural Imagery and Women's Agency* (Oxford, Oxford University Press, 2002).

Minow, M 'Interpreting Rights: An Essay for Robert Cover' (1987) 96 *Yale Law Journal* 1860.

—— 'Justice Engendered' (1987) 101 *Harvard Law Review* 10.

—— *Making All the Difference: Inclusion, Exclusion and American Law* (Itacha, Cornell University Press, 1990).

—— 'Incomplete Correspondence: An Unsent Letter to Mary Joe Frug' (1992) 105 *Harvard Law Review* 1096.

Bibliography

—— *Not Only for Myself: Identity, Politics and the Law* (New York, New Press, 1997).

Minow, M & **Shanley**, M 'Relational Rights and Responsibilities: Revisioning the Family in Liberal Political Theory and Law' (1996) 11 (1) *Hypatia* 4.

Minow, M & **Spelman**, E 'Passion for Justice' (1989) 10 *Cardozo Law Review* 37.

—— 'In Context' (1990) 63 *California Law Review* 1597

Mitchell, J & **Oakley**, A (eds) *What is Feminism?* (Oxford, Blackwell, 1986).

Moss, J (ed) *The Later Foucault: Politics and Philosophy* (London, SAGE, 1998).

Mossman, M 'Feminism and Legal Method—The Difference It Makes' (1986) *Australian Journal of Law and Society* 103.

Mullally, S *Gender, Culture and Human Rights: Reclaiming Universalism* (Oxford, Hart Publishing, 2006).

Mulhall, S *Inheritance and Originality: Wittgenstein, Heideffer, Kierkegaard* (Oxford, Clarendon Press, 2003).

Munro, V 'Legal Feminism and Foucault: A Critique of the Expulsion of Law' (2001) 28 (4) *Journal of Law and Society* 546.

—— 'Square Pegs in Round Holes: The Dilemma of Conjoined Twins and Individual Rights' (2001) 10 (4) *Social and Legal Studies* 459.

—— 'On Power and Domination: Feminism and the Final Foucault' (2003) 2 (1) *European Journal of Political Theory* 79.

Naffine, N (ed) *Gender and Justice* (Aldershot, Ashgate, 2002).

—— 'In Praise of Legal Feminism' (2002) 22 (1) *Legal Studies* 71.

—— 'Shocking Thoughts: A Reply to Anne Bottomley' (2004) 12 *Feminist Legal Studies* 175.

Naffine, N & **Owens**, R (eds) *Sexing the Subject of Law* (London, Sweet & Maxwell, 1997).

Nagel, J *Race, Ethnicity and Sexuality: Intimate Intersections. Forbidden Frontiers* (Oxford, Oxford University Press, 2003).

Nedelsky, J 'Reconceiving Rights as Relationship' (1993) 1 *Review of Constitutional Studies* 1.

Nicholson, D & **Sanghvi**, R 'Battered Women and Provocation: The Implications of *R v Ahluwalia*' (1993) *Criminal Law Review* 728.

Nicholson, L (ed) *Feminism / Postmodernism* (London & New York, Routledge, 1990).

Norris, C 'Law, Deconstruction and the Resistance to Theory' (1988) 15 (2) *Journal of Law and Society* 166.

Nussbaum, M *The Fragility of Goodness: Luck and Ethics in Greek Tragedy and Philosophy* (Cambridge, Cambridge University Press, 1986).

—— *Love's Knowledge—Essays on Philosophy and Literature* (Oxford, Oxford University Press, 1990).

—— 'Human Functioning and Social Justice: In Defence of Aristotelian Essentialism' (1992) 20 *Political Theory* 202.

—— 'Capabilities and Human Rights' (1997) 66 *Fordham Law Review* 273.

—— *Sex and Social Justice* (Oxford, Oxford University Press, 1999).

—— *Women and Human Development: The Capabilities Approach* (Cambridge, Cambridge University Press, 2000).

—— *Upheavals of Thought: The Intelligence of Emotions* (Cambridge, Cambridge University Press, 2003).

Bibliography

Nussbaum, M *Frontiers of Justice: Disability, Nationality and Species Membership* (Cambridge, Harvard University Press, 2006).
Nussbaum, M & **Glover**, J (eds) *Women, Culture and Development* (Oxford, Clarendon Press, 1995).
Nussbaum, M & **Sen**, A *The Quality of Life* (Oxford, Clarendon Press, 1993).
O'Brien, M *The Politics of Reproduction* (London, Routledge & Kegan Paul, 1981).
O'Donovan, K 'Defences for Battered Women Who Kill' (1991) 18 *Journal of Law and Society* 219.
O'Neill, O 'Friends of Difference' (1989) 11 (7) *London Review of Books* 20.
Okin, S 'Reason and Feeling in Thinking About Justice' (1989) 99(2) *Ethics* 229.
—— *Justice, Gender and the Family* (New York, Basic Books, 1989).
—— 'Political Liberalism, Justice and Gender' (1994) 105 (1) *Ethics* 23.
—— 'Poverty, Well-Being and Gender: What Counts, Who's Heard?' (2003) 31 (3) *Philosophy and Public Affairs* 280.
—— 'Justice and Gender: An Unfinished Debate' (2004) 72 *Fordham Law Review* 1537.
Olsen, F 'Statutory Rape: A Feminist Critique of Rights Analysis' (1984) 63 *Texas Law Review* 387.
—— 'Unravelling Compromise' (1989) 103 *Harvard Law Review* 105.
—— *Feminist Legal Theory* (Aldershot, Dartmouth, 1995).
Owen, D *Maturity and Modernity: Nietzsche, Weber, Foucault and the Ambivalence of Reason* (London & New York, Routledge, 1994).
Pateman, C *The Sexual Contract* (Cambridge, Polity Press, 1988).
Pateman, C & **Gross**, E (eds) *Feminist Challenges: Social and Political Theory* (London, Allen & Unwin, 1986).
Pears, D *The False Prison: A Study of the Development of Wittgenstein's Philosophy, Volume I* (Oxford, Oxford University Press, 1987).
—— *The False Prison: A Study of the Development of Wittgenstein's Philosophy, Volume II* (Oxford, Oxford University Press, 1988).
Peters, C 'Equality Revisited' (1997) 110 *Harvard Law Review* 1210.
—— 'Outcomes, Reasons and Equality' (2000) 80 *Boston University Law Review* 1095.
Phillips, A (ed) *Feminism and Equality: Readings in Social and Political Theory* (New York, New York University Press, 1987).
—— (ed) *Feminism and Politics* (Oxford, Oxford University Press, 1998).
—— 'Feminism and Liberalism Revisited: Has Martha Nussbaum Got It Right?' (2001) 8 (2) *Constellations* 249.
Pitkin, H *Wittgenstein and Justice* (Berkeley, University of California Press, 1972).
Post, R (ed) *Law and the Order of Culture* (Berkeley, University of California Press, 1991)
Rabinow, P (ed) *The Foucault Reader* (New York, Pantheon, 1984).
—— (ed) *Ethics—Michel Foucault's Essential Works 1954–85* (London, Penguin, 2000).
Ramazanoglu, C *Up Against Foucault: Explorations of Some Tensions Between Foucault and Feminism* (London & New York, Routledge, 1993).
Rawls, J *A Theory of Justice* (Oxford, Clarendon Press, 1971).
—— *Political Liberalism* (New York, Columbia University Press, 1996).
—— 'The Idea of Public Reason Revisited' (1997) 64 (3) *University of Chicago Law Review* 765.

Bibliography

—— *The Law of Peoples* (Cambridge, Harvard University Press, 1999).
—— *A Theory of Justice* (revised edition) (Oxford, Oxford University Press, 2000).
Raz, J *The Morality of Freedom* (Oxford, Oxford University Press, 1986).
—— *Ethics in the Public Domain: Essays in the Morality of Law and Politics* (Oxford, Clarendon Press, 1994).
Réaume, D 'What's Distinctive About Feminist Analysis of Law?' (1996) 2 *Legal Theory* 265.
—— 'Comparing Theories of Sex Discrimination: The Role of Comparison' (2005) 25 (3) *Oxford Journal of Legal Studies* 547.
Rhode, D *Justice and Gender* (Cambridge, Harvard University Press, 1989).
—— 'Feminist Critical Theories' (1990) 42 *Stanford Law Review* 617.
—— *Theoretical Perspectives on Sexual Difference* (New Haven, Yale University Press, 1990).
—— 'Feminism and the State' (1994) 107 *Harvard Law Review* 1181.
—— *Speaking of Sex: The Denial of Gender Inequality* (Cambridge, Harvard University Press, 1997).
Richardson, J 'Feminist legal Theory and Practice: Rethinking the Relationship' (2005) 13 (3) *Feminist Legal Studies* 275.
Richardson, J & Sandland, R (ed) *Feminist Perspectives on Law and Theory* (London, Cavendish Publishing, 2000).
Rorty, R *Philosophy in the Mirror of Nature*, Oxford, Basil Blackwell, 1983
—— *Contingency, Irony and Solidarity* (Cambridge, Cambridge University Press, 1989).
Rundle, B *Wittgenstein and Contemporary Philosophy of Language* (Oxford, Blackwell, 1990).
Sandel, M *Liberalism and the Limits of Justice* (Cambridge, Cambridge University Press, 1982).
Sandland, R 'Between Truth and Difference: Poststructuralism, Law and the Power of Feminism' (1995) 3 *Feminist Legal Studies* 2.
—— 'Seeing Double? Or, Why 'To Be or Not To Be' Is (Not) The Question For Feminist Legal Studies' (1998) 7 (3) *Social and Legal Studies* 307.
Sartre, J *Critique of Dialectical Reason I: Theory of Practical Ensemles* (trans A Sheridan-Smith) (London, New Left Books, 1976).
Sawicki, J *Disciplining Foucault—Feminism, Power and the Body* (London & New York, Routledge, 1991).
Scales, A 'The Emergence of Feminist Jurisprudence' (1986) 95 *Yale Law Journal* 1373.
Scheffler, S 'Equality as the Virtue of Sovereigns' (2003) 31 (2) *Philosophy and Public Affairs* 199.
—— 'What is Egalitarianism?' (2003) 31 (1) *Philosophy and Public Affairs* 5.
Scheman, N & O'Connor, P (eds) *Feminist Interpretations of Ludwig Wittgenstein* (Pennsylvania, Pennsylvania State University Press, 2002).
Schor, N & Week, E (eds) *The Essential Difference* (Bloomington, Indiana University Press, 1994).
Schott, R (ed) *Feminist Interpretations of Immanuel Kant* (Pennsylvania, Pennsylvania State University Press, 1997).
Schulhofer, S *Unwanted Sex: The Culture of Intimidation and the Failure of the Law* (Cambridge, Harvard University Press, 1998).

Bibliography

Segal, L *Is the Future Female?—Troubled Thoughts on Contemporary Feminism* (London, Virago, 1987).
Sen, A *Inequality Re-Examined* (Oxford, Oxford University Press, 1992).
Sevenhuijsen, S *Citizenship and the Ethic of Care: Feminist Considerations on Justice, Morality and Politics* (London, Routledge, 1998).
Shanley, M & **Narayan**, U (eds) *Reconstructing Political Theory: Feminist Perspectives* (Pennsylvania, University of Pennsylvania Press, 1997).
Shanley, M & **Pateman**, C (eds) *Feminist Interpretations and Political Theory* (Cambridge, Polity Press, 1994).
Sheridan, A *Michel Foucault—The Will to Truth* (London & New York, Tavistock, 1980).
Shrage, L *Moral Dilemmas of Feminism* (London & New York, Routledge, 1994).
Smart, C *Feminism and The Power of Law* (London & New York, Routledge, 1989).
—— 'Law's Power, the Sexed Body and Feminist Discourse' (1990) 17 *Journal of Law and Society* 194.
—— (ed) *Regulating Womanhood: Historical Essays on Marriage, Motherhood and Sexuality* (London & New York, Routledge, 1992).
—— *Law, Crime and Sexuality: Essays in Feminism* (London, SAGE, 1995).
Smith, D *Texts, Facts and Femininity: Exploring the Relations of Ruling* (London, Routledge, 1990).
Sohrab, J 'Avoiding the Exquisite Trap: A Critical Look at the Equal Treatment / Special Treatment Debate in Law' (1993) 1 *Feminist Legal Studies* 141.
Spelman, E *Inessential Woman: Problems of Exclusion in Feminist Thought* (London, Women's Press, 1990).
Spivak, G *In Other Worlds: Essays in Cultural Politics* (New York, Methuen, 1987).
Stone, A 'Essentialism and Anti-Essentialism in Feminist Philosophy' (2004) 1 (2) *Journal of Moral Philosophy* 135.
Tadros, V 'Between Governance and Discipline—The Law and Michel Foucault' (1998) 18 *Oxford Journal of Legal Studies* 75.
Tanesini, A *Wittgenstein: A Feminist Interpretation* (Cambridge, Polity Press, 2004).
Taylor, C *Sources of the Self* (Cambridge, Harvard University Press, 1989).
Taylor, D & **Vintges**, K (eds) *Feminism and the Final Foucault* (Chicago, University of Illinois Press, 2004).
Taylor, J *Reclaiming the Mainstream: Individualist Feminist Rediscovered* (New York, Prometheus Books, 1992).
Temkin, J & **Ashworth**, A 'The Sexual Offences Act 2003: Rape, Sexual Assault and the Problems of Consent' (2004) *Criminal Law Review* 328.
Temkin, L 'Egalitarianism Defended' (2003) 113 *Ethics* 764.
—— 'Equality, Priority or What?' (2003) 19 *Economics and Philosophy* 61.
Tushnet, M 'An Essay on Rights' (1984) 62 *Texas Law Review* 1375.
Unger, R 'The Critical Legal Studies Movement' (1983) 96 *Harvard Law Review* 561.
Walby, S *Gender Transformations* (London, Routledge, 1997).
Walter, N *The New Feminism* (London, Virago Press, 1999).
Wasserstrom, R 'Racism, Sexism and Preferential Treatment' (1977) 24 (3) *UCLA Law Review* 581.
Weedon, C *Feminist Practise and Poststructuralist Theory* (Oxford, Basil Blackwell, 1994).

Bibliography

Weir, A *Sacrificial Logics: Feminist Theory and the Critique of Identity* (London, Routledge, 1996).
West, R 'Jurisprudence and Gender' (1988) 55 *University of Chicago Law Review* 1.
—— 'Feminism. Critical Social Theory and Law' (1989) *University of Chicago Legal Forum* 84.
—— *Caring for Justice* (New York, New York University Press, 1997).
—— *Re-Imagining Justice: Progressive Interpretations of Formal Equality, Rights and the Rule of Law* (Aldershot, Ashgate Publishing, 2003).
Westen, P 'The Empty Idea of Equality' (1982) 95 (3) *Harvard Law Review* 537.
—— *Speaking of Equality: An Analysis of the Rhetorical Force of Equality in Moral and Legal Discourse* (Princeton, Princeton University Press, 1990).
Widder, N 'Foucault and Power Revisited' (2004) 3 (4) *European Journal of Political Theory* 411.
Williams, J 'Deconstructing Gender' (1989) 87 *Michigan Law Review* 797.
—— 'Dissolving the Sameness/Difference Debate: A Post-Modern Path Beyond Essentialism in Feminist and Critical Race Theory' (1991) *Duke Law Journal* 296.
Williams, P 'Alchemical Notes: Reconstructing Ideals from Deconstructed Rights' (1987) 22 *Harvard Civil Rights—Civil Liberties Law Review* 401.
—— *The Alchemy of Race and Rights: Diary of a Law Professor* (Cambridge, Harvard University Press, 1991).
Williams W 'The Equality Crisis: Some Reflections on Culture, Courts and Feminism' (1982) 7 *Women's Rights Law Reporter* 175.
—— 'First Generation' (1989) *University of Chicago Legal Forum* 99.
Wishik, H 'To Question Everything: The Inquiries of Feminist Jurisprudence' (1985) 1 *Berkeley Women's Law Journal* 64.
Wittgenstein, L *Tractatus Logico-Philosophicus* (trans D Pears & B McGuinness) (London & New York, Routledge, 1961).
—— *Remarks on the Philosophy of Psychology Volume II* (trans G Von Wright & H Nyman) (Oxford, Blackwell, 1980).
—— *The Philosophical Investigations* (trans G Anscombe) (Oxford, Blackwell, 2000).
Woolf, J 'Fairness, Respect and the Egalitarian Ethos' (1998) 27 (2) *Philosophy and Public Affairs* 97.
Worden, C 'Overshooting the Target: A Feminist Deconstruction of Legal Education' (1984) 34 *American University Law Review* 1141.
Yar, M 'Beyond Nancy Fraser's Perspective Dualism' (2001) 30 (3) *Economy and Society* 288.
Young, I 'The Ideal of Community and The Politics of Difference' (1986) 12 (1) *Social Theory and Practise* 10.
—— *Justice and the Politics of Difference* (Princeton, Princeton University Press, 1990).
—— 'Gender as Seriality: Thinking about Women as a Social Collective' (1994) 19 (3) *Signs* 713.
—— *Intersecting Voices: Dilemmas of Gender, Political Philosophy and Policy* (Princeton, Princeton University Press, 1997).
—— 'Unruly Categories: A Critique of Nancy Fraser's Dual Systems Theory' (1997) 222 *New Left Review* 147.
—— *Inclusion and Democracy* (Oxford, Oxford University Press, 2000).
—— *On Female Body Experience: 'Throwing Like a Girl' And Other Essays* (Oxford, Oxford University Press, 2005).

Index

Aristotle
  The Rhetoric 60
Assimilation model 14–23
  abandonment, proposal for 22–3
  case for and against 15–19
  conformist 19–20
  conservative approach, as 17
  equal opportunities laws 18
  equality, conception of 15–16
  neutrality, and 16–17
  political representation 17–18
  pregnancy 18–19
  strategic advantages 15
  transformational 20
    affirmative action 20–1
    entrenched patriarchal values, and 21
    male norm, and 21–2
    special protection 20–1
  two faces of assimilation 19–23
Asymmetrical power relationships
  emergence of 152–3

Butler, Judith
  postmodernism, and 35

Celebrating difference 23–8
  case for and against 24–8
  changing men's experiences 25
  child-raising, and 25
  criticisms of approach 27–8
  female moral reasoning 23–4
  home keeping, and 25
  internalised gender stereotypes 26
  'relationist' feminist thinking 24–5, 26
  roots of patriarchy, and 24
  women's lives, and 27

Dominance, rise of 28–33
  case for and against 30–3
  criticism of approach 30–1
  determinism, and 31–2
  differences among women, and 31
  equality, theory of, and 30
  'false-consciousness', and 30–1
  feminist reform, and 33
  patriarchy, and 28
  perpetual victim, status of 31–2
  sex inequality, and 29

Dworkin, Ronald
  equality, on 131

Equality as empowerment 136–9
  Davina Cooper on 136–8
Equality, issue of 7–8
Equality, concept of 131–50
  distributive paradigm, and 137
  equality, appeal of concept 149
  equality as empowerment 136–9
  equality beyond comparison 139–141
    'deontic egalitarianism' 140–1
    'substantive comparisons' 139
    'telic egalitarianism' 140
  equality of power, and 150
  force and tenacity of equality paradigm in feminist analysis 150
  formal equality. *See* Formal equality
  re-deployment of concept of equality 132
  respect as alternative moral ideal. *See* Respect
Essentialism 109–30
  difference, and 110–14
  dilemma facing contemporary feminist legal theory 114
  postmodernism, and 113

Feminism, law and liberalism 41–62
Feminist challenge to legal liberalism 43–51
  abstraction 45–9
  'feminine' voice 47
  impartiality, guise of 49–50
  individualism 45–9
  issues of justice and power 48–9
  John Rawls, and 45–6, 48
  law reform 44–5
  marginalisation of women's experiences 45
  masculine voice 47
  'mists of neutrality' 50
  neutrality 49–51
  partial inclusion of women 44
  patriarchal biases and privileges 44
  power relations 48
  prescriptive agenda 51
  rationality 49–51
  'trashing' activity 51

Index

Feminist challenge to rights
  biases inherent in ascriptions of rights 74–5
  complexity of power relations, and 77–8
  conflict-dominated perception of social interaction 76
  Glendon, M, on 75
  rights are too abstract 77–8
  rights are too individualistic 75–7
  separative agenda 76
Feminist commonalities 11–14
  'asking the women question' 13
  'consciousness-raising' 13
  internal debates 13–14
  male/female binary 12
  male predominance 12
  patriarchal society, claim of 12
  'public' and 'private' 13
Feminist contestations 14
Feminist engagement with liberal state 4
Feminist legal and political analysis
  recent dilemmas 151
Feminist legal and political theory
  critical re-appraisal 2–3
Feminist Re-evaluation of Liberalism 51–61
  abstraction 57–9
  community 54–7
  context 57–9
  Cornell, D 55–6
  Dworkin, and 53, 55
  egoism 54–7
  Hart, and 53
  individualism 54–7
  inequality 57–9
  John Rawls, and 54–6
  justice and care 59–61
  Kant, and 60
  masculine mode of rationality 59–60
  Nussbaum, N, and 57–60
  Okin, S, and 54–5, 56
  rationality of emotions 59–61
Feminist reform and women's rights 73–83
  care and connection, contexts of 81
  constraint of negativity, and 82
  duplicity of law, and 73
  feminist challenge to rights 74–8
  reliance on law, and 83–5
  reconstruction of rights 81–3
  rights analysis, approach to 84
  rights and wrong assumptions 78–81
    bluntness of rights as an instrument 80
    collective well-being, and 79–80
    individualism of rights analysis 79
    relationality, assertion of 79
    rights, origin of 80

Feminist scholarship
  'existential crisis' 151
  'new awareness' 152
Formal equality 132–6
  circularity built into concept of 134
  feminist successes, and 133
  legal inequality, and 136
  MacKinnon on 135–6
  new agendas for 153
  re-formulating 134–6
  usefulness of 132–3
  value of paradigm of 133
Foucault, Michel
  categories of sexuality, on 94–6
  conceptual ally to feminism 88
  'disciplinary techniques', on 90
  distinction between 'suggested' and 'imposed' practices 97
  domination, on 106
  essential victimisation, and 105
  female body, and 96
  feminism, and 104–6
  MacKinnon, and 89–106
  mechanism of power, on 100–1
  micro-politics of power, on 90
  political significance of sexuality, on 95
  power as productive phenomenon, on 93
  radical feminism, and 89
  radical feminist theory, and 104
  resistance, and 91–2, 93, 102–3
  sexuality, on 94, 96
  state of domination, on 102
  subversion, on 91–2
  The Ethics of Care of the Self as a Practice of Freedom 103, 104
  The History of Sexuality 102
  transformation of domination, and 103
Frazer, N
  postmodernism, on 1
Fuss, Diana
  strategic essentialism, and 116–17

Gilligan, Carol 23–4
  female moral reasoning, on 23

Haraway, Donna
  Manifesto for Cyborgs 116

Identity
  focus on 1–2

Law
  operation of 41
  patriarchy, and 41
  partially towards masculine values and interests 41–2
  sex inequality, and 42
Legal reform 63–85

172

Index

approaching in third way 70–3
boundary definition 65
de-centering law, case for and against 64–8, 68–70
deconstruction of legal truths 69–70
feminist critique 64–73
feminist reform, resistance to 64
Fineman, M, on 65–6
Foucault, and 66
juridical power 66
MacKinnon on 71–2
non-legal strategies 69
political impetus of feminism, and 73
preservation of role for 73
rule of law ideal, and 64
Smart, C, on 66–70

Liberalism
key failings 42
relationship with feminism 43

MacKinnon, Catharine
assimilation of patriarchal norms, on 92
'authentic' female voice, on 95–6
collective oppression at hands of men, on 111
criticism of 111–12
equality paradigm, on 135–6
essentialism, and 111–12
Foucault, and 89–106
male dominance, on 91
political significance of sexuality, on 95
relevance and role of discourse, on 93
resistance, on 92
sexuality as social construct, on 95

Phillips, A
radical feminism, and 5–6,7
sex differences, on 39
Post-essentialist feminism
call for development of 112–13
Post-feminism 8–9
Postmodernism 33–9
case for and against 36–9
dispersal of power, and 38
effects of 152
essentialism, and 113
feminism, and 36–8
feminist legal analysis, and 129–30
gender identity, and 35–6
influence of 1–2, 33–9

subversion, and 39
women's lives, and 34
Power, domination and patriarchy 87–107
Pregnancy
assimilation model, and 18–19

Radical feminism 87–9
challenge to 87–8
Foucault, and 89. *See also* Foucault
Rawls, John
A Theory of Justice 45–6
Recognition
focus on 1–2
Respect 141–9
'adaptive preferences', and 145–6
caring and self-sacrifice 145
Cornell, D, on 148–9
Frankfurt, H, on 142,144,146–7
Nussbaum, M, on 144, 148–9
Raz, J, on 142
respect beyond equality 146–9
sufficiency, feminism, and 143–6

Sex inequality
law, and 42
Spivak, Gayatari
strategic essentialism 114–15
Strategic essentialism 7, 114–18
collective action, and 115
'the blackmail of essentialism', and 115–16, 118

Wittgenstein, Ludwig 123–8
'family resemblances,'and 125–6, 128
feminist legal analysis, and 129
games, concept of 125
The Philosophical Investigations 124,128
Womenhood, essentialism and identity 109–30
See also Essentialism

Young, Iris Marion 118–23
collectivity of women 122
criticism of 121–3
essentialism, and 121
gender as seriality 118–23
intersectionality, and 120–1
Sartre, and 118–19
social series, concept of 118–20